Indigenous Biography and Autobiography

Indigenous Biography and Autobiography

Peter Read, Frances Peters-Little
and Anna Haebich
(editors)

ANU
THE AUSTRALIAN NATIONAL UNIVERSITY

E PRESS

ANU E PRESS

Published by ANU E Press and Aboriginal History Incorporated
Aboriginal History Monograph 17

National Library of Australia
Cataloguing-in-Publication entry

National Library of Australia Cataloguing-in-Publication entry

Title: Indigenous biography and autobiography / editors: Peter Read, Frances Peters-Little, Anna
             Haebich.
ISBN: 9781921536342 (pbk.) 9781921536359 (pdf)
Series: Aboriginal history monograph ; 17
Notes: Bibliography.
Subjects: Aboriginal Australians--Biography--History and criticism.
             Autobiography.
Other Authors/Contributors:
             Read, Peter, 1945-
             Peters-Little, Frances, 1958-
             Haebich, Anna.
Dewey Number: 809.93592

Contacting Aboriginal History
All correspondence should be addressed to Aboriginal History, Box 2837 GPO Canberra, 2601, Australia.
Sales and orders for journals and monographs, and journal subscriptions: Thelma Sims, email:
Thelma.Sims@anu.edu.au, tel or fax: +61 2 6125 3269, www.aboriginalhistory.org

Aboriginal History Inc. is a part of the Australian Centre for Indigenous History, Research School of Social
Sciences, The Australian National University and gratefully acknowledges the support of the History
Program, RSSS and the National Centre for Indigenous Studies, Australian National University.

**WARNING: Readers are notified that this publication may contain names or images of deceased
persons.**

ANU E Press
All correspondence should be addressed to:
ANU E Press, The Australian National University, Canberra ACT 0200, Australia
Email: anuepress@anu.edu.au, http://epress.anu.edu.au

Cover design by Teresa Prowse
Cover photo: Judi Wickes, aged 6.

Table of Contents

List of Illustrations

Contributors

Susan Ballyn is a senior Lecturer in the English Department at Barcelona University and the Director of the Australian Studies Centre. Her area of research is Hispanic and Lusophone convicts transported to Australia and the surgeons' diaries on the transports.

Francesca Di Blasio has a PhD in English Literature and is *ricercatrice* at the University of Trento. Her areas of research are Modernism, Postmodernism, Indigenous Australian literature and Literary Theory.

Kristina Everett holds a PhD in anthropology. Her main research interests include (re)emergent traditional Indigenous cultural practices in urban settings and the political, cultural and social effects of these practices. Kristina teaches Indigenous Studies at Macquarie University and is keenly interested in Indigenous higher education.

Karen Fox completed her MA at the University of Canterbury in 2005 and moved to Canberra in 2006 to begin doctoral research at The Australian National University. Her interests include 20th-century Australian and New Zealand history, women's and feminist histories, and the transnational histories of settler societies.

Oliver Haag studied History and Political Science at the University of Vienna, Austria. He specialised in the history of autobiography, Indigenous Studies and theories of nation-building, with particular interest in Australia. Oliver is currently working on a collaborative research project entitled 'national unity through diversity'.

Kristyn Harman lectures in Aboriginal Studies at the University of Tasmania where she recently completed a PhD thesis: 'Aboriginal convicts: race, law, and transportation in colonial New South Wales'. Her research interests include contact history in the Australian colonies, New Zealand and the Cape colony; biography; and legal history.

Anna Haebich, a Research Intensive Professor from Griffith University, is Historian in Residence at the State Library of Queensland. Her books include *Broken circles* and *Spinning the dream: assimilation in Australia 1950 to 1970*.

Michael Jacklin is an Associate Research Fellow at the University of Wollongong. His research interests focus on life writing and issues of collaboration.

Aroha Harris, Te Rarawa and Ngapuhi, is a lecturer in history at the University of Auckland. She combines her research interests in the Maori twentieth century and Maori policy with her commitments to Te Rarawa iwi research and development.

Pat Lowe grew up in the UK and came to Australia in 1972, where she spent many years working as a psychologist in Western Australian prisons, mostly in Broome. Pat has written a dozen books, fiction and non-fiction, and is an active environmentalist and a partner in a part-time publishing house.

Simon Luckhurst is a writer, researcher and journalist. He has produced a number of short films and is the author of several plays, as well as *Eddie's country* (Magabala Books 2006). He is currently a doctoral candidate at the University of Technology Sydney.

Frances Peters-Little is a Kamilaroi/Ulalarai woman and PhD student at The Australian National University. She was formerly Deputy Director and Research Fellow at the National Centre for Indigenous History, The Australian National University. Before coming to Canberra, she was a film maker for the Australian Broadcasting Corporation and left in 1995 after producing and directing 10 x 60-minute documentaries. She spends her time writing, and is currently working on her second book, the official biography on the life of her father, Jimmy Little, which is expected to be published by ABC books.

Munzhedzi James Mafela is a professor of African Languages in the School of Arts, Education and Language Communication at the University of South Africa. His field of specialisation is African Literature and Culture, and Lexicography.

Maria Preethi Srinivasan, a research scholar in the Department of English, University of Madras, developed an interest in Australian Aboriginal Literature. Her research towards a PhD is a transnational study of Australian Aboriginal and Indian Dalit and Adivasi Women's literature.

Peter Read is a historian at the University of Sydney and the chairperson of *Aboriginal History*.

Judi Wickes is a Wakka Wakka/Kalkadoon woman from Queensland. She is currently a post-graduate student at the University of Queensland. After qualifying in social work at the University of Queensland in 1997, Judi worked as a Stolen Generations Counsellor. Working with these families in search of their family/identity re-ignited questions about her Aboriginal identity. It resulted in her Honours thesis, '"Never really heard of it": A study of the impact on identity of the Queensland Certificate of Exemption for Aboriginal people' completed in 2005. Since then, Judi has enrolled in a Master of Arts in the School of Social Sciences in the University of the Sunshine Coast to research the lived experience of citizenship among Indigenous Queenslanders granted the Certificate of Exemption.

Introduction

Our volume of reflections on Indigenous biography and autobiography is drawn from selected and refereed papers first presented at an international conference held at the National Museum of Australia in 2007. The principal sponsor was the Humanities Research Centre at The Australian National University (ANU).

Forty-three people presented papers at this four-day conference. Speakers were drawn from Australia, Spain, Austria, New Zealand, South Africa, Botswana, the Ainu Islands and Taiwan. More than half were Indigenous scholars from around the world, and almost a quarter of the speakers were Indigenous presenters from mainland Australia and the Torres Strait islands. The very generous participation of our sponsor organisations enabled us to cover most of the travel and accommodation expenses of all the Indigenous participants.

The conference poster used the work of Roy Kennedy, a Wiradjuri (southern New South Wales) print-maker depicting the Aboriginal settlement of Warangesda, on the Murrumbidgee. He added the caption 'Days of Harmony on Our Mission: I'm going back to the late thirties and forties when Aboriginals had had great times among the elders of those days when you were told to do something you did it without question'. Here were raised many of the issues discussed at the conference: On whose memories do biographers rely? Can autobiographers rely on their own memories? For whom are stories told? How does one resolve disagreements? Who has the right to tell stories about the Indigenous past? Our discussion covered theoretical issues as well as the ethics and practicalities of negotiating these issues with communities – and sometimes one's own family. The conference themes were 'Who Owns the Story?', 'Controversial Lives', 'Who is My Audience?', 'Elusive Relationships', 'Art and Politics', 'Alternative Narratives' and 'Mixed Identities'.

Each of the papers here is drawn from one of these sections. The Maori scholar Aroha Harris, for example, reflects on her writing the life of Joe Hawke and her biographical role as a biographer balancing the demands of the academy against the demands of Joe and his family, the delicacies and indelicacies of Joe's story, and the privileges of the biographer in 'knowing' Joe against the 'rules' of historical method. Discussion of the life of the Sydney entertainer and 'stolen generations' victim Pauline McLeod draws on the author Simon Luckhurst's decision to prioritise Pauline's enormous private writings. By letting the documents speak for themselves, he wishes to portray a character in which he, as biographer, plays a minimal role.

The conference was very generously sponsored by the Humanities Research Centre, ANU; the National Centre for Indigenous Studies, ANU; the Institute of Advanced Studies, University of Western Australia; the Australian Centre for

Indigenous History, ANU; and the Centre for Public Culture and Ideas, Griffith University. The convenors of the conference acted as the editors of the volume Professor Anna Haebich, Ms Frances Peters-Little and Professor Peter Read.

We strongly recommend the contents of this volume both as examples of state of the art Indigenous life writing, and also as an earnest discussion of the complexities and difficulties involved. These no longer are the concern of only non-Indigenous writers. They are of vital concern also, and perhaps more so, to Indigenous scholars.

Professor Peter Read
Sydney, October 2008

Teaching and Researching

This section of the monograph tackles, first, the methodological issues of Indigenous biographical studies in Europe. European students of Australia are often first drawn to Indigenous studies, thence, logically, to Indigenous autobiographies. Oliver Haag provides a most useful list of those works currently available for study. Francesca Di Blasio and Susan Ballyn discuss how these texts are used with students in Italy and Spain. It is not an easy task to explain texts when Sally Morgan's *My place* is translated in Italian as *My Australia,* analogous to Karen Blixen's *Out of Africa* translated as *My Africa*! Possible pitfalls for students who may know very little about Australia are the development of patronising attitudes towards Indigenous people or an exoticisation of their culture. Teaching in Barcelona, Ballyn insists on studying the autobiographical texts first as 'witnesses to and in depth studies of the social history and cultures of the nations concerned'. Literary theory comes later.

Still on methodology, Kristyn Harman argues convincingly for reading public records with their gaps and silences against the grain. She cites the Dharawal man Duall as an example. By tracking early nineteenth century archives from Sydney and Tasmania, she illustrates how a series of one or two sentence references to an individual over a period, in this case of 19 years, can trace not only the individual's career but the fluctuations in government policy. Partly reflecting changing attitudes towards Aborigines generally, Duall was seen first as 'friendly', then as a villain, then in his final archival appearance as 'friendly' again. In the last article in this section, Karen Fox describes her research in a period for which records are much fuller. Writing of Oodgeroo Noonuccal, she uses mainly press reports, some brief, some lengthy, to trace the attitudinal shifts in press coverage in different periods of her life, and the tonal difference in articles written before and after her death.

Naturally, such records are crucial, but as we shall see later in the monograph, collecting and assessing records, in new ways and old, is just a first step in the long biographical process. For many Indigenous writers such records are subservient to the spoken word.

Peter Read and Anna Haebich

From the margins to the mainstream: towards a history of published Indigenous Australian autobiographies and biographies

Oliver Haag

Published Indigenous Australian autobiographies have undergone considerable change over the last five decades.[1] From tentative beginnings between the 1950s and the 1970s, they saw tremendous growth during the 1980s and 1990s. Now, 50 years later, autobiographies have secured their place in overseas markets. This article reconstructs some aspects of this development.[2] More precisely, I first present an extended bibliography and then make a statistical profile to contextualise the statistical findings within a broader historical frame. 'Extended bibliography' is understood to incorporate several variables relevant to the statistical survey, including year of first publication, genre, gender, publisher, and production-authorship.[3]

Compiling a bibliography

Any bibliography must rely on a consistent definition of its sources. In this instance, two ideas require a definition: 'what makes an autobiography an autobiography?' and 'what makes it Indigenous?' The latter idea in particular should be comparable to self-perceptions: 'how do Indigenous authors define their own work?' Anita Heiss elaborates on this question in her seminal analysis *Dhuuluu-Yala*.[4] Following her findings, my principle is that a work must at least be co-authored by an Indigenous person to be identified as Indigenous.[5] Other indicators, such as subject-matter and perspective, are too imprecise to use in constructing a definition and they tend to homogenise what is, more often than not, highly diverse. This definition thus excludes all biographies about Indigenous persons, as well as authors such as Mudrooroo, whose indigeneity is contested.[6]

This definition, however, is complicated by early autobiographies that do not meet the criterion of shared authorships, such as, for example, Hetherington's *Aboriginal queen of sacred song*, Thonemann's *Tell the white man*, or Lockwood's *I, the Aboriginal*.[7] Including them as Indigenous autobiographies is a matter of perspective because the issue of actual authorship was relatively unimportant in these earlier works. I have excluded them from this analysis because their contexts of production and reception are too different from those that I wish to study.

Compared to authorship, genre is a more complex topic. Scholarly literature has applied more than 10 different genres to Indigenous autobiography: autobiography, autobiographical narrative, life history, life story, life writing, testimony, history, Indigenous history, oral history, auto-ethnography, and novel.[8] Most of these genres closely relate to each other because they revolve around life experiences. Their differences, however, can be both subtle and substantial. While some stress the oral background of Indigenous autobiography, others heed the differences in the historical depth of a narrated life, stretching from aspects of a life to an entire life cycle. Further genres gauge a clear distinction between self-productions and 'as-told-to' stories.[9] Yet, it is striking that, while (or exactly because) the autobiography is ranked as one of the most widely used genres, it is also one of the most fiercely criticised. While Rowse, Brewster, and Watson deploy the term autobiography, a considerable number of other researchers use other terms such as life history.[10] Interestingly, this is not the case with the term biography. Moreton-Robinson, for example, prefers life writing and life 'herstories' to autobiography, considering that the Indigenous autobiographical self was not in any sense individualistic but relational, communal, and connected to others through spirituality and/or place.[11] Westphalen holds that the term autobiography has tended to conceal the actual origin of Indigenous life histories, namely, the discourses of the Dreamings.[12] In turn, Mudrooroo decried the autobiography as an individualistic and apolitical 'battler genre'.[13]

Conventional literary definitions of autobiography play a major role in this critique, referring in particular to the understanding that the autobiography presupposes a completely individualised self.[14] From such a perspective, Indigenous autobiographies are indeed fundamentally different. They rest upon a distinctively oral background as well as a wealth of inter-generational story-telling networks. Their presentation is often dialogic rather than purely retrospective, taking the form of direct speech. They are often communal instead of entirely individual. All of this, however, does not mean that the term autobiography as such is unhelpful. For example, (Indigenous) feminist theorists have criticised and expanded the narrow focus on individualism.[15] To me, then, the term autobiography is not necessarily a misnomer for Indigenous life narratives because it finally depends on how the genre itself is defined. Bearing this in mind, I adopt the following working definition: both autobiography and biography can at least be identified as distinct genres of Indigenous literature. While the autobiography is a life-narrative principally narrated by the protagonist(s), the biography is a life-narrative principally narrated about the protagonist(s).

In my bibliography, I do not distinguish between individualised and relational selves, dialogic and descriptive styles, or collaborative and independent works. Nor is it important whether a publication covers an entire life circle or focuses upon select aspects of a life. Furthermore, this bibliography includes published books and excludes manuscripts, journal articles, reports, and ethnographic field studies. I do not consider such forms to be equivalent to books, at least as far as public reception and marketing are concerned. The 'Bulman Oral History Series' are a special case. Although they are added to a separate rubric in the bibliography, they are not part of the sample underlying the statistics.[16] All items included are authored or co-authored by an Indigenous person; authorship follows gender so that men's autobiographies have to be authored by men. Indigenous autobiographies are sometimes a composition of different life stories of different protagonists. In this respect, they bear some similarities to related genres like family or community history. Nevertheless, such genres are different from autobiographies and thus excluded from the bibliography. This bibliography also does not include semi-autobiographies or autobiographical novels. In many cases, this bibliography draws upon the National Library of Australia Cataloguing-in-Publication Data. It also takes into account similar bibliographies, such as those compiled by Heiss, Watson, and Schürmann-Zeggel.[17] Lastly, no bibliography of Indigenous autobiographies should ever be considered definitive.

Retracing the history of Indigenous autobiographies

My goal, then, is to provide an overview. For this purpose, I explored approximately 400 books across different genres, published between 1950 and 2004, before selecting 177 which qualified as published autobiographies for analysis.

I make three general observations relating to authorship, genre, and increase:[18]

(1) Authorship: The overall ratio between female and male authors is 3 to 2, meaning that women have authored around 60 per cent of the 177 books issued between 1950 and 2004. There are signs that this numerical imbalance corresponds to a broader pattern of Indigenous literature: in the survey *To tell my story*, around 66 per cent of Indigenous writers are female.[19] Most of the autobiographies (98 per cent) were published in the period of self-determination (from the late 1960s onwards).[20] Males prevailed by 55 per cent during the first phase, prior to 1988, while women dominated by 64 per cent during the second period. The Indigenous autobiography, it seems, has become a female-dominated genre. David Unaipon (1951) is the first male Indigenous autobiographer, and Theresa Clements (c 1954) is the first female.

(2) Genre: The bulk of Indigenous life writing is autobiographical (81 per cent). A more recent phenomenon, biographies did not gain a foothold until the

mid-1980s. In all, 38 per cent of Indigenous autobiographies are co-authored ('as-told-to' stories). Statistically, both these genres do not show any gender-based differentials. This means that, in contrast to the autobiography, the biography is neither a more male nor female genre and that co-authoring is not specifically gendered. Only anthologies (collections of several distinct contributors) are dominated by female authors (71 per cent).

(3) Increase: Measuring by decade-specific data, the number of publications has continuously increased since the 1960s. That is, the 1970s saw, in nominal terms, more publications than the 1960s, the 1980s saw more than the 1970s, and the 1990s saw more than the 1980s. The number in the 2000s will likely surpass the 1990s. While 6.8 books were published a year on average during the 1990s, 15.2 books were published a year during the period of 2000 to 2004. This steady increase also applies to co-productions and biographies.

In the case of co-authoring and production processes, these changes have been not only quantitative but also qualitative. As scholars such as Jones and McDonell have explored, there are now substantial discourses on how to collaborate, edit, and publish Indigenous autobiographies.[21] This, along with the establishment of Indigenous publishers, has led many publishing houses to maintain Indigenous English and idiomatic styles of expression. Also, while many autobiographies were exclusively transcribed and edited by non-Indigenous persons, they are now increasingly co-produced by Indigenous persons, including *My place*, *When the pelican laughed*, or *Auntie Rita*.[22] Together, these factors suggest a consistent progression of the Indigenous autobiography, due to the consistent increase in publishing in general and the numbers for co-productions and biographies in particular. The history of Indigenous autobiography has indeed followed a linear path of progression.

This history has, however, also been distinguished by uneven developments. I have ascertained two different phases in the evolvement of Indigenous autobiography: from 1951 to 1987 (20 per cent of all items) and from 1988 to 2004. This corresponds with the findings of other scholars such as Brewster and Olijnyk Longley, who also consider the late 1980s as a turning point.[23] There may be at least three reasons for this: publications have increased enormously, the 'publishing landscape' has changed, and Indigenous autobiographies have started to acquire an international reputation.

(1) The Increase in Publications

In spite of the fact that published Indigenous autobiographies date from 1951, rapid expansion did not begin until the late 1980s, after when their growth was dramatic. But, unlike the decade-specific pattern, year-to-year data reveal an uneven growth rate characterised by four major peaks in publications (see Figure 1.1). The first of these occurred in 1977 and 1978, after the first Whitlam reforms, such as the implementation of the (new) Australia Council, had taken effect. The second major peak occurred in the two years following the Bicentenary in 1988. The third occurred in 1995 between the Mabo judgment and the tabling of the *Bringing them home* Report. The final peak was in the year of the Sydney Olympic Games, 2000.

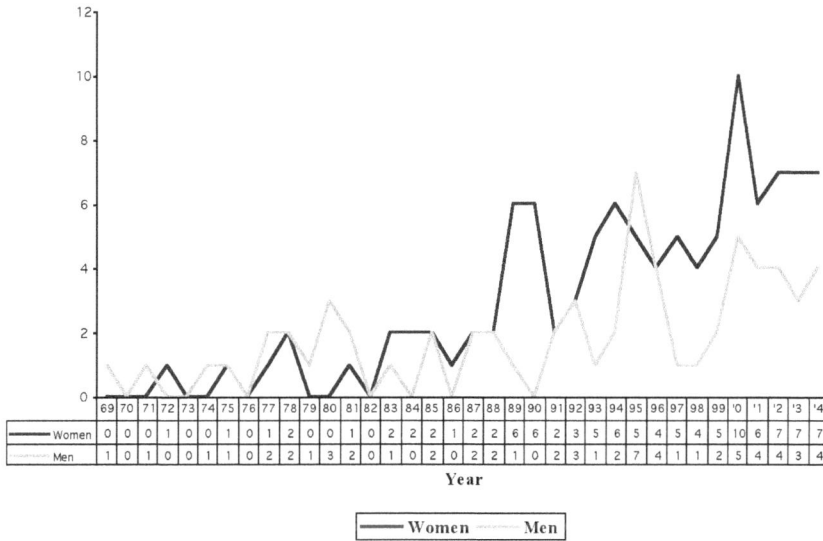

Ratio of Female to Male Autobiographers - Year Specific (1969-2004)

	69	70	71	72	73	74	75	76	77	78	79	80	81	82	83	84	85	86	87	88	89	90	91	92	93	94	95	96	97	98	99	'0	'1	'2	'3	'4
Women	0	0	0	1	0	0	1	0	1	2	0	0	1	0	2	2	2	1	2	2	6	6	2	3	5	6	5	4	5	4	5	10	6	7	7	7
Men	1	0	1	0	0	1	1	0	2	2	1	3	2	0	1	0	2	0	2	2	1	0	2	3	1	2	7	4	1	1	2	5	4	4	3	4

Year

Women ——— Men

Figure 1.1: Diagram representing both graphically and numerically the number of male and female Indigenous autobiographies published per year. The lower two rows of the figure display the numerical data and form a ratio.

This evidence points to a likely correlation between periods of heightened socio-political activity and the rise in publications. Shoemaker has also identified such a nexus,[24] and, indeed, the first wave of published Indigenous autobiographies appeared just at the threshold of what is now often perceived as creative period of change – the late 1960s. Political minorities, including Indigenous Australians, became (not least because of the then nation-wide political activisms) increasingly vocal and, therefore, a subject of intense interest. Some 10 years later, the (anti-)celebrations of 200 years of settlement or invasion in 1988 generated a similar demand for Indigenous stories which publishers were eager to meet.[25] Market demands, in other words, were not steady. Indigenous Australians had become increasingly visible. Audiences and writers followed the trend.

(2) Changes within the national market

The proliferation of Indigenous autobiographies has been closely intertwined with the nature of the publishers. In general, most items have been issued by either local presses or through self-publication, both of which have affected their reception. Significantly, none of the autobiographies that are part of the canon in inter/national scholarship has been published in either of these categories of press. Setting this aside, the publishing infrastructure surrounding Indigenous autobiography can be subdivided into Indigenous and mainstream publishers.

The most prolific publishers of Indigenous autobiographies are the two Indigenous presses, Magabala Books and Aboriginal Studies Press (ASP). The former was inaugurated in 1987, the latter in the 1960s. Though not Indigenous, the University of Queensland Press (UQP) – within the scope of its 1990-launched Black Writers Series – ranks third.[26]

As for the mainstream field, four eminent publishing companies, including imprints, stand out: Fremantle Arts Centre Press (FACP), Allen & Unwin, Angus & Robertson, and Penguin. Together, they make up 20 per cent of the 177 published Indigenous autobiographies (see Figure 1.2).

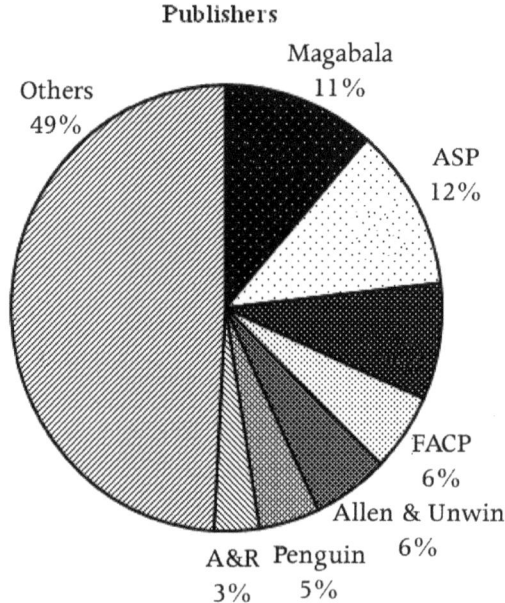

Figure 1.2: Pie chart displaying the relative proportions of the 177 published Indigenous autobiographies each publisher produced.

Interestingly, Australian feminist presses have not played a significant role. Except for Spinifex Press, none of the major feminist presses, such as Sybylla Press, Women's Redress Press, or Artemis Publishing, has issued Indigenous autobiographies. Other presses evidently also supported women's autobiographies, but a possible correlation between the different gender ratios and a corresponding publishing policy demonstrated by these presses reveals a rather hazy picture: the different ratios in the publications of Magabala Books, ASP, and Penguin are too minuscule to draw any serious conclusion. In contrast, while FACP, Allen & Unwin, and UQP published significantly more female than male authors, Angus & Robertson in turn published twice as many male authors.

Mainstream and Indigenous publishers have both produced Indigenous autobiographies. This has not always been true, as the publishing landscape has changed drastically since the late 1980s. Firstly, Magabala Books and, shortly thereafter, the UQP Black Writers Series were established. This new infrastructure led to a proliferation of Indigenous autobiographies and culturally sensitive publishing. Secondly, by the late 1980s, Indigenous autobiographies increasingly attracted the attention of the mainstream publishing industry, presumably triggered by the success of *My place*.[27] Whatever the different causes, two significant events occurred in the late 1980s: Magabala Books was founded, and Indigenous autobiographies entered a mainstream market and, thus, a new phase.

(3) The entry into an international market

When the 1980s, especially the Bicentenary, drew to a close, publications of Indigenous autobiographies became increasingly prolific. Since then they have flourished not only within Australia but overseas. Little, however, is known about this international reception and distribution.

International distribution can be analysed from two perspectives: reception, including both readership and scholarship, and the publication, including the translation. Both have seen an enormous expansion within the last two decades. In particular, increasing interest can be observed within the academic field. Indigenous autobiographies have become an intense subject of academic study, demonstrated by an increasing number of university theses. At Austrian universities alone, at least six have been written since 1998. Moreover, Rühl, Schürmann-Zeggel, Zierott, and Duthil have published their studies on Indigenous autobiographies.[28] These monographs, however, have received only minor attention within Australia.

Indigenous autobiographies have also been taken on by overseas presses. The UK edition of *My place* was published by Virago Press, a leading publisher of women's literature. The German translation, entitled *Ich hörte den Vogel rufen*, was published by the feminist press Orlanda Frauenverlag.[29] The German version of Morgan's *Wanamurraganya* was released by the mainstream Swiss company

Unionsverlag.[30] The Finnish edition of Langford Ginibi's *Don't take your love to town, Bonalbon Musta Ruby*, was published by Kääntöpiiri, a Christian press.[31] *Long walk home*, the German translation of *Follow the rabbit-proof fence*, was issued by mainstream publisher Rowohlt.[32] It appears that, in overseas contexts, it is primarily mainstream and feminist presses that have published Indigenous autobiographies. The existence of such a strong commitment on the side of feminist publishing is in stark contrast to the situation in the Australian market. This contrast in part suggests why predominantly, if not exclusively, women authors have been published overseas.

Lastly, I would like to present a note on the complexity of translating Indigenous autobiographies. Translations are an unmistakable sign of success, but also pose a string of critical questions: How is it possible to properly consult with Indigenous authors once a text is rendered into an unfamiliar language? How can a distinctive speech pattern – like dialogic utterance – be maintained in a foreign language? For instance, *My place* was rendered into a very rough version of Northern German, which sounds extremely artificial to most German speakers. To mention yet another difficulty, the German equivalent of race, *Rasse*, denotes a purely biological conception of race. Meanwhile, *Rasse* has become an indubitably racist word that is either substituted for ethnicity (*Ethnizität*) or avoided completely. Ethnicity, however, does not correspond with current discourses on race and racisms in Australia. How, then, does one translate this word?

Conclusion

Published Indigenous autobiographies span five decades, during which they have undergone some drastic changes. They have changed from 'male' to 'female', from 'local' to 'global', and from the 'margins' to the 'mainstream'. Particularly since the Bicentenary, they have seen several decisive increases in publication. As I have argued, the late 1980s indeed marks a watershed in the history of published Indigenous autobiography, separating two different phases from one another, and it is in the second phase that they have became an internationally recognised phenomenon.

Table 1: Extended Bibliography (1951-2004)

Author	Year	Author	Year
Unaipon/**M**	1951	Cohen*__F__	<u>1990</u>
Clements/**F**	1954	Morgan*__F__	1990a
Rose*__M__	1969	Morgan*__F__	1990b
Roughsey/**M**	1971	Morgan*__F__/ __B__	1990c
Noonuccal/**F**	1972	Pring/**F**	<u>1990</u>
Lamilami*__M__	1974	Woodrow/**F**	1990
Cawley/**F**	1975	Davis/**M**	1991
Perkins/**M**	1975	McGinness/**M**	1991
<u>Tatz/**M&F**</u>	<u>1975</u>	*Pilkington/**F***	1991
<u>Jangala/**M**</u>	<u>1977</u>	Ward/**F**	1991
Tucker*__F__	1977	Dodd/**M**	1992
*Clare/**F***	1978	Edmund/**F**	1992
McKenna*__M__	1978	Langford/**F**	1992
Mirritji*__M__	1978	Nannup*__F__	1992
Simon/**F**	1978	Saunders/**M**	1992
Dhoulagarle/**M**	1979	Sing*__M__	1992
Bropho/**M**	1980	Chryssides/**F**/ __B__	1993
Pepper/**M**/ __B__	1980	Crawford*__F__	1993
Raggett*__M__	1980	Goolagong/**F**/ __B__	1993
MumShirl*__F__	1981	Lester/**M**	1993
Ngabidj*__M__	1981	Prior/**F**/ __B__	1993
Thaiday/**M**	1981	Sykes/**F**	1993
McKenzie/**F**	1983a	Anderson/**F**/ __B__	1994
McKenzie/**F**	1983b	Harrison/**M**	1994
Sullivan*__M__	1983	Huggins/**F**/ __B__	1994
Roughsey*__F__	1984	Langford/**F**	1994
West/**F**	1984	McPhee*__M__	1994
Kennedy/**F**	1985	Morgan/**F**	1994
Neidjie*__M__	1985	<u>Somerville/**F**</u>	<u>1994</u>
Rosser/**M**/ __B__	1985	van den Berg/**F**/ __B__	1994
<u>White/**F**</u>	<u>1985</u>	Bohemia*__M__	1995
Coe/**F**/ __B__	1986	Camfoo*__F__	1995
Cohen/**M**	1987	Camfoo*__M__	1995
Morgan/**F**	1987	Gibbs/**M**	1995
Ward/**F**	1987	Marika*__M__	1995
Willmot/**M**/ __B__	1987	McAdam*__M__	1995
Chesson/**M**/ __B__	1988	Medcraft/**F**	1995
Langford/**F**	1988	Moran/**M**/ __B__	1995
Lowah/**M**	1988	*Nungurrayi*__*F__	<u>1995</u>
Thancoupie*__F__	1988	Pedersen*__M__	1995
Gaffney/**F**	1989	<u>Vaarzon-Morel*__F__</u>	<u>1995</u>
Hamilton*__F__	1989	Wood/**F**/ __B__	1995
McKenzie*__F__	1989	Edmund/**F**/ __B__	1996
Morgan/**F**/ __B__	1989	Harney*__M__	1996
*Thomson*__*F__	1989	King/**M**	1996
Walker*__F__	1989	Lennon*__F__	1996
Wilson/**M**/ __B__	1989	Mabo*__M__/ __B__	1996
		McDonald*__F__	1996

Author	Year	Author	Year
Munro*M	1996	Mallett/F	2001
Pilkington/F/ **B**	1996	Pilbara Aboriginal Centre*F	2001
Appo/F	1997	Riley/F/ **B**	2001
Bell/F/ **B**	1997	Sykes/F	2001
Chittick/M/ **B**	1997	Taylor/M	2001
Lovett-Gardiner/F	1997	Wright/F/ **B**	2001
Napanangka*F	1997	Bayet-Charlton/F	2002
Sykes/F	1997	Brodie*F	2002
Corrigan*F	1998	Diwurruwurru-jaru* M&F	2002
Fraser/ F	1998	Grant/M	2002
Pryor*M	1998	Harrison*M	2002
Sykes/F	1998	Lowe*M	2002
Wilson/F	1998	Pilbara Aboriginal Centre/F	2002
[n.a]/F	1999	Pilkington/F	2002
Hegarty/F	1999	Purcell/F	2002
J.K.*F	1999	Rubuntja*M	2002
Langford/F/ **B**	1999	Russell/F/ **B**	2002
Read/Coppin*M	1999	Smith*F	2002
Walgar*M	1999	Aboriginal Community/M&F	2003
Williams*F	1999	Brown/F	2003
Lenoy*F	200(?)	Clarke*M	2003
Barnes/F	2000	Collard/F	2003
Bin-Sallik/F	2000	Crombie/F/ **B**	2003
Burgonye/F	2000	Freeman*F	2003
Camfoo*M&F	2000	Hegarty/F	2003
Daley/M	2000	Kinnane/M	2003
Dodd/M	2000	Peris*F	2003
Kartinyeri/F	2000	Randall*M	2003
Lalor*M	2000	Schilling/F	2003
Lennon*F	2000	Beetson*M	2004
McKellar*F	2000	Bent/F	2004
Meehan/F	2000	Flick*F	2004
Moriarty*M	2000	Hamilton*/F	2004
Onus/M/ **B**	2000	Marshall*F	2004
Smith/F	2000	Moran*M	2004
Sykes/F	2000	Muir/F	2004
Chalarimeri/M	2001	Ngarta et al./F	2004
Decker*F	2001	Schilling/F	2004
Havnen/M&F	2001	Tovey/M	2004
Holt/M	2001	Wilson*M	2004
Latham/M	2001	Wyllie/F/ **B**	2004

Annotation to coding: F(emale) and M(ale) refer to the gender of main author. If not indicated as **B** (= biography), all items are autobiographies. Asterisk* after name means 'as-told-to' story or editor/transcriber/assistant is named as additional author. All borderline cases (history/semi-autobiography) are italicised. Joint productions (anthologies) are underlined. Roberta Sykes is included. Mudrooroo has been omitted.

Bibliography of published Indigenous autobiographies

Aboriginal Community Elders Service and Kate Harvey 2003, *Aboriginal Elders' voices: Stories of the 'tide of history' – Victorian Indigenous Elders' life stories & oral histories*, Aboriginal Community Elders Service, Melbourne.

Appo, Josephine and Joyce Summers 1997, *Wajehla Dubay: Women speakin – Aboriginal women's essays, stories and poems*, Keeaira Press, Southport.

Barker, Jimmie and Janet Mathews 1977, *The two worlds of Jimmy Barker: The life of an Australian Aboriginal 1900–1972*, Aboriginal Studies Press, Canberra.

Barnes, Nancy 2000, *Munyi's Daughter: A spirited brumby*, Seaview Press, Henley Beach.

Bayet-Charlton, Fabienne 2002, *Finding Ullagundahi Island*, Allen & Unwin, Crows Nest.

Beetson, Arthur et al. 2004, *Big Artie. The autobiography*, ABC, Sydney.

Bin-Sallik, Mary Ann (ed) 2000, *Aboriginal women by degrees: Their stories of the journey towards academic achievement*, University of Queensland Press, St Lucia.

Bohemia, Jack and William McGregor 1995, *Nyibayarri: Kimberley tracker*, Aboriginal Studies Press, Canberra.

Brodie, Veronica and Mary-Anne Gale 2002, *My side of the bridge: The life story of Veronica Brodie*, Wakefield Press, Kent Town.

Bropho, Robert 1980, *Fringedweller,* Alternative Publishing Co-operative, Sydney.

Brown, Eileen Kampakuta 2003, *Anangu: An Anangu-Aboriginal love story – My young life*. Nyiri Publications, Murray Bridge.

Burgoyne, Iris [Yumadoo Kochallalya] 2000, *Mirning: We are the whales – A Mirning-Kokatha woman recounts life before and after dispossession*, Magabala Books, Broome.

Camfoo, Nellie and Gillian Cowlishaw 1995, *Nellie Camfoo: Her story*. Barunga Press, Katherine.

—— and Gillian Cowlishaw 1995, *Tex Camfoo: His story*, Barunga Press, Katherine.

Camfoo, Tex, Nellie Camfoo and Gillian Cowlishaw 2000, *Love against the Law: The autobiographies of Tex and Nellie Camfoo*, Aboriginal Studies Press, Canberra.

Cawley, Evonne and Bud Collins 1975, *Evonne!: On the move*, Dutton, New York.

Chalarimeri, Ambrose Mungala 2001, *The man from the sunrise side*, Magabala Books, Broome.

Clare, Monica 1978, *Karobran: The story of an Aboriginal girl,* Alternative Publishing Cooperative, Chippendale.

Clarke, Banjo and Camilla Chance 2003, *Wisdom Man,* Viking, Camberwell.

Clements, Theresa c.1954, *From Old Maloga: The memoirs of an Aboriginal woman,* Fraser & Morphet, Prahran.

Cohen, Bill 1987, *To My Delight: The Autobiography of Bill Cohen, a grandson of the Gumbangarri,* Aboriginal Studies Press, Canberra.

Cohen, Patsy and Margaret Somerville 1990, *Ingelba and the five black matriarchs,* Allen & Unwin, Sydney.

Collard, Dot and Beryl Hackner 2003, *Busted Out Laughing: Dot Collard's Story as told to Beryl Hackne,* Magabala Books, Broome.

Corrigan, Florence and Loreen Breahut 1998, *Miles of post and wire,* Magabala Books, Broome.

Crawford, Evelyn 1993, *Over my tracks,* Penguin, Ringwood.

Daley, Laurie and David Middleton 2000, *Laurie: Always a winner,* HarperCollins Publishers, Pymble.

Davis, Jack 1991, *A boy's life,* Magabala Books, Broome.

Decker, Diane and Marjorie Woodrow 2001, *Long time coming home: As recalled by Marjorie Woodrow,* Marjorie Woodrow, Lake Haven.

Dhoulagarle, Koorie [Roy Simon] 1979, *There's more to life,* Alternative Publishing Co-operative, Chippendale.

Diwurruwurru-Jaru Aboriginal Corporation and Lana Quall 2002, *So far from home: Oral histories of the Stolen Generations,* Diwurruwurru-Jaru Aboriginal Corp., Katherine.

Dodd, Bill 1992, *Broken dreams,* University of Queensland Press, St Lucia.

Dodd, Martin 2000, *They liked me, the horses, straightaway,* Ginninderra Press, Charnwood.

Edmund, Mabel 1992, *No regrets,* University of Queensland Press, St Lucia.

Flick, Isabel and Heather Goodall 2004, *Isabel Flick: The life story of a remarkable Aboriginal leader,* Allen & Unwin, Crows Nest.

Fraser, Rosalie 1998, *Shadow child: A memoir of the Stolen Generation,* Hale & Iremonger, Sydney.

Freeman, Cathy and Scott Gullan 2003, *Cathy: Her own story,* Penguin, Camberwell.

Gaffney, Ellie 1989, *Somebody now: The autobiography of Ellie Gaffney, a woman of Torres Strait,* Aboriginal Studies Press, Canberra.

Gibbs, Jack 1995, *Son of Jimmy,* Historical Society of the Northern Territory, Darwin.

Grant, Stan 2002, *The tears of strangers: A memoir,* HarperCollins, Pymble.

Hamilton, Fiona et al. 2004, *Aboriginal women's heritage: Brungle & Tumut,* Department of Environment and Conservation, Hurstville.

Hamilton, Jean, Joan McKenzie and Katherine McKenzie 1989, *Just Lovely,* J. McKenzie, Coonamble.

Harney [Yidumduma], Bill and Jan Wositzky 1996, *Born under the paperbark tree: A man's life,* ABC, Sydney.

Harrison, Shorty 1994, *All hearts bleed the same: Reflections, recollections and memories, an autobiography*, Bill Harrison, Nowra.

Harrison, Harald John, Jack Miller and Michele Miller 2002, *Living in two cultures: Memories of Harold Harrison,* Bournda Environmental Education Centre, Kalaru.

Havnen, Peg and Leonie Norrington 2001, *Under the mango tree: Oral histories with Indigenous people from the Top End*, NT Writers' Centre Inc., Darwin.

Hegarty, Ruth 1999, *Is that you Ruthie?,* University of Queensland Press, St Lucia.

—— 2003, *Bittersweet journey,* University of Queensland Press, St Lucia.

Holt, Albert 2001, *Forcibly removed,* Magabala Books, Broome.

J.K., Janine Clancy and Sisters Inside 1999, *My prison experience*, Sisters Inside, South Brisbane.

Jangala, Abie et al. 1977, *Stories from Lajamanu,* NT Department of Education, Darwin.

Kartinyeri, Doris 2000, *Kick the tin,* Spinifex Press, North Melbourne.

Kennedy, Marnie 1985, *Born a half-caste,* Aboriginal Studies Press, Canberra.

King, Wayne 1996, *Black hours,* Angus & Robertson, Sydney.

Kinnane, Stephen 2003, *Shadow lines,* Fremantle Arts Centre Press, Fremantle.

Lalor, Myles and Jeremy Beckett 2000, *Wherever I go: Myles Lalor's 'oral history',* Melbourne University Press, Carlton.

Lamilami, Lazarus and JM Bolton 1974, *Lamilami speaks: The cry went up, a story of the people of Goulburn Islands*, North Australia, Ure Smith, Sydney.

Langford, Ruby 1988, *Don't take your love to town,* Penguin, Ringwood.

—— 1992, *Real deadly,* Angus & Robertson, Pymble.

—— 1994, *My Bundjalung people,* University of Queensland Press, St Lucia.

Latham, George 2001, *Copper Wire George,* Yamaji Language Centre, Geraldton.

Lennon, Jessie et al. 1996, *And I Always Been Moving! The early life of Jessie Lennon,* Jessie Lennon and Michele Madigan, Coober Pedy.

Lennon, Jessie and Michele Madigan 2000, *I'm the one that know this country: The story of Jessie Lennon and Coober Pedy,* Aboriginal Studies Press, Canberra.

Lenoy, Norma, Angela Zammatora et al. 200[?], *Norma's story,* Creative Support, Cairns.

Lester, Yami 1993, *Yami: The autobiography of Yami Lester,* Institute for Aboriginal Development, Alice Springs.

Lovett-Gardiner, Iris 1997, *Lady of the lake: Aunty Iris's story,* Koorie Heritage Trust, Melbourne.

Lowah, Thomas and Ray Crooke 1988, *Eded mer (my life),* Rams Skull Press, Kuranda.

Lowe, Robert and Framlingham Mission 2002, *The Mish,* University of Queensland Press, St Lucia.

McAdam, Charlie and Elizabeth Tragenza 1995, *Boundary lines: A family's story of winning against the odds,* McPhee Gribble, Ringwood.

McDonald, Connie [Nungulla] and Jill Finnane 1996, *When you grow up,* Magabala Books, Broome.

McGinness, Joe 1991, *Son of Alyandabu: My fight for Aboriginal rights,* University of Queensland Press, St Lucia.

McKellar, Hazel 2000, *Woman from nowhere: Hazel McKellar's story* [as told to Kerry McCallum], Magabala Books, Broome.

McKenna, Clancy and Kingsley Palmer 1978, *Somewhere between black and white: The story of an Aboriginal Australian,* Macmillan, South Melbourne.

McKenzie, Janet 1983a, *Ebenezer,* New Creation Publications, Blackwood.

—— 1983b, *Fingal tiger,* New Creation Publications, Blackwood.

McKenzie, Ruth 1989, *Molly Lennon's story: That's how it was* [as told to Jen Gibson], Aboriginal Heritage Branch, Adelaide.

McPhee, Jack and Patricia Konigsberg 1994, *Bee Hill River Man: Kandulangu-bidi. Memories of Jack McPhee,* Magabala Books, Broome.

Mallett, Molly 2001, *My past – their future: Stories from Cape Barren Island,* Blubber Head Press, Sandy Bay.

Marika, Wandjuk and Jennifer Isaacs 1995, *Wandjuk Marika: Life story,* University of Queensland Press, St Lucia.

Marshall, Lucy and Colleen Hattersley 2004, *Reflections of a Kimberley woman*, Madjulla Inc., Broome.

Medcraft, Rosalie and Valda Gee 1995, *The sausage tree,* University of Queensland Press, St Lucia.

Meehan, Donna 2000, *It is no secret,* Random House, Milsons Point.

Mirritji, Jack et al. 1978, *My people's life: An Aboriginal's own story,* Milingimbi Literature Centre, Milingimbi.

Moran, Charles Harold and Glennys Moran 2004, *Talk softly, listen well: Profile of Bundjalung elder, Charles Moran,* Southern Cross University Press, Lismore.

Morgan, Eileen 1994, *The calling of the spirits,* Aboriginal Studies Press, Canberra.

Morgan, Sally 1987, *My place,* Fremantle Arts Centre Press, Fremantle.

Morgan, Sally and Barbara Ker Wilson 1990a, *Sally's story.* Fremantle Arts Centre Press, Fremantle.

—— 1990b, *Mother and daughter: The story of Daisy and Gladys Corunna,* Fremantle Arts Centre Press, Fremantle.

Moriarty, John and Evan McHugh 2000, *Saltwater fella,* Viking, Ringwood.

Mumshirl and Bobbi Sykes 1981, *MumShirl: An autobiography with the assistance of Bobbi Sykes*, Heinemann, Richmond.

Muir, Hilda Jarman 2004, *Very big journey: My life as I remember it,* Aboriginal Studies Press, Canberra.

Munro, Morndi and Mary-Anne Jebb 1996, *Emerarra: A Man of Merarra,* Magabala Books, Broome.

n.a. 1999, Holding Up the Sky. *Aboriginal women speak*, Magabala Books, Broome.

Nannup, Alice, Lauren Marsh and Stephen Kinnane 1992, *When the pelican laughed,* Fremantle Arts Centre Press, Fremantle.

Napanangka, Tjemma Freda, Pamela Lofts and Sonja Peter 1997, *Yarrtji: Six Women's Stories from the Great Sandy Desert,* Aboriginal Studies Press, Canberra.

Neidjie, Bill, Stephen Davis and Allan Fox 1985, *Kakadu Man: Bill Neidjie,* Mybrood, Queanbeyan.

Ngabidj, Grant and Bruce Shaw 1981, *My country of the pelican dreaming: The life of an Australian Aborigine of the Gadjerong, Grant Ngabidj, 1904–1977 — as told to Bruce Shaw*, Australian Institute of Aboriginal Studies, Canberra.

Ngarta, Bent et al. 2004, *Two sisters: Ngarta & Jukuna,* Fremantle Arts Centre Press, Fremantle.

Nungurrayi, Lumu and Jordan Crugnale 1995, *Footprints across our Land: Short stories by senior desert women,* Magabala Books, Broome.

Noonuccal, Oodgeroo [Kath Walker] 1972, *Stradbroke Dreamtime,* Angus & Robertson, Sydney.

Pederson, Howard and Banjo Woorrnmurra 1995, *Jandamarra and the Bunuba resistance,* Magabala Books, Broome.

Peris, Nova and Ian Heads 2003, *Nova: My story: The autobiography of Nova Peris,* ABC, Sydney.

Perkins, Charles 1975, *A bastard like me,* Ure Smith, Sydney.

Pilbara Aboriginal Language Centre et al. 2002, *Thalanjyi gujurunyjarri: Jarburda Thalanyjigu guliyarriyarra ngarrarigu* (Thalanyi Stories: thinking about Thalanyji country), Wangka Maya Pilbara Aboriginal Language Centre, South Hedland.

Pilbara Aboriginal Language centre and Rose Murray 2001, *Wumun turi: Pilbara Aboriginal women's stories,* Wangka Maya Pilbara Language Centre, Port Headland.

Pilkington, Doris [Nugi Garimara] 1991, *Caprice: A stockman's daughter,* University of Queensland Press, St Lucia.

—— 2002, *Under the Wintamarra tree,* University of Queensland Press, St Lucia.

Pring, Adele (ed) 1990, *Women of the Centre,* Pascoe, Apollo Bay.

Pryor, Boori and Meme McDonald 1998, *Maybe tomorrow,* Penguin, Ringwood.

Purcell, Leah (ed) 2002, *Black chicks talking,* Hodder Headline, Sydney.

Raggett, Obed and Bill Marshall-Stoneking 1980, *Stories of Obed Raggett,* Alternative Publishing Co-operative, Sydney.

Randall, Bob and Paul Newbury 2003, *Songman: The story of an Aboriginal Elder of Uluru,* ABC, Sydney

Read, Jolly and Peter Coppin 1999, *Kangkushot: The life of Nyamal Lawman Peter Coppin,* Aboriginal Studies Press, Canberra.

Rose, Lionel Edmund 1969, *Lionel Rose: Australian — The life story of a champion — As told to Rod Humphries,* Angus & Robertson, Sydney.

Roughsey, Dick [Goobalathaldin] 1971, *Moon and rainbow: The autobiography of an Aboriginal,* Reed, Sydney.

Roughsey, Elsie [Labumore] and Paul Memmot 1984, *An Aboriginal mother tells of the old and the new,* McPhee Gribble/Penguin, Fitzroy/Ringwood.

Rubuntja, Wenten, Tim Rowse and Jenny Green 2002, *The town grew up dancing: The life and art of Wenten Rubuntja,* Jukurrpa Books, Alice Springs.

Saunders, Keith 1992, *Learning the ropes,* Aboriginal Studies Press, Canberra.

Schilling, Kath et al. 2003, *Aboriginal women's heritage: Nambucca,* NSW National Parks and Wildlife Service, Hurstville.

—— 2004, *Aboriginal women's heritage: Nowra,* NSW National Parks and Wildlife Service, Hurstville.

Simon, Ella 1978, *Through my eyes: Autobiography of a part Aborigine,* Rigby, Adelaide.

Sing, (Sabu) Peter and Pearl Ogden 1992, *From humpy to homestead: The biography of Sabu,* Pearl Ogden, Darwin.

Smith, Alice [Bilari], Anna Vitenberg and Loreen Brehaut 2002, *Under a Bilari tree I born: A story of Alice Bilari Smith,* Fremantle Arts Centre Press, Fremantle.

Smith, Ollie and Diana Plater 2000, *Raging partners. Two worlds, one friendship,* Magabala Books, Broome.

Somerville, Margaret, Marie Dundas et al. 1994, *The sun dancin': People and place in Coonabarabran,* Aboriginal Studies Press, Canberra.

Sullivan, Jack and Bruce Shaw 1983, *Banggaiyerri: The story of Jack Sullivan as told to Bruce Shaw,* AIAS, Canberra.

Sykes, Roberta (ed) 1993, *Murawina: Australian women of high achievement,* Doubleday, Sydney.

—— 1997, *Snake cradle,* Allen & Unwin, Crows Nest.

—— 1998, *Snake dancing,* Allen & Unwin, Crows Nest.

—— 2000, *Snake circle,* Allen & Unwin, Crows Nest.

—— 2001, *Snake dreaming: Autobiography of a black woman,* Allen & Unwin, Crows Nest.

Tatz, Colin and Keith McConnochie (eds) 1975, *Black viewpoints. The Aboriginal experience.* Australia and New Zealand Book Co., Sydney.

Taylor, Alf 2001, *Long time now: Stories of the Dreamtime, the here and now,* Magabala Books, Broome.

Thaiday, Willie 1981, *Under the act,* N.Q. Black Publishing, Townsville.

Thancoupie and Ulli Beier 1988, *I keep my head above my shoulders, and I try to keep him strong and high,* Long Water.

Thomson, Judy 1989, *Reaching back, Queensland Aboriginal people recall early days at Yarrabah Mission,* Aboriginal Studies Press, Canberra.

Tovey, Noel 2004, *Little black bastard: A story of survival,* Hodder Headline, Sydney.

Tucker, Margaret and Kim Beazley 1977, *If everyone cared: Autobiography,* Ure Smith, Sydney.

Unaipon, David 1951, *My life story,* Aborigines Friends Association, Melbourne.

Vaarzon-Morel, Petronella, Molly Nungarrayi et al. 1995, *Warlpiri karnta karnta-kurlangu yimi* (Warlpiri women's voices: our lives our history), IAD Press, Alice Springs.

Walgar, Monty and Cloud Shabalah 1999, *Jinangga: On my tracks,* Magabala Books, Broome.

Walker, Della and Tina Coutts 1989, *Me and you: The life story of Della Walker,* Aboriginal Studies Press, Canberra.

Ward, Glenyse 1987, *Wandering Girl,* Magabala Books, Broome.

—— 1991, *Unna You Fullas,* Magabala Books, Broome.

White, Isobel and Betty Meehan 1985, *Fighters and singers: The lives of some Australian Aboriginal women,* Allen & Unwin, Sydney.

West, Ida 1984, *Pride Against prejudice: Reminiscences of a Tasmanian Aborigine,* Aboriginal Studies Press, Canberra.

Williams, Magdalene and Pat Torres 1999, *Ngay janijirr ngank: This is my word,* Magabala Books, Broome.

Wilson, Dulcie 1998, *The cost of crossing bridges,* Small Poppies Publishing, Mitcham.

Wilson, Garnet Ian and Anne Bartlett 2004, *The chairman: The story of Garnett Ian Wilson,* Australian Scholarly Publishing, Melbourne.

Woodrow, Marjorie 1990, *One of the Lost Generation,* Marjorie Woodrow, Narromine.

Bibliography of published Indigenous biographies

Anderson, Barbara 1994, *Think before you judge,* Barbara Anderson, Frankston.

Bell, Jeanie 1997, *Talking About Celia: Community and family memories of Celia Smith*, University of Queensland Press, St Lucia.

Chesson, Keith 1988, *Jack Davis: A life-story,* Dent, Melbourne.

Chittick, Lee and Terry Fox 1997, *Travelling with Percy: A South Coast journey,* Aboriginal Studies Press, Canberra.

Chryssides, Helen 1993, *Local heroes,* Collins Dove, North Blackburn.

Coe, Mary and Isabell Coe 1986, *Windradyne: A Wiradjuri Koorie,* Blackbooks, Glebe.

Crombie, Eileen [Unkari] 2003, *He was a South Australian film star: My life with Billy Pepper,* Nyiri Publications, Murray Bridge.

Edmund, Mabel 1996, *Hello, Johnny!: Stories of my Aboriginal and South Sea Islander family.* Central Queensland University Press, Rockhampton.

Goolagong Cawley, Evonne and Phil Jarrat 1993, *Home!: The Evonne Goolagong story.* Simon & Schuster, East Roseville.

Huggins, Rita and Jackie Huggins 1994, *Auntie Rita,* Aboriginal Studies Press, Canberra.

Langford, Ginibi 1999, *Haunted by the past,* Allen & Unwin, St Leonards.

Mabo, Koiki Edward and Noel Loos 1996, *Edward Koiki Mabo: His life and struggle for land rights,* University of Queensland Press, St Lucia.

Moran, Rod 1995, *Icon of the north: The legend of Tom Gray,* Access Press, Northbridge.

Morgan, Sally 1989, *Wanamurraganya: The story of Jack McPhee,* Fremantle Arts Centre Press, Fremantle.

Morgan, Sally and Barbara Ker Wilson 1990c, *Arthur Corunna's story,* Fremantle Arts Centre Press, Fremantle.

Onus, Lin, Michael Eather, Margo Neale et al. 2000, *Urban dingo: The art and life of Lin Onus, 1948–1996,* Craftsman House in association with the Queensland Art Gallery, South Brisbane.

Pepper, Phillip 1980, *You are what you make yourself to be: The story of a Victorian Aboriginal family 1842–1980,* Hyland House, Melbourne.

Pilkington, Doris [Nugi Garimara] 1996, *Follow the rabbit-proof fence,* University of Queensland Press, St Lucia.

Prior, Renarta 1993, *Straight from the Yudaman's mouth: The life story of Peter Prior before, during and after Robert Curry days, never told before,* Department of History and Politics, James Cook University, Townsville.

Riley, Linette and Riley, Samantha 2001, *The life of Riley,* Random House, Milsons Point.

Rosser, Bill 1985, *Dreamtime nightmares: Biographies of Aborigines under the Queensland Aborigines Act,* Australian Institute of Aboriginal Studies, Canberra.

Russell, Lynette 2002, *A little bird told me: Family secrets, necessary lies,* Allen & Unwin, Crows Nest.

van den Berg, Rosemary 1994, *No options, no choice! The Moore River experience: My father, Thomas Corbett, an Aboriginal half-caste*, Magabala Books, Broome.

Willmot, Eric Paul 1987, *Pemulwuy, the rainbow warrior*, Weldons, McMahons Point.

Wilson, Graham 1989, *Pilbara bushman: The life experience of W. Dunn*, Hesperian Press, Victoria Park.

Wood, Roma 1995, *The young soldier from the Goldfields*, Hesperian Press, Carlisle.

Wright, Edie 2001, *Full circle: From mission to community – A family story*, Fremantle Arts Centre Press, Fremantle.

Wyllie, Diana 2004, *Dolly Dalrymple*, Diana Wyllie, Childers.

'Bulman oral history series'

13 books published by Barunga Press, Katherine, 1995; co-authored by Gillian Cowlishaw.

References

Unpublished sources

Haag, Oliver 2006, 'Histories of Survival. Australian Indigenous Women's Auto/Biographies, Past and Present', Thesis (*Diplomarbeit*), University of Vienna, Vienna.

Watson, Christine 2001, '"My own eyes witness": Australian Aboriginal women's autobiographical narratives', PhD Thesis, University of Queensland, St Lucia.

Westphalen, Linda 2002, 'Deadly Lives: Palimpsests in Aboriginal Women's Life-Histories', PhD Thesis, Flinders University of South Australia, Adelaide.

Translated autobiographies (select)

Langford, Ruby 2000, *Bonalbon Musta Ruby,* Kääntöpiiri, Päivi Paapanen.

Morgan, Sally 1991, *Ich hörte den Vogel rufen. Roman,* Orlanda, Berlin.

—— 2002, *Wanamurraganya. Die Geschichte von Jack McPhee*, Unionsverlag, Zürich.

Pilkington, Doris [Nugi Garimara] 2003, *Long Walk Home: Die wahre Geschichte einer Flucht quer durch die Wüste Australiens*, Rowohlt, Reinbek.

Published sources

Anderson, Ian 2000, 'Post-colonial Dreaming at the end of the whitefella's 'millennium', in *The Oxford companion to Aboriginal art and culture,* Sylvia Kleinert and Margo Neale (eds), Oxford University Press, Melbourne: 427–437.

Anderson, Linda 2001, *Autobiography*, Routledge, London.

Angrosino, Michael 1989, *Documents of interaction: Biography, autobiography, and life history in social science perspective*, University of Florida Press, Gainesville.

Attwood, Bain and Fiona Magowan (eds) 2001, *Telling stories: Indigenous history and memory in Australia and New Zealand,* Bridget William Books, Wellington.

Blackburn, Regina 1980, 'In search of the black female self: African-American women's autobiographies and ethnicity', in *Women's autobiography: Essays in criticism*, Estelle Jelinek (ed), Indiana University Press, Bloomington, London: 133–148.

Brettel, Caroline 1997, 'Blurred Genres and Blended Voices: Life History, Biography, Autobiography, and the Auto/Ethnography of Women's Lives' in *Auto/ethnography: Rewriting the self and the social,* Deborah Reed-Danahay (ed), Berg, Oxford, London: 223–246.

Brewster, Anne 1996, *Reading Aboriginal women's autobiography,* Sydney University Press in association with Oxford University Press, South Melbourne.

Cooper, Judi et al. 2000, 'To tell my story. A study of practising professional Indigenous writers of Australia', Research report, Australia Council for the Arts, Sydney.

Duthil, Fanny 2006, *Histoire de femmes Aborigènes,* Presses Universitaires des France, Paris.

Ferrier, Carole 1992 [1988], 'Aboriginal women's narratives' in *Gender, politics and fiction: Twentieth century Australian women's novels,* Carole Ferrier (ed), University of Queensland Press, St Lucia: 200–218.

Geiger, Susan 1986, 'Women's life histories: method and content', *Signs* 11(2): 334–351.

Grossman, Michele (ed) 2003, *Blacklines: Contemporary critical writing by Indigenous Australians*, Melbourne University Press, Carlton.

Gusdorf, Georges 1980, 'Conditions and Limits of Autobiography', in *Autobiography: Essays theoretical and critical,* James Olney (ed), Princeton University Press, Princeton: 28–48.

Hamilton, Paula 1990, 'Inventing the self. Oral history as autobiography', *Hecate* 16(1/2): 128–133.

Heiss, Anita 2003, *Dhuuluu-Yala: To talk straight – Publishing Indigenous literature*, Aboriginal Studies Press, Canberra.

Hetherington, Isabella 1929, *Aboriginal queen of sacred song: Her life story*, Saxton & Buckie, Melbourne.

Jones, Jennifer 2003, 'Oodgeroo and her editors. The production of Stradbroke Dreamtime', *Journal of Australian Studies* 76: 47–56.

Koolmatrie, Wanda 1994, *My own sweet time*, Magabala Books, Broome.

Korporaal, Glenda 1990, *Project Octopus: The publishing and distribution ownership structure in the book industry, in Australia and internationally – Implications of the changes for Australian authors*, Australian Society of Authors, Redfern.

Langton, Marcia 1993, *'Well, I heard it on the radio and I saw it on the television…': An essay for the Australian Film Commission on the politics and aesthetics of filmmaking by and about Aboriginal people and things*, Australian Film Commission, Woolloomooloo.

Lockwood, Douglas 1962, *I, the Aboriginal*, Rigby, Adelaide.

McCooey, David 1996, *Artful histories: Modern Australian autobiography*, Cambridge University Press, Melbourne.

—— 2006, 'Going public: a decade of Australian autobiography', *Australian Book Review* 281, May 2006: 25–31.

McDonell, Margaret 2004, 'Protocols, political correctness and discomfort zones: Indigenous life writing and non-Indigenous editing', *Hecate* 30(1): 83–95.

Moreton-Robinson, Aileen 2002 [2000], Talkin' up to the white woman. Indigenous women and feminism, University of Queensland Press, St Lucia.

Mudrooroo 1990, *Writing from the fringe: A study of modern Aboriginal literature*, Hyland House, Melbourne.

Olijnyk Longley, Kateryna 1992, 'Autobiographical storytelling by Australian Aboriginal Women', in *De/Colonizing the Subject: The politics of gender in women's autobiography*, Sidonie Smith and Julia Watson (eds), University of Minnesota Press, Minneapolis: 370–384.

Phillips, Sandra 1997, 'Aboriginal women's writing today', *Hecate's Australian Women's Book Review* 9: 40–42.

Rowse, Tim 2004, 'Indigenous autobiography in Australia and the United States', *Australian Humanities Review* August-October, Accessed 25 June 2007, http://www.lib.latrobe.edu.au/AHR/archive/Issue-August-2004/rowse.html/

Rühl, Christiane 1997, *Die autobiographische Literatur australischer Aborigines-Frauen: Eine ethnologische Studie*, Lang, Frankfurt.

Schürmann-Zeggel, Heinz 1997, *Black Australian literature: A bibliography of fiction, poetry, drama, oral traditions and non-fiction, including critical commentary, 1900–1991*, Lang, Bern.

—— 1999, *Life Writing: Literarische Identitätskonstruktionen in schwarzaustralischen Autobiographien und Lebensgeschichten*, Lang, Bern.

Shaw, Bruce 1982–1982, 'Writing Aboriginal history for the East Kimberley: methodology and themes', *Oral History Association of Australia Journal* 5: 75–83.

Shoemaker, Adam 1995, 'Does paper stay put? The politics of Indigenous literature in Canada and Australia', in *Speaking positions: Aboriginality, gender and ethnicity in Australian cultural studies*, Penny van Toorn and David English (eds), Victoria University of Technology, Melbourne: 73–89.

Thonemann, Harold Eric 1949, *Tell the white man: The life story of an Aboriginal Lubra*, Collins, London.

Zierott, Nadja 2005, *Aboriginal women's narratives: Reclaiming identities*, Lit Verlag, Münster.

ENDNOTES

[1] I thank Peter Read for his feedback on the earlier version of this article. I am also grateful to Frances Peters-Little, Jackie Huggins, and Maria Preethi Srinivasan for expanding my thinking on Indigenous autobiography.

[2] This paper is based on a fuller empirical documentation, see Haag 2006. In stark contrast to articles and theses, little monographic literature addresses Indigenous (Australian) autobiography. Brewster 1996 is hitherto the only Australian-originated book entirely devoted to the topic. Other books, such as McCooey 1996, Attwood and Magowan 2001, and Grossman 2003 deal only partially with *published* Indigenous autobiographies. See Rowse 2004 for an assessment of this literature.

[3] Production-Authorship refers to the relation between single- and co-authored items.

[4] This study uses a plenitude of interviews conducted with Indigenous writers. See Heiss 2003: 26.

[5] The current definition of an Indigenous person is threefold: descent, self-identification, and community acceptance. See Langton 1993: 29.

[6] This includes Koolmatrie/Carmen and Mudrooroo, but not Sykes. Koolmatrie 1994 is a forged Indigenous woman's autobiography. Heiss 2003: 8-9 does not include Sykes' and Mudrooroo's books in her bibliography. I include Sykes' with a special annotation because the debates surrounding Sykes are not clear-cut.

[7] Hetherington 1929; Thonemann 1949; Lockwood 1962.

[8] Due to length restrictions, I cannot reference all these cases. For a fuller survey, see Haag 2006: 14-15. A few examples should suffice. For *fiction*, see Ferrier 1992; for *lifestory*, see Phillips 1997: 40.

[9] There is no consistent definition and usage of these genres in international scholarship. Often, life story and oral history are understood as an account of select life experiences. See Brettel 1997: 224, 227.

Hamilton 1990, however, regards oral history as a form of autobiography. Life history in turn is often seen as an 'as told to story'. See Angrosino 1989: 3; Geiger 1986: 336. For a discussion of these terms in the Australian context, see Shaw 1982-1983.

[10] See Rowse 2004; Brewster 1996; Watson 2001: 12-17.

[11] See Moreton-Robinson 2002: 1, 16.

[12] See Westphalen 2002: 12-13, 22, 29-31, 73, 78-88, 105, 227-228.

[13] See Mudrooroo 1990: 14-15, 149, 158-161, 163.

[14] See Gusdorf 1980: 29-30.

[15] See Anderson 2001: 86; Blackburn 1980: 133-134.

[16] These are 13 booklets (between seven and 19 pages in length), all published in 1995 by Barunga Press. They are transcribed and co-authored by Cowlishaw. Including them would falsify the statistics due to their arithmetic extremes (that is, their shortness and the circumstance of their having been published by the same press within a group project).

[17] Most bibliographies are unpublished, fragmentary, or dated. Here, I can reference only a few: Heiss 2003: 222-228; Watson 2001: 242-250; Schürmann-Zeggel 1997: 131-155.

[18] Unless otherwise indicated, the findings are taken from the extended bibliography.

[19] This survey is based upon the responses of 215 Indigenous writers. It shows women dominating most genres, including family history and academic writings. See Cooper et al. 2000: 3, 12, 42.

[20] For this policy, see Anderson 2000: 431-432. Rowse 2004 discusses the usefulness of a periodisation of Indigenous autobiographies along the policies towards Indigenous peoples.

[21] See Jones 2003; McDonell 2004.

[22] See Morgan 1987; Nannup et al. 1992; Huggins and Huggins 1994.

[23] See Brewster 1996: 7; Olijnyk Longley 1992: 376-377.

[24] See Shoemaker 1995: 75.

[25] This is the case not only with Indigenous autobiography but also with Australian non-fictional writing in general that has amassed throughout the last decades. Consequently, Indigenous autobiography should not be treated as an isolated phenomenon. See McCooey 2006: 26; Korporaal 1990: 12-13.

[26] Statistically, the third of the three major Indigenous presses, IAD Press, including its imprint Jukurrpa Books, has not been decisive as regards the autobiographical genre. For a good overview of publishers, see Heiss 2003: 51-65.

[27] Morgan 1987.

[28] See Rühl 1997; Schürmann-Zeggel 1999; Zierott 2005; Duthil 2006.

[29] See Morgan 1991.

[30] See Morgan 2002.

[31] See Langford 2000.

[32] See Pilkington 2003.

A path of words: the reception of autobiographical Australian Aboriginal writing in Italy

Francesca Di Blasio

To the Memory of my Father Luigi

The trodden paths, and new paths for the future

The words of Indigenous Australian women took me to Australia several years ago, and one could, therefore, take my title literally, and say that I reached this wondrous continent by following 'a path of words'. However, being fully aware of the fact that 'the syllables / on the page are not / the land beneath the name', as Patricia Sykes puts it, I knew I had to see the *land*.[1] When I did see it, I had the extraordinary good fortune of meeting Jackie Huggins, whose works I had read, and whom I now consider my 'guiding light' in my journey through Aboriginal literature.

I started studying Aboriginal women's autobiographies in 1999 and they remain one of the main interests in my research activity. My work in this area is obviously situated in one or more specific cultural and political contexts, primarily in the Italian contemporary ambit, where my immediate audiences are my students, colleagues and friends. I also intend my activity as a dialogue with colleagues and friends in the antipodes, that is, in Australia. From this position, in the pages that follow, I will provide an account of the state of the reception of Aboriginal literature in Italy today, in areas that include translation, publishing and the academic community.

Creating an Italian audience through translation, publishing and academic discourse

In the Italian context very few Aboriginal texts are known, because they are not translated and disseminated by Italian publishers. Among those one is Sally Morgan's bestseller *My place*, translated as *La mia Australia*[2] [My Australia], a title echoing Karen Blixen's Italian edition of *Out of Africa* translated as *La mia Africa*.[3] Market strategies here clearly overlook the political and epistemological differences among texts which relate to very different contexts, and are spoken from widely different, and even essentially antithetical perspectives.

While Sally Morgan's book is easily found in Italian bookshops, other translated texts, which I deem very interesting and valuable, are quite rare or virtually non-existent. Paradoxically, Mudrooroo is considered 'an Aboriginal writer' in

Italy, while his standing as an Indigenous author is essentially denied in Australia. His work *Wild cat falling*, *Gatto Selvaggio cade*, was translated into Italian as part of the emerging Indigenous canon.[4] Even more frustratingly, the fake Aboriginal world created by Marlo Morgan in *Mutant message down under* [in Italian, *E venne chiamata due cuori*] is very popular, and it is difficult to convince people that Marlo Morgan's fiction is not 'Aboriginal literature' by any means.[5]

Clearly in the mainstream Italian cultural world there is much to be done in terms of wider, deeper, and better knowledge and circulation of Australian Aboriginal literature, while other forms of art such as music, visual art and cinema[6] have in general a wider recognition, although often in a stereotypical way. The notion that dot painting and didgeridoo are *all* the 'Aboriginal art' that exists is fairly common. In this respect it is interesting to witness the reception of a volume on Aboriginal art edited by myself and Franca Tamisari.[7] The text includes contributions by several Aboriginal artists, including Fiona Foley and Jenny Fraser and is published in Italian in order to inform a wide Italian audience about the vitality of Aboriginal art in the realm of visual arts, music, literature and film. It offers an overview of the complexity of Indigenous creativity in Australia and usually provokes surprise in the Italian reader, as it is meant to shatter commonplace perceptions of Aboriginal culture as exclusively 'traditional', 'timeless' and unchanging, by focusing on the prominent 'urban' dimension of contemporary Indigenous art in painting, multimedia installations, autobiographical writing, poetry, cinema and music.

In Italian university curricula, Australian Aboriginal fiction, poetry and drama are uncommon. Anthropological and historical studies are more widespread, and in this respect the University of Venice has a leading role. As far as literature is concerned, apart from some universities where academics have occasionally shown some kind of interest (for example, the Universities of Padua and Lecce), the Indigenous literature of Australia is presented generically as the problematic 'post-colonial literature', and is not in any case thoroughly examined as a specific cultural phenomenon. The University of Trento is an interesting exception, since in the last few years the study of Aboriginal literature has become a relevant curricular activity. Indeed, I taught three courses for our PhD students specifically on Aboriginal literature, focusing in particular on autobiographical writing. The reception of the courses has been very positive. The students have shown great interest and were very excited by the topic. A relevant and meaningful feature of this positive reception is again the element of surprise: students are always very surprised, and shocked when learning about Australian contemporary history through Aboriginal literature.

Although at undergraduate level curricula do not involve Australian Aboriginal literature institutionally, several of our undergraduate and graduate students show interest in this kind of literary production. Some wrote their final dissertation on the topics 'Australia and Aboriginal culture'; '"While the stories came out of his eyes and nestled among the coals": Archie Weller's *Pension day* and Australian Aboriginal literature'; 'Aboriginal culture and its expression in women's autobiographical writing'; '"Murries speak, not migloos": Melissa Lucashenko's *Steam pigs* and Australian Aboriginal literature'; '*Follow the rabbit-proof fence*: a reading'.

When I discuss literary works, I invite my students to ponder on the fact that although Australian Indigenous texts do not belong to our cultural traditions, they can, nonetheless, be studied and understood with the same means we employ when reading Italian, French, German or British authors, because literature is an intrinsically trans-cultural practice. This means that the criteria according to which we judge these literary works are always at least double: at one level they are valuable because they convey a political message which needs to be uttered and to be heard; at another level, they must be judged on their relevance in the realm of 'world literature', that is, for their artistic merit. Of course such 'merit' is always relative to the community of readers and their times, so that while all readers may perceive the political message (and accept it or refuse it for political reasons, but the message is indisputable for all of them), not all readers would be prepared to grant the same artistic value to a specific novel or poem. For example, Dr Johnson despised the metaphysical poets and they had to wait for TS Eliot to be fully valorised.

The hermeneutical instruments of my readings of autobiographical Aboriginal writing range from the philosophy of Deleuze and Heidegger, to the works of bell hooks and Audre Lorde, in a dialogic dimension which is intended to be inter-cultural and cross-cultural. In my interpretative activity, I also try to foreground the ethical and political dimension of literature, bearing in mind Lisa Bellear's words: 'Hold me sister / I need your strength / got to keep believing / that somewhere someone / cares'.[8] What follows is to say that *here*, but also elsewhere, we and others, *do* care.

Indigenous autobiography as/(is) literature

Reading Indigenous autobiographical writing *as* literature is a challenging and rewarding activity. The recent debate over the literary canon has produced a widespread, new awareness of what I would now call the 'literature of identity', be it ethnic, gender, or class oriented. In this sense, researching Aboriginal women's writings is an essentially political activity, concerning, as it does, the representations of both cultural and social difference. Yet it is more than that: a number of autobiographies by Indigenous women whose stories and whose literary status is widely different, share common roots and a common struggle to represent the bond to their own land and culture as marks of authentic selfhood, and constitute at the same time a precise literary phenomenon.

Starting from my previous investigations in the field of the gaze and literature, and specifically on the gaze on/of women in biographical and autobiographical writings,[9] I will now explore some hybrid autobiographical narratives[10] by Aboriginal women whose stories deserve to gain visibility in the context of a belated, but growing interest in ethnic studies, in particular, three works which have appeared over a little less than a decade, between 1994 and 2002. They are Rita and Jackie Huggins' *Auntie Rita*, Ruth Hegarty's *Is that you Ruthie?*, and Nugi Garimara's *Under the Wintamarra tree*.[11] These writers aim at articulating their own experience in the Australian context of the 1920s, and up to the 1960s. Their task in contemporary culture is that of achieving a new recognition of their formerly suppressed and denied 'indigenality'. The political circumstances in which these women grew up did not allow sufficient cultural space to express themselves fully as Indigenous subjects, and furthermore prevented their cultural and political recognition. Writing helps them recover from such cultural loss of visibility, and to claim back a history that was either entirely obscured, or largely misrepresented by government bureaucrats in racist and patronising narratives and reports. These stories are *both* family memoirs and Australian history, their status is therefore inevitably a hybrid condition between literary narrative and historiography.

Rita and Jackie Huggins' words are exemplary in defining the nature and purpose of these autobiographies:

> We want the book [*Auntie Rita*] to be a record for my children and their children and other members of my family. Hopefully it will speak to other people, too, including those white people who want to know what the story looks like from the Aboriginal side.[12]

Besides their purpose, and their private and public form of address, we should note Rita Huggins' statement: 'These are my own recollections. I speak only for myself and not how others would expect me to speak'.[13] She intends to tell her story in her own voice, a sure sign of a recovered identity and self confidence, but also an invitation to the reader to place her utterance in the context of other voices, which can be different, and perhaps even antagonistic.

Whether the so called 'literature of identity' represents a specific literary genre is a question that depends on one's definition of genre, either in terms of theme or in any other terms (including style, structure, chronotope).[14] As I have said above, the recent debate over the literary canon, and the necessity of its expansion beyond traditional parameters of 'high literature', eurocentric and male categories certainly favours a new apprehension of literary forms that are concerned with the issues of race, gender, class and language.

'My eyes fix on a face / a time / a space':[15] some considerations on time and space

One of the main topics in Indigenous autobiographical narratives is the relevance of the issue of the relationship of the protagonists and narrators with the land.[16] This implies an articulation of the category of 'space', which in the literary chronotope is inextricably linked to 'time'. In Rita Huggins' *Auntie Rita*, the relationship with the land is linked to the trauma of deportation. Her story recalls that 'land' and 'home' have a strong and specific sense in Aboriginal consciousness. Despite the lacerating experience of deportation, which Rita Huggins underwent at a very young age, the land remains for her a bedrock of Indigenous existence: 'It will always be home, the place I belong to'.[17] The recollection of the times that Rita had spent in harmony with the wilderness of the bush, and within her clan, gives an edenic overtone to the representation of the wildest of territories, recalling Bakhtin's definition of idyllic landscapes and times.[18] This does not mean that the life in the bush was easy and smooth, we know that Indigenous people often did suffer severe hardship, but in this particular case the landscape is pictured as edenic because it implies the symbolic connotation of a time of past childood happiness. Huggins feels and evokes the call of this 'paradise lost', and she establishes an ideal and vital connection with her cultural past, which goes back to times immemorial:

> Our people lived in this land since the time began. In our land are waterfalls, waterholes and creeks where we swam and where the older people fished. Our mob always seemed cool, even on the hottest days, because the country was like an oasis. There were huge king ferns. I believe they have been described as living fossils because their form has not changed for thousand of years.[19]

The political consequences of this type of literature are immediately obvious; less obvious and more subtle are its epistemological implications. The Aboriginal gaze on the land has a specificity that must be discerned before and beyond the problem of legal rights. The land as space to conquer, or the land as commodity, that is the land in the gaze of the colonisers, fails to account for the mythical perception of the land as a sacred and vital space, an entity, a force, and even a human condition, that is the land in the Aboriginal gaze. Cultural difference is fully at stake in the different epistemological perspectives, which can provide, when made visible, the opportunity of a true cultural encounter and exchange. I believe that we need to look at Aboriginal writings in order to create a dialogical return of the gaze. Our reading of these texts cannot be a merely voyeuristic look at something outside, and a sad reduction of other utterances to fashionable 'exotism' or 'orientalism'. Rita Huggins' story is probably the most significant because the most 'typical' in Lukács' sense.[20] In fact, it reflects the experience of most Aboriginal people in the twentieth century, whose lives were closely intertwined, and always painfully so, with the history of the Australian government policies towards Indigenous people.

Likewise, Ruth Hegarty's *Is that you Ruthie?* is the representation of an experience that is not exclusively personal, but rather the common lot of Aboriginal women, victimised by a system created by the invaders, and by its disruptive effect on a millennial culture. Hegarty's book is both the story of a 'dormitory girl' and a historical document on the minute organisation of the government-established Indigenous settlements, and in particular of the sections that were reserved for the children when they were separated from their families and their single mothers.

The story seems to freeze, at a certain point, significantly when the protagonist comes of age at 21, and it begins to revolve around a repetitive and impersonal destiny:

> I was twenty-one when I had my second child. [...] I was back to the babies dormitory. [...] 'Can you see the pattern continuing?' I asked myself. It was frightening, and we were all becoming victims of the system and moving back to where most of us started from. Our children, through no fault of their own, could end up making the same journey as we made, and achieving nothing. Caught in the same victim trap, without the ability to fulfil their dreams and goals.[21]

In this narrative, and in others of this kind, Indigenous people's philosophical categories, that is the conception of time and space that, in Heidegger's sense, are the 'original structures' of our human 'being in the world', are totally obscured and repressed. Aboriginal time and space are completely shattered by the disruptive force of an alien gaze, which gives shape to the real in forms that become uncontrollable by Indigenous people. In Hegarty's narrative what was to be 'just a little while' in the camp, due to an economic crisis imported by the colonisers, turns out to be a repeated expropriation of self and culture, across different Aborigines generations. Not surprisingly, the unconfined space of life in the bush exists only in Hegarty's mother's memory, since the space the daughter experiences is limited by barbed wire or by bureaucratic provisions that send her to specific, and still confined places outside the camp.[22]

Hegarty's decision to articulate the story of her Aboriginal identity in a novel shows her desire to commit it to the memory of readers. Her writing is clearly meant as a re-appropriation and redemption. In fact, through her mother's accounts, she is able to re-appropriate times and spaces that are now present only in cultural memory, and despite this fact, or perhaps precisely because of this, she writes her story so that it may become a vehicle of shared and living cultural heritage.

'I know that I don't speak the language of my ancestors':[23] the role of language

Nugi Garimara's *Under the Wintamarra tree* is a novel about the return to one's origins, after the experience of deportation and alienation imposed on the natives by colonial rule in Australia. Nugi Garimara's ancestors, belonging to the Mardu tribes of Western Australia, were driven away from their territory in the desert and forced into the 'white' settlements at its fringe. Garimara's mother, Molly, was taken away from her family and place, and regimented into Moore River Native Settlement, from which she eventually escaped, with two young girls, thus accomplishing an unbelievable counter-migration and returning to her homeland. This story is told in *Follow the rabbit-proof fence*, a narrative which has gained international reputation as the film, *Rabbit-Proof Fence*, directed by Phillip Noyce in 2002.[24] *Under the Wintamarra tree* tells a story which is once again a vivid representation of the same cruel destiny for several generations of Australian Indigenous people, and of their resilient spirit of rebellion and survival. The articulation of Aboriginal identity in its deep complexity is exquisitely represented in the following passage which highlights the central role of language in shaping cultural and ethnic identity:

> When the sun was high and the heat uncomfortable, the Mardudjara women returned to camp, their *wirnis* filled with *wamula*. Tjirama Garimara and his sons arrived with a cooked kangaroo and a couple of *bungarras* to add to their collection. After the meal of kangaroo meat, *bungarra* and *wamula* everyone rested, as was the custom.
>
> 'Who's that?' old Bambaru Banaka asked.
>
> 'I don't know, I can't see them clearly yet,' her husband Tjirama replied. As the group came closer, he recognised them. 'It's old man Bayuka, my brother, and his family,' he announced happily. As his family watched the visitors approach they could not know this meeting would lead to a decision that would change their lives forever.
>
> Bayuka and his family were on their way to Jigalong, the government depot for the maintenance teams that travelled up and down the rabbit-proof fence.
>
> Bayuka informed them that everything had run out in their country. There was no food left north of the river. 'We're all starving up there.'
>
> Many clans in the region were migrating to Jigalong because their traditional food sources were disappearing. They were coming to depend on the Government rations from the depot.[25]

The passage opens the novel and tells about an experience of forced migration and of uprooting from the land which is the beginning of the loss of original identity. From here stems the need of the protagonist of this *Bildungsroman* of recovering the past, after innumerable hardships and suffering. The symbol of the wintamarra tree, under which her mother gave birth to her, has sacral connotations and literally represents the tree of life.

The colloquial and immediate tone of the passage, which is typical of most Aboriginal autobiographical writings, is a precise and self-conscious literary style, which is far from being assimilable to any form of 'primitivism'. A supposed 'primitivism' in Aboriginal writings and art has often been presented as a mark of 'anthropological authenticity'; on the contrary, it actually represents the basis of too many aberrant readings of Aboriginal texts. Garimara's text demonstrates that these readings are offensively oversimplified and epistemologically wrong, since it is a text that is highly conscious of its literary devices. Let us consider, for example, the inclusion of many words in an Aboriginal language (*wirnis*, *wamula*, *bungarras*). These words are obscure for most 'western' readers, and they both signal and provoke a sense of exclusion of the invaders, not for the relevance of their meanings (they probably have their correspondence in botanical, scientific words in English), but at a symbolic level. The use of such phrases, in this and other Indigenous texts, invite a perception of cultural difference and a salutary resistance to easy appropriations. 'Western' readers are not part of the community represented in the novel, and language is the deliberate instrument of this exclusion. This evokes Gilles Deleuze and Felix Guattari's concept of 'minor language', that is a language which inscribes in the hegemonic idiom identity marks which are able to obscure commonplace meaning, and thus derail mainstream discourse.[26] Deleuze and Guattari define Kafka's writing as 'a minor literature', that is a literature that deviates from the hegemonic language, but belongs to a community and becomes irrevocably political. It goes without saying that 'minority' here does not mean that the language or literature is simply non-canonical or non-canonised. This is the current use of the term 'minority', that is minority as a synonym of 'marginality'. I do not deny that Aboriginal literature has often been relegated to such a marginal cultural space. However, what I am suggesting is quite another idea involving 'minority' in a specific philosophical sense. The fact that Deleuze and Guattari call 'minor' the language and literature of a canonised and celebrated author like Kafka illustrates the meaning of the term in their discourse as being different from 'marginal' or 'less important'. As already stated, 'minor literature' is for them always collective, deterritorialising, and directly political. The issue is not about canonicity but about the capacity of such literature to compel re-thinking about both politics and literature.

In many Aboriginal novels, Indigenous language skillfully obliterates the linearity of English, in its refusal to use a hegemonic language when presenting a subaltern condition. This linguistic strategy once again accounts for the intrinsic complexity of Indigenous utterances, and foregrounds the necessity of a non-naive dialogic attitude, that is a confrontation with alterity within a cultural awareness of difference.

In the previous pages I have advocated a 'return of the gaze' between Aboriginal and Italian culture. A lot still needs to be done to disseminate the knowledge of Aboriginal literature and art in Italy, but the initial work carried out so far, and here illustrated, seems to be promising a wider understanding and deeper appreciation of the meaning and value of Indigenous culture beyond Anglophone cultures.

References

Bakhtin, Mikhail 1981, *The dialogic imagination: Four essays*, Michael Holquist (ed), University of Texas Press, Austin.

—— 1997, *Estetica e romanzo*, Einaudi, Torino.

Bellear, Lisa 1996, *Dreaming in urban areas*, University of Queensland Press, St Lucia.

Blixen, Karen 1954, *Out of Africa*, Penguin, Hammondsworth. Italian edition 1986, *La mia Africa*, Feltrinelli, Milano.

Deleuze, Gilles and Felix Guattari 1975, *Kafka*, Minuit, Paris. English edition 1986, *Kafka: Toward a Minor Literature*, University of Minnesota Press, Minneapolis.

Di Blasio, Francesca 2001, *Teoria e pratiche dello sguardo: Percorsi nella letteratura inglese e americana*, Sestante, Bergamo.

—— 2003, 'Riti e passaggi in My Place di Sally Morgan', in *Rites of Passage, Atti del XX Convegno dell'Associazione Italiana di Anglistica*, C Nocera, G Persico, R Portale (eds), Rubbettino, Soveria Mannelli: 75–85.

—— 2005b, 'Nativeness and/as otherness: the female gaze in autobiographical Aboriginal Writings', in *Cross-cultural encounters: Identity, gender, representation*, Marc Silver, Giovanna Buonanno (eds), Officina Edizioni, Roma: 97–108.

—— 2005, *The pelican and the Wintamarra tree: Voci della letteratura Aborigena Australiana*, Collana Labirinti, Università di Trento, Trento.

—— 2006, 'Moving to a strange place: spazio coloniale e spazio esistenziale nella letturatura aborigena australiana', in *Spazi/o: Teoria, rappresentazione, lettura*, Francesca Di Blasio and Carla Locatelli (eds), Collana Labirinti, Università di Trento, Trento: 195–209.

—— 2006b, '"Post-Colonial – NOT!": defining Aboriginality in contemporary/(post-?)colonial Australia', in *Postcolonial studies: Changing perceptions*, Oriana Palusci (ed), Collana Labirinti, Università di Trento, Trento: 275–287.

Garimara, Nugi /Doris Pilkington 1996, *Follow the rabbit-proof fence,* University of Queensland Press, St Lucia.

—— 2002, *Under the Wintamarra tree,* University of Queensland Press, St Lucia.

Hegarty, Ruth 1999, *Is that you, Ruthie?,* University of Queensland Press, St Lucia.

Heiss, Anita 2007, *I'm not racist, but…: A collection of social observations,* Salt, Cambridge.

Huggins, Rita and Jackie Huggins 1994, *Auntie Rita,* Aboriginal Studies Press, Canberra.

Locatelli, Carla 2000, 'Passaggi obbligati: la differenza (auto)biografica come politica co(n)testuale', in *Co(n)texts: Implicazioni testuali,* Carla Locatelli (ed), Collana Labirinti, Università di Trento, Trento: 151–196.

—— 2002, 'Lo sguardo autobiografico e l'ignoto della scrittura', in *Sguardo e raffigurazione,* Anna D'Elia (ed), Adriatica Editrice, Bari: 154–124.

Lukács, György 1969, *The historical novel,* Penguin, Harmondsworth.

Morgan, Marlo c1994, *Mutant message down under,* Harper Collins Publishers, New York. Italian edition 1998, *E venne chiamata due cuori,* It. Transl. Maria Barbara, Sonzogno, Milano.

Morgan, Sally 1998, *La mia Australia,* Teoria, Napoli.

Mudrooroo 2003, *Gatto Selvaggio Cade,* It. transl. Lorenzo Perrona, Le Lettere, Firenze.

Sykes, Patricia 2005, *Modewarre: Home ground,* Spinifex Press, Melbourne.

Tamisari, Franca 1999, 'L'immagine dell'orma. Della cosmogonia indigena australiana', *Quaderni di semantica,* XX(2): 281–310.

Tamisari, Franca and Francesca Di Blasio (eds) 2007, *La sfida dell'arte indigena australiana: Tradizione, innovazione, contemporaneità,* Jacabook, Milano.

Tuccio, Silvana (ed) 2002, *Sguardi australiani: Cortometraggi e registi che raccontano la metropoli e la lontananza,* Le Mani Editore, Recco.

ENDNOTES

[1] Sykes 2005: 5.

[2] Morgan 1998. A second edition of the novel has been published by Bompiani, one of the major Italian publishers, in 2000. On Morgan's book see Di Blasio 2003.

[3] Blixen 1954.

[4] Mudrooroo 2003.

[5] Morgan c1994.

[6] In this respect see, for example, the Film Festival *Sguardi australiani* [Australian perspectives] and its catalogue, Tuccio 2002.

[7] Tamisari and Di Blasio 2007.

[8] Bellear 1996: 23.

[9] Di Blasio 2001.

[10] On the concept of 'autobiography' and 'autobiographical gaze' see Carla Locatelli 2002, 2000.

[11] Huggins and Huggins 1994; Hegarty 1999; Garimara 2002. I have discussed them elsewhere. See Di Blasio 2005, 2005b, 2006b.

[12] Huggins and Huggins 1994: 1.

[13] Huggins and Huggins 1994: 1.

[14] Bakhtin 1981.

[15] Heiss 2007: 31.

[16] Tamisari 1999.

[17] Huggins and Huggins 1994: 7.

[18] Bakhtin 1997.

[19] Huggins and Huggins 1994: 7.

[20] Lukács 1969.

[21] Hegarty 1999: 128.

[22] For a more extensive discussion of the concept of 'space' in Indigenous literature see Di Blasio 2006.

[23] Heiss 2007: 39.

[24] Garimara 1996; Noyce, Phillip, *Rabbit-Proof Fence*, 89 min, Jabal Films Pty Ltd.

[25] Garimara 2002: 1–2, italics added.

[26] Deleuze and Guattari 1975.

Ethical approaches to teaching Aboriginal culture and literature in Spain

Susan Ballyn

The teaching of any subject, regardless of discipline, at whatever level of education, involves a teacher taking an ethical stance both towards the subject matter and the students. There has to be a commitment by the teacher to an application of what he or she believes to be the best, most honest, ethical approach in the classroom and to enable open constructive discussions among students. Furthermore, the ethics to which a teacher subscribes should, I believe, always be at the forefront of any teaching and clearly visible to the students. There is often discussion regarding the fact that at tertiary level there is room for little else other than cramming knowledge and preparing the individual to enter the labour market, to find their 'niche' as some call it. This is not so. And if it is so, then the educational system has lost its way and purpose. These are the crucial years when a young person will make many decisions which will have a lasting effect on both themselves and often their families. These are the years of putting to use the art of reasoning, of philosophic debate, of questioning the already learnt and opening horizons to new areas of thought and study. In short, of consolidating and grounding the individual, thus enabling him or her to take a responsible active role in society.

Although one tries to have an ethical base when teaching, my present concern with both did not actually crystallise until I began to teach Aboriginal culture and literature especially biography.

I was born and educated in England within a cultural background in which the British Empire and its history held the central role in what we learnt. Many of my generation will well remember the world map, which took prominent place in any classroom, with a proliferation of 'British' pink on it. Thus I was conditioned to conceptualise the world and its relationship to me in a very traditional British way. However, in my late teens I reversed the usual process of 'school to university' by going to live in Spain and have remained there ever since. I qualified as a secondary school teacher of English as a foreign language and worked in the private sector for several years before finally graduating in English at Barcelona University. It was here that the rest of my academic life was focused under the tutelage of my PhD supervisor, Doireann MacDermott, who had started 'Commonwealth Studies' at Barcelona in the 1960s. I became absorbed in studying Australian culture and literature, finally moving into the area of Postcolonial Studies, as it had then become, as a lecturer in the late 1980s. As Aboriginal culture formed part of three of the courses, I found myself questioning how I could actually teach this to Spanish students when I was neither Australian nor Aboriginal but British. It seemed to me that I was threefold removed from the subject I was going to teach. Did I in fact have an authoritative position from which I could actually approach the subject? It became quite clear to me then, that I had to work out some viable ethical approach which would allow me to open up Aboriginal culture and literature to students without academically re-colonising and perpetuating what I saw as the continued colonial situation in Australia with regard to its Indigenous people.

But what of my audience? Today the English Department has a fully developed postcolonial stream on its syllabus. To obtain a BA in English a student must undertake a four year undergraduate course. For first and second year students, 'An introduction to the Anglophone postcolonial world' is an obligatory course with modules on Africa, Australia, Canada, the Caribbean, India and New Zealand. The course is taught by various lecturers who cover the geographical areas of their expertise plus visiting lecturers. The set texts used in the course are looked at not so much from a theoretical literary point of view but rather as witnesses to and in depth studies of the social history and cultures of the nations concerned. For third and fourth year students each of these regions becomes a separate in depth optional subject, in the case of Australia titled 'The global village: the Pacific in film and literature'. The course takes Australia as its core and then moves out to compare and contrast with other Pacific nations, particularly New Zealand. At Postgraduate level we have a visiting Australian lecturer incorporated into our Masters course each year and there is also an online virtual Masters, independently run by the university, called 'The Asia Pacific region' in which Aboriginal Australia is part of a compulsory module in 'An introduction to the Pacific'. Of all the courses mentioned this is the only one taught in either Spanish or Catalan. The English Department teaches exclusively in English.

The bulk of the students come from Catalonia, an autonomous region with its own rich cultural heritage and language, and from the rest of Spain, often as part of the Seneca internal mobility programme. Other students are drawn from all parts of Europe under the European Erasmus Exchange scheme, from exchange programmes with North and South American universities and also from two Australian universities, La Trobe University and Southern Cross University. To date, Barcelona University has the largest number of Erasmus students in Spain. Increasingly and interestingly, we are now getting a small core of migrant students moving into tertiary education. Thus there is frequently a rich cultural diversity in the classes which often facilitates a range of cultural debates.

So what ethics can be applied in dealing with Aboriginal culture and texts in such a class? Students can be surprisingly Eurocentric in their outlook, frequently reading autobiographies as windows on a world which they look at and judge from a Euro-western-theoretical perspective, displaying a disturbing tendency to remain within the comfort zone of the European. This euro-centrism needs to be constantly challenged by questioning their innate assumptions regarding their own identity together with the place and role of Europe in the world. When talking about *Dreaming*, for example, students will, albeit unwittingly, use terms such as 'myth' or 'legend', taking for granted that western terminology can easily connote and equate to Aboriginal belief systems. A whole debate must ensue from this in which views and opinions must be discussed and challenged, preferably by the students themselves, in order to right this skewed look at indigenous belief systems across the world. An ideological and responsible repositioning has to take place if we are to understand Aboriginal culture to any degree.

Spain is in essence an ideal place to work. Very little historic revision of Spanish colonialism has actually taken place in Spanish schools. Therefore the classroom can become a dynamic space of colonial and postcolonial repositioning in terms of the students' own national history. Working within an already culturally and linguistic plural environment such as Catalonia, can often serve as the trampoline for debate on the relationship between Catalonia and Spain, spreading out to take on reconsiderations of the colonisation of South America and the important parallels that can be drawn between the two systems of colonial invasion and consequent physical and cultural genocide. A discussion of the invasion of Australia and its consequences together with the increasingly retrograde policies of Prime Minister John Howard in Aboriginal affairs can lead to an invigorating insight into where we are today when we look at the situation in Chiapas, or the dispossession caused by intense logging and burning in the Amazon. It is this wealth of cross cultural possibilities that makes the Spanish classroom an ideal place for debate, for mapping out the need for social awareness, tolerance and an attempt at understanding where we have and are going wrong and what we can do about it. A student in Barcelona need only look at the rapidly changing demographic composition of their own society to realise that being at a tertiary institution has to involve more than sitting in an ivory tower and debating within the walls of academia. My objective is to get them to become outwardly thinking individuals able and willing to take on a responsible role as world citizens.

Each year I sit with the new texts and films we are going to watch and begin an ongoing monologue about how I am going to deal with this material. Each year old and new problems pop up. I am coming at Aboriginal culture right from the outside, three times removed and only able to make short yearly visits to the country. While I can read unlimited sources at home there is, I believe, no substitute for being on the land, for developing a bond with it in my own peculiar way and, most importantly, for those long personal conversations of learning with others. Certainly a valuable amount can be done through constant email contact but it is in no way a substitute for being in the country, meeting people, and having doors, previously unknown to one, opened. However, 'teaching from the outside' does enable me to help the students not to fall into some of the pitfalls I myself may have encountered along my way.

Student reactions to the Aboriginal texts and films used in class surface very rapidly. They tend to home in on the Aboriginal work, especially autobiographies, because it is all new and, in their words, 'exciting' to them. This can be and often has been problematical, leading students to want to do all their term work on Aboriginal film and writing. While this is no bad thing, it can lead to an exoticisation of the Aboriginal, a 'recolonising' from a European reading/seeing perspective and on rare occasions to a deeply worrying paternalistic attitude. All of these tendencies have to be contained and redirected. A statement made by a student recently when reading a non-Aboriginal author that '[t]he book was not Australian literature because it was not authored by an Aboriginal and did not contain Aboriginal characters' is just the sort of remark which will lead to the debate as to how we should approach the texts and films, as to whether we as Europeans are in a position to categorise the material we are studying and finally to question the notion of the constant drive to categorise everything as we do in Europe.

I approach the Aboriginal texts/films within the European history of invasion, dispossession, genocide and on-going trauma. The students have access to a huge amount of electronic information in the form of articles, press links, reviews, journals and I impress upon them that any engagement with the work we are doing must move through a social-historical approach to a well documented analysis of current government intervention. As far as I am concerned any theoretical approach must wait.

Our first task, once the socio-historical background has been dealt with, is to attempt to come to the work with a clean slate. We need to *listen* if we are to understand, we need to realise that enabling ourselves to leap the cultural abyss that lies between us and Aboriginal culture, indeed that of any indigenous group around the world, has to be based on listening, absorbing, taking the texts away with us and thinking profoundly about what they are saying about themselves and us as outsiders. We must tread carefully across the bridge of cultural difference to establish a degree of intercultural understanding.

Respect, diffidence and, perhaps paradoxically, unencumbered positive engagement have become keywords in my approach. If we have listened to and understood as much as we can, then a responsible position of knowing can be reached. My own awareness of what I term 'responsible knowing' first surfaced on hearing Lauretta Ncobo speak to a crowded auditorium at Barcelona University many years ago. At the end of her talk there was a stunned silence. Eventually a student asked her what it was that she would wish us to take away from her talk. The reply was quick: 'You can never say you did not know!' Positive engagement with a culture signifies becoming proactive regarding that culture and the misconceptions that are so often bandied about, but always with an awareness that we can neither speak for the indigenous community concerned nor adopt a 'know it all' approach. We do not *know it all*, especially as outsiders, but what we *do know and understand* is what we can bring to bear on those who, for whatever reason, do not know. Television audiences in Spain are often offered documentaries about Aboriginal painting, dancing, traditional ways of life, but little or nothing comes across about contemporary art, urban environments, land rights or the political climate Aboriginal people are currently enduring. That is the arena where I would hope that students would indeed become proactive with what knowledge they have, not just with regard to Aboriginal culture, but across the board where injustice and lack of solidarity raises its head.

It may appear to the reader that what I am doing is throwing literary theory, social theory, *all* theory out of the window and merely indulging in a close reading of film and autobiographical and other texts. This is not actually the case, I believe that first we have to materialise, physicalise the text to later be able to approach in various theoretical ways. The theoretical approaches may be applied in term projects, in the electronic debating forum, in small group seminar work. I ask time and again: how can we use theory to come at a culture about which, initially, we know little or nothing? It seems to me that in coming to Aboriginal work from the very outside the text must be privileged over theory.

Multiple subjectivities: writing Duall's life as social biography

Kristyn Harman

The colonial archive is replete with accounts of the intimacies of life at the frontier in early New South Wales. In reading these records, it is readily apparent that the scribes who mentioned an Indigenous presence had a habit of situating such people at the periphery of colonial society. More often than not, Aboriginal people were cast as supporting actors to the white male leads valorised in accounts of early exploration and settlement. Despite their textual marginalisation, such archival records remain a rich resource for those wanting to appreciate more fully Indigenous contributions to early colonial New South Wales.

Reading archival records against the grain has in recent years been embraced as a practice that holds out the potential to resituate indigenes in more active roles, allowing an increasingly complex and nuanced picture of frontier life to emerge. At the same time, this practice raises a methodological issue as to how such lives might best be reinterpreted and represented for a present-day readership. Before discussing how I have dealt with this conundrum in a recently completed research project, let me set the scene with a brief illustrative example. The three anecdotes that follow are sourced from archival records describing a series of events that unfolded in New South Wales between 1814 and 1819. Their inter-relationship will be made evident shortly.

In 1814 a party of young men returned to an area to the west of Sydney known as the Cowpastures from an overland journey to a tract of country renamed Argyle by the settlers. One of the youthful companions had travelled across this landscape numerous times. Aged about 17, he was a local Dharawal man whose knowledge and relationships to country and people enabled the expeditionary party to traverse the landscape with confidence. One of the men accompanying him was Hamilton Hume. This journey has since been venerated as Hume's first voyage of 'discovery'.[1] At the time of the expeditionary party's return, the Cowpastures was afflicted by drought.[2] Rising tensions over competing land use practices were exacerbated by an influx of settlers that saw increasing numbers of Indigenous people displaced from their tracts of country. Other indigenes were seeking to negotiate some kind of accommodation with the newcomers. Conflict between settlers and Indigenous peoples escalated, reaching a crisis point in 1816. A report in the *Sydney Gazette* identified one of the local Indigenous people as a leader amongst his people, a man who 'excited and encouraged' others in 'committing various atrocious acts of robbery, depredation, and barbarity'.[3] Named on a list of 10 most wanted Aborigines circulated by Governor Macquarie, this leader was arrested by the military during a punitive expedition and sentenced to death.[4] A reprieve was granted, and he was instead transported to Van Diemen's Land as a convict sentenced to seven years banishment.[5] Three years later, in 1819, another of the many exploratory expeditions originating from the Cowpastures was co-ordinated by the colonial surgeon and administrator Charles Throsby, a man later celebrated as the first white person to negotiate a direct route from the Cowpastures to Bathurst. Indigenous guides and interpreters accompanied, and indeed led, Throsby just as they had Hume and other celebrated white explorers.[6] Following the successful completion of the journey, these Indigenous men were awarded brass breastplates and blankets for their services while Throsby and his white retinue received substantial land grants.[7]

These various colonial representations – the figure of the Indigenous guide on Hume's inaugural expedition, the resistance leader banished to Van Diemen's Land, and the recipient of a brass breastplate and blanket – converge in the body of a man known to the Cowpastures settlers as Duall or Dewal. The rapidly changing subject position allocated Duall by colonial scribes reflects the flux associated with life at the frontier as viewed from settlers' standpoints. Ambiguity is also evident in the range of variant spellings used to inscribe him into the colonial records. Ranging from Duall, Dual, and Doual to Dicall (the latter being a transcription error), careful reading of the contextual information within which these proper nouns are embedded is required in order to be sure that they refer to one and the same person. Writing around Duall's life has posed the challenge of identifying a methodology that allowed exploration and explication of some of the complexities and subtleties inherent in the network of colonial relations within which representations of Duall and other Indigenous convicts were embedded. This article elaborates some of the challenges faced in dealing with various diverse colonial representations of Duall as part of a wider project in which I have focused on Indigenous convicts transported from and within New South Wales during the first half of the nineteenth century.[8]

I am intrigued by 'histories from below'. This influenced me at the outset of this research project to imagine a process whereby it might be possible to recover the life stories of Indigenous convicts. It soon became apparent that, at best, one might anticipate catching the occasional glimpse of them as refracted through the lenses of nineteenth century colonial scribes. Duall, like other Indigenous convicts, was captured in the colonial records only at those moments where his life was considered remarkable in the original sense of the word. Remarks about him reflect those instances when his life events attracted colonial attention, whether favourable or unfavourable. Given that I can never know Duall or claim to be able to represent his lived experiences, it begs the question as to why I have proceeded with this particular project? The short answer is that while the colonial records reveal more about the people and society that compiled them than they do about Duall himself, the project is nevertheless important as the colonial forces that shaped this archive are the very same forces that impacted on Duall's lived experiences and shaped his destiny. In addition, as Blaze Kwaymullina recently pointed out, colonial policies and practices in the past have had lasting impacts on Aboriginal families who 'are still bearing the scars today'.[9] Given that 'the reality of the past [is] inescapably entwined in the present', it is necessary to engage with the past on its own terms in order to understand better its emanations in present-day Australia.[10]

The process of researching and writing Duall's life has not been without its temptations. Within the context of early colonial New South Wales the possibility of casting Duall solely in the role of Indigenous resistance fighter or leader holds a certain appeal. Over recent decades a number of other significant Indigenous figures have enjoyed a similar appellation that would not be inconsistent with elements of Duall's colonial career.[11] Such representations have also been contested. This was particularly evident in the ongoing debate between Keith Windschuttle and Naomi Parry during the 'history wars' over whether the Gai-marigal man Musquito was an 'outlaw … engaged in a minor crime wave' in 1820s Van Diemen's Land, or was instead a 'prisoner of war' when he was hanged in Hobart Town in 1824 at the onset of the Black War.[12] In any case, a greater understanding of Duall's importance as an historical actor has emerged through considering the range of subject positions he adopted, or was represented as adopting, at the colonial interface. In aiming to portray something of this complexity, I was inspired by Ian Clark's recent journal article in which he sought to reconcile varying depictions of the well-known Port Phillip personality Derrimut. Taking as his starting point the competing characterisations crafted by Massola, Christie, Christiansen, Griffiths and Barwick, Clark presented what might be termed a 'social biography' of Derrimut in which he highlighted the complex nature of this man's interactions both within colonial society and with Indigenous people. Clark's article is indicative of a shift in the historiography towards more nuanced approaches to the treatment of Indigenous subjects.[13]

When I began researching Duall's life and the lives of other Indigenous convicts I wanted the material uncovered about them to remain central. Rather than dispersing fragments of their recorded lives throughout my writing as pieces of 'evidence', I aimed to adopt a methodology that allowed the men's lives as represented in the archival materials to remain intact. This was intended both as a gesture of respect and to highlight the extent to which such men exercised agency at the colonial interface. The presentation of the research findings therefore became informed by social biography as a methodology, a practice best described as a confluence of biography and social history. In a nutshell, it means using biography as a form of historical writing. The principal advantage of social biography in relation to this project is that, as Nick Salvatore has pointed out, it 'treats equally seriously both the subject and the context that shapes that life … it creates the possibility of a broader understanding of the interplay between an individual and social forces beyond one's ability to control'.[14] Aiming to achieve that broader understanding has been integral to my research project.

One of the challenges in writing around Duall's life has been an absence of much material relating specifically to him. This issue is common to all the Aboriginal convicts in whom I am interested. This necessitated writing these social biographies as what has been termed 'short lives'. Such biographies achieve what Lytton Strachey described as a 'becoming brevity' but nevertheless serve to illuminate various social and historical processes at work in shaping representations of individual lives.[15] At times, Duall has received only a passing mention as in the instance of his having been Hume's guide on his inaugural journey of discovery.[16] On other occasions, events in which he was involved have been elaborated more fully.

Fortunately, the colonial records dealing with the 1816 conflict at the Cowpastures are quite extensive. Investigating this aspect of Duall's life revealed something interesting about the particularities of the relationships in which he was embedded at the Cowpastures frontier. For example, it became evident that while the elite troops from the colonial garrison ordered out by Macquarie were patrolling the district in search of so-called 'hostile natives', some of the settlers at the Cowpastures were willing to risk the hangman's noose by harbouring Indigenous men and their families who were both friends and fugitives.[17] Throughout this troubled period, Duall was sheltered by John Kennedy, who was none other than an uncle to Hamilton Hume and an explorer in his own right.[18] Kennedy's willingness to shelter several fugitives, including Duall, demonstrates amongst other things that life at the Cowpastures frontier cohered around a different set of social and economic relationships than those imagined by the colonial administration in Sydney. For example, Kennedy claimed that rather than the murderers that they were characterised as being by the colonial administration, the Aboriginal men he sheltered were 'harmless, innocent men' who protected his farm as well as his neighbour Broughton's property. Were the military to arrest these men, Kennedy claimed, it would result in his having to 'abandon the country'.[19] Throsby, another Cowpastures resident, was also willing to put himself on the line for local Aboriginal people. His lengthy letters to the Governor to complain about the treatment meted out to indigenes earned Throsby a place on a list of malcontents secretly compiled by Macquarie and sent to England in 1817.[20]

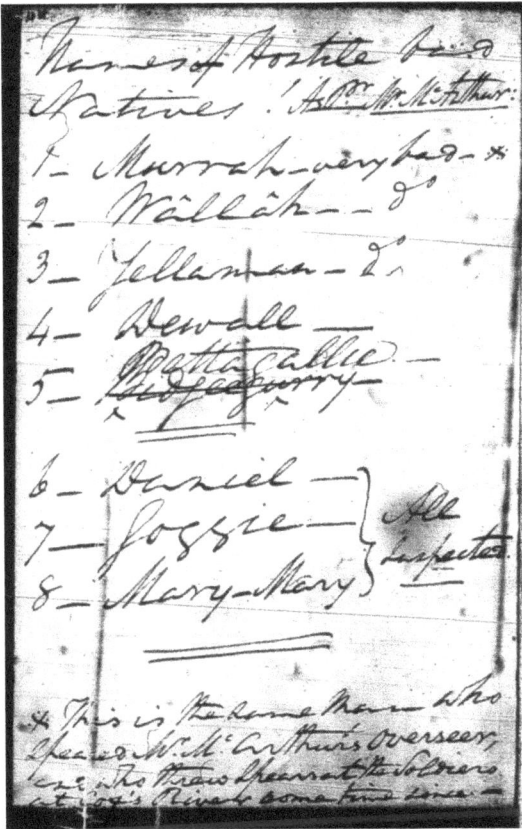

Figure 4.1: Lachlan Macquarie. 'List of hostile natives', *New South Wales Colonial Secretary's Office Correspondence*, Reel 6005: 44. Reproduced with the kind permission of State Records New South Wales.

Following his capture during the Cowpastures conflict and his subsequent transportation to Van Diemen's Land, Duall simply vanished for a while from the historical record. I know, for example, that his sentence of banishment to Van Diemen's Land was carried out as he is listed as having arrived in the penal colony on the 28 April 1816, on board the *Kangaroo*.[21] Unfortunately Duall's convict conduct record for the years he spent in Van Diemen's Land is no longer extant. Contextual material pertaining to this period therefore takes on a heightened significance as it provides a more complete backdrop against which Duall's captivity took place. He was in Van Diemen's Land at a time when local Indigenous peoples still inhabited tracts of their original country and bushrangers were a significant issue to indigenes and the colonial administration alike.[22] Duall is commonly supposed to have volunteered to work as a blacktracker[23] alongside Musquito with the 46th regiment to help capture bushrangers during the administration of Lieutenant-Governor William Sorell, although only Musquito is mentioned as a blacktracker in primary sources.[24] Characterised as 'bloodhounds',[25] men such as Duall and Musquito were admired for their tracking skills with the latter being particularly hated by Van Diemen's Land convicts for his involvement in apprehending a number of escapees.[26]

Life in Van Diemen's Land was particularly difficult during the period in which Duall was in exile. Increasing competition over land use led to heightened conflict between Van Diemen's Land settlers and indigenes. At the same time, some of the colonial garrison were openly rebellious and robbed some of the local authorities around Port Dalrymple as well as setting fire to the picket fence surrounding their own accommodation. The administration itself was also fraught by conflict. Convict life during this era was made all the more difficult through a gross shortage of clothing and blankets in conjunction with inclement weather.[27]

While I concur with Salvatore that '[i]t is not enough … to hang the burden of a traditional social or institutional history upon the inert form of the chosen one, occasionally evoking that body to highlight an interpretative point', it has not proved possible to follow this maxim to the letter. Rather, I have aimed to 'grant the individual his particularity in all its dimensions … and … explore these byways wherever they may lead'.[28] One significant byway involved Charles Throsby's 1819 expedition from the Cowpastures to Bathurst. When a letter arrived in Van Diemen's Land in 1819 from the Colonial Secretary's Office requesting Duall's early return to Sydney, his repatriation was probably sought so that Duall could accompany Throsby as an interpreter.[29] While researching this expedition might seem tangential, doing so was significant for several reasons not the least of which being, as Terry Goldie so succinctly put it, that 'the role of the white "discoverer" has become a vexing problem for historians in recent years in deciding how a land with an existing population can be discovered'.[30] I am also interested in working towards redressing one of the silences Henry Reynolds identified in the historiography. While Aboriginal advisers played a crucial role in the white exploration and settlement of Australia 'their role has rarely been fully appreciated in the innumerable historical works which have celebrated the achievements of the explorers who "discovered" inland Australia'.[31]

Considering the journey between the Cowpastures and Bathurst shed light upon some of the broader concerns informing the exile of key Indigenous men. The most obvious of these was competition over land use. From reading records relating to Macquarie's instructions to explorers like Throsby, it became clear that the Governor was single-minded about ascertaining the suitability or otherwise of the country being explored for pastoral and agricultural expansion. This was inextricably linked to a desire to assess the extent to which local Indigenous inhabitants might hamper expansion into such terrain.[32] With such concerns foremost in their minds, men like Throsby traversed landscape virgin to white explorers but well known to their Indigenous guides and interpreters. While doing so, they kept journals detailing their new discoveries. Throsby also wrote letters to the Governor, describing aspects of the journey and recommending rewards for his Indigenous guides and interpreters.[33] It remains possible to catch glimpses of Duall framed within these pages, although his response to receiving a breastplate and blanket as his reward for participating in the expedition is not recorded. One is left to wonder whether and to what extent he drew a correlation between the bestowal of these items upon his person and the subsequent seizure of further Indigenous lands.

Regardless of how Duall might have viewed the process, transporting Indigenous men from New South Wales to Van Diemen's Land and elsewhere followed a particular pattern in that their exile into captivity followed closely the expropriation of their lands. This was predicated on the notion that such men were British subjects and therefore under the protection of, as well as subject to, colonial law. In the absence of any formal declaration of war or recognition of Aboriginal sovereignty, their acts of political resistance were transmuted into criminal activity. As well as banishment into exile at the behest of earlier colonial governors, from the 1824 inception of the Supreme Court of New South Wales this resulted in sentences of death, imprisonment, or transportation for those who appeared before the colonial judges. Others of course were dealt with summarily under the euphemistically termed method of 'frontier justice'.[34]

To conclude, following as much as can be elucidated about Duall's life-course from the colonial records and contextualising this through utilising social biography as a methodology provided a useful approach. Engaging with some of the by-ways in the records about Duall's life elucidated not only aspects of his individual experiences but also revealed some interesting dynamics driving broader colonial society. That has been one of the key benefits in utilising social biography to inform my methodology in writing around Duall's life. Obviously this exploration has been hampered by considerable constraints, not the least of which being the sparse records relating to Duall that are extant. The most conspicuous absence, though, is any material relating to Duall's life beyond the colonial interface. His Indigenous life beyond the parameters of the frontier remains as inaccessible as his interiority. Captured by the colonial garrison with traces remaining in colonial newspapers, journals, official correspondence, and convict records, Duall as an historical actor remained elusive. He stayed an ephemeral figure who managed to escape detailed scrutiny.

As closing vignettes, I would like to linger for a moment over several images of an older Duall, restored to his people and place. In 1826, Duall was recorded as being one of the 'chiefs' who enjoyed 'roast and boiled beef, soup, plum pudding, and grog' at the annual gathering hosted by the Governor at Parramatta.[35] The following decade, in 1833 and aged around 40, Duall was living at the

Cowpastures with his wife and their child. When the distribution of blankets took place that year, he was provided for as he had been a so-called 'good native' throughout the proceeding year. Duall was thus reinscribed in the subject position 'friendly native' that characterised his first recorded interactions with some of the colonists as a young expeditionary guide to Hamilton Hume, and to which he was restored when working as a translator in New South Wales following his early recall from exile.[36]

References

Primary Sources

Archival files, Archives Office of Tasmania:

Assignment Lists and Associated Papers, CON13/1: 65.

New South Wales Colonial Secretary's Correspondence, 1788–1825, Reel 6006: 188; Reel 6020: 238, 248; Reel 6034: 77–89; Reel 6038: 47–50; Reel 6045: 50–62; Reel 6065: 44.

Historical Records of Australia, Series I, Volume IX, Library Committee of the Commonwealth Parliament, Canberra.

—— Series III, Volume II, Library Committee of the Commonwealth Parliament, Canberra.

Newspapers

Sydney Gazette

Sydney Morning Herald

The Australian

Secondary Sources

Bethall, Llewelyn 1957, *The story of Port Dalrymple: Life and work in northern Tasmania*, Government Printer, Hobart.

Bonwick, James 1969 [1870], *The last of the Tasmanians; or, the Black War of Van Diemen's Land*, Libraries Board of South Australia, Adelaide.

Branagan, Jack 1994, *The historic Tamar Valley: Its people, places and shipping, 1798–1990*, Regal Publications, Launceston.

Clark, Ian 2005, '"You have all this place … no good have children" Derrimut: traitor, saviour, or a man of his people?', *Journal of the Royal Australian Historical Society* 91(2): 107–132.

Goldie, Terry 1989, *Fear and temptation: The image of the Indigene in Canadian, Australian and New Zealand literatures*, McGill-Queen's University Press, Kingston.

Harman, Kristyn 2008, 'Aboriginal convicts: race, law, and transportation in colonial New South Wales', PhD Thesis, University of Tasmania, Hobart.

Kwaymullina, Blaze 2007, 'Introduction: listening through the heart', in *Speaking from the heart: Stories of life, family and country*, Sally Morgan, Tjalaminu Mia and Blaze Kwaymullina (eds), Fremantle Arts Centre Press, Fremantle.

Liston, Carol 1988, 'The Dharawal and Gandangara in colonial Campbelltown NSW 1788–1830', *Aboriginal History* 12(1): 48–62.

Lowe, David 1994, *Forgotten rebels: Black Australians who fought back*, Permanent Press, Melbourne.

Parry, Naomi 2004a, '"Many deeds of terror": Windschuttle and Musquito', *Labour History* 85: 207–212.

—— 2004b, '"Many deeds of error": response to Windschuttle's defence of his view of Musquito', *Labour History* 87: 236–238.

—— 2005, 'Musquito c1780–1825', Australian Dictionary of Biography, Supplementary Volume, Melbourne University Press, Melbourne: 299.

—— 2007, '"Hanging no good for Blackfellow": looking into the life of Musquito', *Transgressions: critical Australian Indigenous histories*, accessed on 9 May 2008, <http://epress.anu.edu.au/aborig_history/transgressions/html/ch07.html>

Perry, Thomas 1963, *Australia's first frontier: The spread of settlement in New South Wales 1788–1829*, Melbourne University Press, Kingsgrove.

Reynolds, Henry 1990, *With the white people*, Penguin, Ringwood.

Salvatore, Nick 2004, 'Biography and social history: an intimate relationship', *Labour History* 87: 178–192.

Sargent, Clem 1996, *The Colonial Garrison 1817–1824*, TCS Publications, Canberra.

Walter, James 2006, 'The utility of short lives', *Biography* 29(2): 329–337.

Windschuttle, Keith 2004, 'Guerrilla warrior and resistance fighter? The career of Musquito', *Labour History* 87: 221–235.

Wise, Christine 1983, 'Black Rebel Musquito' in *Rebels and Radicals*, Eric Fry (ed), Allen & Unwin, Sydney: 1–7.

ENDNOTES

[1] Liston 1988: 60.

[2] *Historical Records of Australia* [hereafter *HRA*], Series I, Volume IX, Macquarie to Bathurst, 18 March 1816: 52–53.

[3] *Sydney Gazette*, 3 August 1816: 1.

[4] Macquarie 1816, 'List of Hostile Natives', *New South Wales Colonial Secretary's Correspondence*, Reel 6065: 44, Archives Office of Tasmania [hereafter AOT]. The other Aboriginal people named on this list were Murrah (who was said to have been 'the same man who speared W. McArthur's overseer, and

who threw spears at the soldiers at Cox's River some time since'), Wallah (alias Warren), Yellaman, Bettagalie, Daniel, Coggie (Cogie), and Mary-Mary.

[5] *Sydney Gazette*, 3 August 1816: 1.

[6] Charles Throsby 1819, 'Journal of a Tour to Bathurst Through The Cow Pastures Commencing on April 25th 1819', *New South Wales Colonial Secretary's Correspondence*, Reel 6034: 88–89, AOT [Hereafter Throsby 1819]. Duall was a member of this expeditionary party in the official capacity of interpreter.

[7] Government and General Orders, Civil Department, 31 May 1819, *New South Wales Colonial Secretary's Correspondence*, Reel 6038: 47–50, AOT.

[8] Harman 2008.

[9] Kwaymullina 2007: 20.

[10] ibid.

[11] See, for example, depictions of Windradyne, Musquito, Yagan, Jack Napoleon (Tunnerminnerwait), Dundalli, and Jandamurra in Lowe 1994.

[12] See Parry 2004, 2005. See also Windschuttle 2004.

[13] Clark 2005. Such a shift is also indicated by Naomi Parry's recently published nuanced interpretation of Musquito's life. See Parry 2007.

[14] Salvatore 2004: 187.

[15] Cited in Walter 2006: 330.

[16] Liston 1988: 60.

[17] Report of Lt. Parker of the 46th Regiment, concerning his detachment's operations at Appin and Journey to the Five Islands, *New South Wales Colonial Secretary's Correspondence*, Reel 6045: 60–62, AOT.

[18] Death Notice for John Kennedy, *Sydney Morning Herald*, 3 April 1843: 3.

[19] Report of Captain James Wallis of the 46th Regiment, to Governor Macquarie concerning his operations against the hostile natives in the Airds and Appin Districts, 9 May 1816, *New South Wales Colonial Secretary's Correspondence*, Reel 6045: 50–59, AOT.

[20] *HRA*, Series I, Volume IX, Macquarie to Bathurst, 1 December 1817: 500.

[21] 'Government Public Notice and Order: Civil Department', *Sydney Gazette*, 3 August 1816: 1; Assignment Lists and Associated Papers, CON13/1: 65, AOT.

[22] Sargent 1996: 60. See also Branagan 1994: 3–4; and Bethall 1957: 15.

[23] Wise 1983: 3. Duall working as a blacktracker was mentioned by Christine Wise but was not footnoted. Despite searching all Wise's references as well as undertaking exhaustive archival research, I am yet to find any evidence that supports the assertion that Duall worked as a blacktracker whilst in Van Diemen's Land.

[24] For a succinct biography of Musquito, see Parry 2005: 299. See also Parry 2007.

[25] Bonwick 1969 [1870]: 93.

[26] *HRA*, Series III, Vol II, Sorell to Macquarie, 13 October 1817: 283–284.

[27] *HRA*, Series III, Vol II, Sorell to Macquarie, 8 December 1817: 289.

[28] Salvatore 1987: 190.

[29] 'Transfer of Dicall (Dual) from Port Dalrymple to Sydney', *New South Wales Colonial Secretary's Correspondence*, Reel 6006: 188, AOT.

[30] Goldie 1989: 42.

[31] Reynolds 1990: 5.

[32] Macquarie's Memorandum, April 1816, *New South Wales Colonial Secretary's Correspondence*, Reel 6065, AOT.

[33] Throsby 1819.

[34] Perry 1963: 99.

[35] 'The Corroborie at Parramatta', *The Australian*, 19 January 1826: 3.

[36] 'Return of the Cowpasture Aborigines for 1833', AONSW 4/6666.3, cited in Liston 1988: 58–59.

Oodgeroo Noonuccal: media snapshots of a controversial life

Karen Fox

Many voices swirl around a famous life. Some of this complexity can be grasped through exploring those voices that leave traces on paper or microfilm in articles, quotes and letters in the pages of major daily newspapers. This paper focuses on one famous life in particular, that of Oodgeroo Noonuccal (formerly Kath Walker).[1] Such biographical snapshots of Oodgeroo, often challenged by Oodgeroo herself, reveal the lack of coherence in popular narratives of one famous life while it was still being lived. While biography can appear to impose a fixed narrative shape upon a life that was experienced as fluid and shifting by both the biographical subject and outsiders, exploring such biographical fragments re-emphasises that fluidity. Narrative fragments about Oodgeroo often appeared in large-circulation newspapers in relation to controversial events and issues, as well as in more specialised forums such as literary journals. I narrate several controversial incidents or issues Oodgeroo was involved in which featured in the pages of Australia's large-circulation daily newspapers. I contrast these narratives of controversies in Oodgeroo's life, and selected representations of her in the media, with her own views and understandings of the events and of herself. I demonstrate the way in which she both used the media to convey her message of Aboriginal rights and challenged media portrayals of herself and her work, publicly articulating her own understandings of her life.

Snapshots of a controversial life: Oodgeroo in the media

After Oodgeroo published her first collection of poems in 1964, titled *We are going*, she became famous more or less immediately. Her fame was based firstly on her status as the first published Aboriginal poet, but her writing was also deeply entwined with her politics and activism. She became well-known nationally to those with an interest in Aboriginal affairs, as well as to those with an interest in literature. Oodgeroo first became politically active in the 1940s through involvement with the Communist Party, and was deeply involved in the Aboriginal civil rights movement for much of her life.[2] She became the secretary of the Queensland Council for the Advancement of Aborigines and Torres Strait Islanders (QCAATSI), became involved in the Federal Council (FCAATSI), and was a key figure in the campaign for the 1967 referendum, the 40th anniversary of which was celebrated in 2007.[3] Her writing thus was part of her political efforts on behalf of Aboriginal people, in a period in which Aboriginal issues became more visible to the wider population.[4] It is, as Kathie

Cochrane noted, 'impossible ... to separate the poet from the activist for Aboriginal rights'.[5] In her terms, perhaps, Oodgeroo's writing was part of her project of educating the white population of Australia.[6] Later in life, Oodgeroo returned to Stradbroke Island to live, running a cultural and education centre, Moongalba. Over 8000 children visited the centre between 1972 and 1977, staying in tents and learning Aboriginal approaches to gathering food.[7]

Oodgeroo's efforts for Aboriginal civil rights made her a public figure both through her poetry and through campaigning. Roberta Sykes remembered Oodgeroo having been angry about sometimes being 'misquoted' and 'betrayed' by the press.[8] At the same time, the media, like her poetry, provided a channel to convey her message to the wider population. For example, several newspapers in late 1970 reported the possibility that Oodgeroo might abandon the struggle for Aboriginal rights in Australia and emigrate. She was quoted in *The Australian* explaining that she felt her poetry had done nothing but 'cause the Australian people to duck for cover with a guilty conscience', and she felt unable to remain and 'wait for the Aboriginal to die'.[9] Described in the *Sun News-Pictorial* as 'an angular, tensely aggressive and dignified figure', she was reported to be making the decision because she was 'tired of her fight to get and retain dignity' for herself and for all Aboriginal people.[10] The *Australian* reported in 1979 that she had 'given her new book to a German publisher as a protest at Australia's treatment of Aborigines' and the country's policies relating to uranium.[11]

A controversial issue is one which is publicly and often acrimoniously debated, and Oodgeroo lived a life dedicated to controversial issues of Aboriginal rights. Though not usually explicitly described as herself controversial, Oodgeroo was often featured in large-circulation daily newspapers in relation to controversial events or issues, several times relating to events in the conservative state of Queensland, her home state. Although she observed in an interview published in edited form in 1987 that she considered herself 'fairly conservative', it was often made clear to her that others saw her as controversial.[12] For instance, she was quoted in 1986 in the *Sunday Mail* telling the following story:

> I have not forgotten that when I was one of six finalists in the 1981 Queenslander of the Year contest [Queensland Premier Joh] Bjelke-Petersen shook the hands of the other five and ignored me. ... No Australian paper has ever printed that, although I have told plenty.[13]

When the organiser of the contest followed Bjelke-Petersen and persuaded him to return, he 'went through the motions of the shortest handshake in history'.[14] In 1984, Oodgeroo was quoted in the *Sydney Morning Herald* commenting on the continuing refusal of the Queensland government to change the tenure of the land at Moongalba so as to allow her to take up a Federal grant for developing an 'Aboriginal educational and cultural centre'. The refusal, she said, was 'bloody-minded revenge' and '[t]hey are out to get me because I am an Aboriginal and because I was a thorn in their side last year'.[15] As these instances suggest, Oodgeroo was a more controversial figure in Queensland than may have been the case elsewhere in Australia. Under Bjelke-Petersen from 1968 until 1987, oppressive legislation continued to circumscribe the lives of Aboriginal people, and attempts were made to suppress protest. Change came slowly and erratically, as a consequence of increasing pressure from Indigenous groups and from wider public opinion, both within Queensland and nationally.[16] By the time Bjelke-Petersen ceased to be premier in 1987, the society in which Oodgeroo lived and worked had changed in crucial ways.

Expo '88, the Bicentenary and becoming Oodgeroo

One of Oodgeroo's most visible and widely commented upon gestures of protest, which she publicised through the media, related to the celebration of the Bicentenary in 1988. Made a Member of the Order of the British Empire (MBE) in 1970, Oodgeroo suggested that same year that she might take the controversial step of returning the award.[17] Almost two decades later, at the end of 1987, she did so, expressing her relief after having handed the award back.[18] The shifts occurring in Queensland society may also have made her decision to return the award an easier one. Oodgeroo wrote a piece for *The Age* explaining her reasons for returning the award, and for changing her name. As 'a protest against what the Bicentenary "celebrations" stand for', she asserted that she could 'no longer, with a clear conscience, accept the English honor [sic] of the MBE', and would return it to Queen Elizabeth II, via the Queensland Governor, Sir Walter Campbell.[19] She had accepted the award in the first place, she said, only after Aboriginal people with whom she discussed the offer considered that it might help to break barriers that continued to restrict Aboriginal people.[20] Seeing the Bicentenary as an anniversary of '200 years of rape and carnage', she now asked, 'what is there to celebrate?'[21]

While it is difficult to judge accurately public responses to these actions, letters to the editor published in the Brisbane *Courier-Mail* provide some clues, both reflecting and contesting Queensland's conservative and repressive approach to Aboriginal affairs. One letter-writer focused on the return of the MBE, arguing that the award was granted 'by the people for her services – regardless of color [sic], politics or religion' and that Oodgeroo had 'in many ways, profited through the so-called white policy'.[22] Another writer, failing to understand Oodgeroo's work and beliefs, saw her actions as a 'decision to relinquish her status in the white community', which he found 'disturbing to those Queenslanders who have admired her work and her tireless effort to uplift her race in the battle for assimilation'.[23] Most letters focused on the name change. One writer sarcastically offered 'congratulations' to Oodgeroo 'for her stand against "the great white menace"' and suggested she also leave behind 'all things in her life that are white man-made' such as spectacles, or printing her books in English 'on a white man's invention'.[24] This letter provoked several responses supporting Oodgeroo. One author questioned whether such technological advances were worth the loss of land, disease and 'bloodshed' brought by colonisation.[25] The responses of Aboriginal leaders as reported in the press also varied. Gary Foley reportedly suggested that other Aboriginal people might take similar actions, and Chicka Dixon pointed out that he did not think such awards should be accepted in the first place. He had himself refused one.[26] Neville Bonner, on the other hand, said that although he had no desire to celebrate the Bicentenary he would not take similar actions.[27]

Also in 1988, Brisbane hosted an International Exposition, or World's Fair, known as Expo '88. Oodgeroo agreed to script a short theatrical piece for Expo '88, acknowledging Aboriginal people as the first inhabitants of Australia, since she did not want this task done by an outsider.[28] She was described in the *Sydney Morning Herald* as someone who 'personifies [the] tragedy' of division among Aboriginal people as some accepted involvement in Bicentenary celebrations and others rejected it, although the two events were actually separate.[29] Oodgeroo responded that 'I am not celebrating' and that:

> I don't give a stuff for Expo, or the Bicentenary. I will pick up the blood money because for the last 200 years that is all we have been given by the white people and I will use it to the best of my ability. I am giving at least 14 of my people six months' work.[30]

It was later reported that Queen Elizabeth had wanted to meet Oodgeroo when she attended Expo '88. Considering it 'just a little too risky to have the Queen of the Commonwealth sipping tea with one of Australia's best-known Aboriginal activists', protocol officers presumably told the Queen Oodgeroo was not 'available', although she was in the vicinity.[31] The Queen was reported to be 'furious', having found Oodgeroo's return of the MBE understandable, and being a reader of her work.[32]

Poetry for a purpose: a controversial endeavour

Oodgeroo's poetry also led her into controversy, this time played out in the pages of literary journals as well as newspapers. *We are going* was the first published collection of poetry in English by an Aboriginal writer. The book was popular, selling over 10,000 copies in seven editions.[33] It became a common refrain in the popular media that Oodgeroo was the first published Aboriginal poet. As John Collins put it, she 'immediately became a public person'.[34] Oodgeroo sometimes suggested that her Aboriginality increased interest in her poetry. She commented in an interview in 1988 that *We are going* 'sold mainly out of curiosity value', a remark she had also made in the foreword to *The dawn is at hand*, her second book of poetry, in 1966.[35] Ian Turner also suggested this, reviewing *We are going* for the *Australian* in 1964. Like the painter Albert Namatjira, he suggested, 'Mrs Walker is having a *succes de surprise*', which he thought reflected 'on the audience, not on the poet'.[36] Even by 1971, SE Lee, writing in *Southerly*, described her as 'something of a curiosity (an aborigine [sic] who is also a poet)'.[37]

Oodgeroo had joined the Realist Writers' Group in Brisbane. These groups existed throughout Australia, and aimed 'to promote the discussion and production of socialist realism in literature'.[38] She had also first become politically active through a brief involvement with the Communist Party, because of the party's opposition to discrimination towards Aboriginal people, leaving when she discovered other members wished to write her speeches for her.[39] As she recalled in a speech given in 1993, close to the end of her life, one of the early criticisms of her poetry when she began writing was that it was not her work, but that a 'well-known Communist' was 'writing it for her'.[40] As well, she recalled:

> ... then when they said 'She must be writing these poems', they said 'Well, the reason why she writes good poems is because she's not a full-blood, you know. She's got white man's blood coming out in her'.[41]

Similarly, Oodgeroo was quoted in *Woman's Day/Woman's World* in 1980 observing that her work was first said to be the work of a 'white person', and later, 'when it became widely known it was my poetry they said it must be the white genes giving her the brilliance'.[42]

Yet a further controversy surrounding Oodgeroo's poetry was literary, as many reviewers denigrated her poetic skills, sometimes suggesting that any merit her work possessed stemmed only from its message, providing a voice for Aboriginal people which was authenticated by her own Aboriginality. Reviewing *We are going*, poet Jill Hellyer wrote in *Hemisphere* in 1964 that Oodgeroo's poetry had 'considerable and definite promise' but that the collection's 'quality' was 'uneven' and that 'an attitude of preaching' sometimes weakened the poems.[43] Oodgeroo's poetry was subject to considerable criticism as being mere propaganda rather than literature.[44] For instance, Katharine England, in the Adelaide *Advertiser*, commented in 1971 that Oodgeroo 'is no poet'.[45] England considered that her '*forte* is protest: she is a militant and dedicated fighter for social justice'.[46] Likewise, Hellyer suggested Oodgeroo's focus on 'the theme of her race' was something that 'must limit her eventually unless she ceases to regard herself as a propagandist for her people', and argued that her 'pleadings are most powerful when they do not become obvious'.[47] In 1967, Lee's review in *Southerly* suggested that 'it is difficult to imagine' that even those of her poems best in poetic terms would be 'considered for publication' if it were not that 'their author happens to be an aborigine [sic] passionately concerned about a very great social wrong ... currently troubling many consciences in the white community'.[48]

Oodgeroo herself at times referred to her poems as simple or as propaganda. She said in a 1990 interview, after agreeing with the interviewer that her poems were 'propaganda', that this was because of the need to get 'seventh generation white Australians' to listen, which required 'shock tactics', and she added that 'I'd rather hit them with my words than pick up a gun and shoot them'.[49] Judith Wright later noted that '[i]f there was one forbidden territory in poetry' in the era in which Oodgeroo began writing 'it was "propaganda and protest" literature, especially in verse'.[50] In this context, Oodgeroo's poetry became contested in terms of its literary merit. Moreover, defining what was political poetry was not always straightforward. In *The dawn is at hand*, Oodgeroo considered only one poem to be 'propaganda-like stuff', a view with which Lee emphatically disagreed.[51] Confusion among literary critics about how to understand Oodgeroo's poetry suggests the variety of ways in which a life may be controversial. In these criticisms, the demand for civil rights for Aboriginal people was not explicitly questioned, as the criticisms were framed in terms of literary merit. Yet such criticisms carried the potential to suppress Oodgeroo's political message, by arguing that politics did not belong in literature, and by denying Oodgeroo literary acceptance while she used her poetry to carry her message.

Representations of a 'poet and activist'

In the first decades after the publication of *We are going*, Oodgeroo was often described in the print media as an 'Aboriginal poet' or 'Aboriginal poetess', rather than simply as a poet, although this description became less common in articles about her from the mid-1980s. In one article in the *Australian* in 1969, she was termed '*the* Aboriginal poet', a description that served to emphasise representations of her as a first and a path-breaker.[52] She was a strong advocate of Aboriginal rights and felt that her poetry gave a voice to Aboriginal people. In one interview she stated that she felt that the 'success' of *We are going* was 'inevitable ... because for the first time the Aboriginals had a voice, a written voice'.[53] However, she also wished to be considered as an individual writer without such labels being applied.[54] She commented that:

> When I'm written up in the papers or the media or whatever, they always call me an 'Aboriginal poet'; they always tag me with that. And I don't see myself as an 'Aboriginal poet' ... I see myself as a poet who is proud to be of Aboriginal descent.[55]

Many other such labels were applied to her in newspaper articles across her career, shifting as she became involved in a variety of different activities. For instance, she appears to have only been described as an 'actress' around the time when she appeared in Bruce Beresford's *The Fringe Dwellers* (1986). Jennifer Jones has argued that Oodgeroo's 'earlier profile as "Kath Walker, poet and pan-Aboriginal activist" persistently eclipse[d] her important later work as an educator and children's author'.[56] Jones suggested that 'white Australia was not ready to acknowledge the vitality of contemporary Aboriginality that she attempted to communicate'.[57] Labelling Oodgeroo in these ways not only summed up her activities quickly for a skim-reading public, but potentially shaped understandings of her life and work, denying her public adoption of her own definition of herself and her activities.

Oodgeroo was often depicted in the print media as having a fiery temperament. Even in an article describing her as having 'become more a do-er than a shouter', this perception of her was evident:

> Put down poet and civil rights person Kath Walker's lack of fire yesterday to one of those dreaded Melbourne colds. That's not to say the fires have gone out – with just a minimum of stoking she can flare up as she has done so often throughout her lifetime.[58]

Newspaper articles that profiled Oodgeroo or reported upon her work and public statements often included words such as 'fierce', 'intense', 'outspoken' or 'forthright'. Interestingly, these descriptions appeared in many newspapers across Australia, despite their different contexts and political leanings. This representation of Oodgeroo also recurred in a variety of analogies in other mediums. For instance, Shelly Neller wrote in the conservative *Bulletin* in 1985 that Oodgeroo 'brandishes her passionate views with the force and accuracy of a stockwhip'.[59] Oodgeroo herself observed that she was 'very angry' in the years in which her early poems were written, and observed that 'I used to have to tone myself down a lot'.[60] As well as being fiery, however, Oodgeroo was sometimes also described as dignified and graceful, and her dislike of violence in protest was reported on several occasions.[61] When she received the award of Aboriginal of the Year in 1985, she was described by the *Sun Herald* as receiving it 'with her accustomed soft-spoken grace, edged with hard-nosed home truths about the lot of her race in Australia'.[62] However she was portrayed, such descriptions carried baggage which could shape readers' understandings of both Oodgeroo and her message.

Conclusion

Oodgeroo's work, speeches and actions as mediated through newspaper coverage reveal many snapshots of controversy, moments when her actions and words provoked criticism and debate. Perhaps this was inevitable for one who so openly challenged the society in which she lived, who was so obviously willing to be a visible and vocal Aboriginal woman in a society with a white male norm. During her lifetime she was often represented in the media as an 'Aboriginal poet', a propagandist rather than a real poet, or a fiery activist. At her death in 1993 she was lauded as 'a great Australian',[63] 'one of Australia's finest citizens',[64] 'a battler' and 'a national treasure'.[65] Such tributes, genuine though they may have been, potentially transformed her from a controversial figure, a challenger of society, to an embodiment of an idealised nation, one of its canonised heroes. One wonders what she would have had to say about that, and what controversy she would have begun.

References

Anonymous 1969, 'Aboriginal poet sees black revolt as inevitable', *The Australian*, 17 September: 2.

Anonymous 1970, '"I won't watch the Aboriginals die out": Kath Walker talks about deserting', *The Australian*, 21 November: 5.

Anonymous 1970, 'Kath Walker is giving up her battle', *Sun News-Pictorial*, 23 November: 13.

Anonymous 1970, 'May return MBE, says native leader', *The Age*, 27 July: 10.

Anonymous 1971, 'Poet hits at "Black Power" violence', *Sydney Morning Herald*, 1 December: 11.

Anonymous 1979, 'Kath closes the book on local publishers', *The Australian*, 5 October: 2.

Anonymous 1993, 'Nation mourns tenacious mother figure', *The Australian*, 17 September: 2.

Aubin, Tracey 1987, 'A celebration with a bitter taste for some', *Sydney Morning Herald*, 18 August: 17.

Barnes, Mick 1980, 'Kath Walker and the bridge to the Dreamtime', *Woman's Day/Woman's World*, 13 August: 58–9.

—— 1985, 'Kath's devoted herself to survival', *Sun-Herald*, 15 September: 53.

Bicknell, Graham 1977, 'Kath's fire still has heat', *Daily Telegraph*, 19 July: 13.

Blyth, Tracey 1987, 'Is she really serious?', *Courier-Mail*, 21 December: 8.

Box, RR 1987, 'Shame on us', *Courier-Mail*, 30 December: 8.

Cochrane, Kathie 1994, *Oodgeroo*, University of Queensland Press, St Lucia.

—— 1994, 'Oodgeroo', in *Oodgeroo*, Kathie Cochrane (ed), University of Queensland Press, St Lucia: 3–158.

—— 2000, 'Noonuccal, Oodgeroo', in *The Oxford companion to Aboriginal art and culture*, Sylvia Kleinert and Margo Neale (eds), Oxford University Press, Melbourne: 664.

Collins, John 1994a, 'A mate in publishing', *Australian Literary Studies* 16: 9–23.

—— 1994b, 'Oodgeroo of the Tribe Noonuccal', *Race and Class* 35 April-June: 77–87.

Craven, Rhonda 1994, 'Oodgeroo: An educator who proved one person could make a difference', *Australian Literary Studies* 16: 121–30.

Dwyer, Nan 1986, 'Aboriginal poet seeks peace with visit to Moscow', *Sunday Mail*, 21 December: 9.

—— 1987, 'Support for black poet's name change', *Sunday Mail*, 27 December: 5.

England, Katherine 1971, 'Kath Walker: a fighter in verse', *Advertiser*, 1 May: 26.

Evans, Raymond 2007, *A history of Queensland*, Cambridge University Press, Cambridge and Port Melbourne.

Green, Jonathan 1987, 'In the blacking of a name is a struggle for a "humiliated race"', *Herald*, 17 December: 2.

Hamilton, Fiona 1993, 'Oodgeroo buried beneath the paperbarks: tributes flow for "Grand Old Lady"', *Canberra Times*, 21 September: 3.

Hellyer, Jill 1964, 'Aboriginal poet', *Hemisphere*, December: 17–8.

Jones, Jennifer 2004, 'Deemed unsuitable for children: the editing of Oodgeroo's *Stradbroke Dreamtime*', *Papers,* 14 May: 5–14.

Lee, SE 1967, 'Poetic fisticuffs', *Southerly*: 60–71.

—— 1971, 'Old verse', *Southerly*: 227–40.

Lucas, M 1987, 'Shortchanged?', *Courier-Mail*, 28 December: 8.

Mackenzie, Ian 1987, 'Oodgeroo keeps culture alive', *Courier-Mail*, 29 December: 8.

McLaren, John 1996, *Writing in hope and fear: Literature as politics in postwar Australia*, Cambridge University Press, Cambridge.

Mitchell, Susan 1987, *The Matriarchs: Twelve Australian women talk about their lives to Susan Mitchell*, Penguin, Ringwood.

Monk, Sylvia 1988, 'Understanding', *Courier-Mail*, 5 January: 8.

Neller, Shelly 1985, 'Kath Walker, activist, artist, finds a new medium for her cause', *Bulletin*, 3 December: 88–90.

Noonuccal, Oodgeroo 1987, 'Why I am now Oodgeroo Noonuccal', *The Age*, 30 December: 11.

Noonuccal, Oodgeroo and Turcotte, Gerry 1988, 'Recording the cries of the People', in *Aboriginal Culture Today*, Anna Rutherford (ed), Dangaroo, Sydney: 16–30.

Paskins, Alfred 1987, 'White man's only crime', *Courier-Mail*, 24 December: 8.

Roberts, Greg 1984, 'It's "bloody-minded revenge", says Kath Walker', *Sydney Morning Herald*, 10 May: 16.

—— 1989, 'And now to settle a royal score, by Malcolm Williamson', *Sydney Morning Herald*, 19 October: 3.

Rushtone, J 1987, 'Honour was deserved', *Courier-Mail*, 22 December: 8.

Sherman, Paul 1987, 'Understanding the name change', *Courier-Mail*, 23 December: 8.

Shoemaker, Adam 2004, *Black words white page*, ANU E Press, Canberra.

Smith, David 1993, 'Goss leads tributes to "Remarkable Australian" ', *Gold Coast Bulletin*, 17 September: 2.

Smith, Elizabeth 1990, 'Are you going to come back tomorrow?', *The Queensland Writer*, July-August: 13–16.

Sykes, Roberta B 1994, 'While my name is remembered ... ' *Australian Literary Studies,* 16(4): 35–41.

Turner, Ian 1964, 'Colour seeks justice', *Australian*, 26 September: 13.

Van Toorn, Penny 2000, 'Indigenous texts and narratives', in *The Cambridge companion to Australian literature*, Elizabeth Webby (ed), Cambridge University Press, Cambridge: 19–49.

Walker, Kath 1966, *The dawn is at hand*, Jacaranda, Brisbane.

Wright, Judith 1994, 'The poetry', in *Oodgeroo*, Kathie Cochrane (ed), University of Queensland Press, St Lucia: 163–183.

ENDNOTES

[1] I refer to her throughout as Oodgeroo, the name she chose.

[2] Cochrane 1994: 17–18 .

[3] Cochrane 1994: 32 .

[4] This point is also made by Penny Van Toorn. Van Toorn 2000: 29–30.

[5] Cochrane 2000: 664.

[6] Several writers acknowledged after her death that her poetry was part of a mission to educate white Australians. For instance, see Craven 1994: 122.

[7] Cochrane 1994: 93.

[8] Sykes 1994: 38.

[9] Anonymous, *Australian*, 21 November 1970: 5.

[10] Anonymous, *Sun News-Pictorial*, 23 November 1970: 13.

[11] Anonymous, *Australian*, 5 October 1979: 2 .

[12] Mitchell 1987: 203 .

[13] Dwyer, *Sunday Mail*, 21 December 1986: 9 .

[14] Dwyer, *Sunday Mail*, 21 December 1986: 9.

[15] Roberts, *Sydney Morning Herald*, 10 May 1984: 16 .

[16] Evans 2007: 232 .

[17] The *Age* reported that she wished the National Tribal Council's requests be put in place, and quoted her suggesting that if they were not, she could write to the Queen about her concerns and return her award. Anonymous, *Age*, 27 July 1970: 10 .

[18] Collins 1994a: 19.

[19] Noonuccal, *Age*, 30 December 1987: 11 .

[20] Noonuccal, *Age*, 30 December 1987: 11.

[21] Noonuccal, *Age*, 30 December 1987: 11

[22] Rushtone, *Courier-Mail*, 22 December 1987: 8.

[23] Paskins, *Courier-Mail*, 24 December 1987: 8 . Oodgeroo, however, had consistently opposed assimilation, as she had made clear in a pair of poems respectively titled 'Assimilation, No!' and 'Integration, Yes!': Walker 1966: 7–8.

[24] Blyth, *Courier-Mail*, 21 December 1987: 8.

[25] Lucas, *Courier-Mail*, 28 December 1987: 8. Others that were supportive of Oodgeroo's name change appeared in: Box, *Courier-Mail*, 30 December 1987: 8; Mackenzie, *Courier-Mail*, 29 December 1987: 8; Monk, *Courier-Mail*, 5 January 1988: 8; Sherman, *Courier-Mail*, 23 December 1987: 8.Oodgeroo also received letters personally, reportedly telling the *Courier-Mail* that she had received both 'hate mail' and letters 'written to offer support' for her name change. Dwyer, *Sunday Mail*, 27 December 1987: 5.

[26] Green, *Herald*, 17 December 1987: 2.

[27] Green, *Herald*, 17 December 1987: 2.

[28] Cochrane 1994: 134.

[29] Aubin, *Sydney Morning Herald*, 18 August 1987: 17.

[30] Aubin, *Sydney Morning Herald*, 18 August 1987: 17.

[31] Roberts, *Sydney Morning Herald*, 19 October 1989: 3.

[32] Roberts, *Sydney Morning Herald*, 19 October 1989: 3.

[33] Cochrane 1994: 37.

[34] Collins 1994b: 79.

[35] Noonuccal and Turcotte 1988: 19; Walker 1966: foreword.

[36] Turner, *Australian*, 26 September 1964: 13.

[37] Lee 1971: 233.

[38] McLaren 1996: 33.

[39] Cochrane 1994: 17– 18.

[40] Noonuccal, 'Writers of Australia, "I dips me lid"', Goossens Lecture, delivered at the Sydney Opera House, 9 June 1993, reprinted in Cochrane 1994: 229.

[41] Noonuccal, 'Writers of Australia, "I dips me lid"', Goossens Lecture, delivered at the Sydney Opera House, 9 June 1993, reprinted in Cochrane 1994: 229.These aspects of the controversy around her poetry were remarked on by Cochrane and by Collins. Cochrane 1994: 40; Collins 1994b: 79.

[42] Barnes, *Woman's Day/Woman's World*, 13 August 1980: 59.

[43] Hellyer 1964: 17–18.

[44] Many writers have noted the dismissal of her work on literary grounds and by terming it merely propaganda. See for instance: Shoemaker 2004: 182–185.

[45] England, *Advertiser*, 1 May 1971: 26.

[46] England, *Advertiser*, 1 May 1971: 26.

[47] Hellyer 1964: 17–18.

[48] Lee 1967: 64.

[49] Smith 1990: 14.

[50] Wright 1994: 168.

[51] Walker 1966: foreword; Lee 1967: 64.

[52] Anonymous, *Australian*, 17 September 1969: 2 . Emphasis is mine.

[53] Noonuccal and Turcotte 1988: 19.

[54] See Adam Shoemaker on this point. Shoemaker 2004: 188.

[55] Personal interview with Oodgeroo Noonuccal, conducted by Cliff Watego, Stradbroke Island, August 1982, quoted in Shoemaker 2004: 188.

[56] Jones 2004: 5.

[57] Jones 2004: 5.

[58] Bicknell, *Daily Telegraph*, 19 July 1977: 13.

[59] Neller, *Bulletin*, 3 December 1985: 90.

[60] Smith 1990: 13–14.

[61] For example: Anonymous, *Sydney Morning Herald*, 1 December 1971: 11.

[62] Barnes, *Sun-Herald*, 15 September 1985: 53.

[63] Queensland Premier Wayne Goss, quoted in Smith, *Gold Coast Bulletin*, 17 September 1993: 2.

[64] Minister for Aboriginal and Torres Strait Islander Affairs Robert Tickner, quoted in Anonymous, *Australian*, 17 September 1993: 2.

[65] Hamilton, *Canberra Times*, 21 September 1993: 3.

Indigenous Storytelling

It is a difficult process to publish papers from a conference and try to recapture the event, the impact, the mood, the vast exchange of knowledge and friendships that were developed and load it all into one stand-alone monograph. Some may argue for starters that the faces are missing; voices cannot be heard and thousands of words have been cruelly left out. Some may even go so far as to say that there are some things in life that can only be lived and that no amount of writing can account for experience. Some may say it, but try telling an indigenous biographer or an autobiographer and see how far you will get.

In putting this monograph together it was important for the editors to divide the monograph into sections. Section Two focuses on four of the papers presented by Indigenous biographers and autobiographers. Just as it was difficult to put the monograph together, it was just as complex trying to organise an international gathering of biographers and autobiographers who came from such a broad spectrum of academic disciplines, educational backgrounds and cultures from across the globe. One of the many concerns we had was to ensure that speakers would not be made to feel detached from the main thrust of the conference because they themselves were yet to be published authors. So as a precautionary measure, the first thing we communicated at the opening was that what we hoped would emerge from out of the conference was a sense of 'heart'.

In the days ahead that 'heart' was freely delivered; particularly by those who talked about their own communities or family members and even their own life's stories. Jenni Caruso, an Arrernte woman, presented a powerful paper about how she as an academic has to constantly juggle with a multiple identity between her ways of communicating and western academic modes of understanding. Samantha Faulkner talked about how she as a Torres Strait Islander writer, copes with writing about what she calls the 'bumps and joys' of her grandfather's biography; as with Professor John Maynard who has just recently undergone the process of publishing a book about his grandfather Fred Maynard. Then there were those like Margo Neale from the National Museum of Australia who talked about why it was important to write about Aboriginal role models like Aboriginal artist Emily Kngwarreye; while Aboriginal curator Barrina South from the Australian Museum in Sydney gave a talk centred on the narratives of a number of Aboriginal women from New South Wales. In the same vein was Dale Kerwin a proud Biripi Man who talked about his project on Aboriginal resistance fighters in nineteenth century Queensland.

Adding to the spirit of the conference were indigenous speakers from overseas such as Taiwanese lecturer Hau-Ren Bradley Hung who talked about the value of indigenous literature and the autobiographies of Native American author Joseph Bruchac and indigenous Taiwanese autobiographer Ahronglong Sakinu. Also contributing was New Guinean writer and Senior Lecturer Sam Kiama, who discussed what had been some of the more prickly problems one deals with when recording and publishing the stories of the local people in the Morobe Province while Kuela Kiama a musician and mathematician from Botswana gave a touching presentation entitled 'Tears for my land'. Conversely Dr George Mukuka from the University of Johannesburg offered an insight into the rich history on the early developments of the indigenous clergy of South Africa; while Mina Sakai, a leader of the 'Ainu Rebels' in Tokyo not only shared a heartfelt message as 'one Ainu woman to the rest of society' at the conference, but gave a traditional Ainu musical performance at the conference dinner.

Nevertheless, the final four papers selected for Section Two of the monograph were chosen ultimately on the basis of their diversity. The first paper in this section is written by Waka Waka/Kalkadoon elder Judith Wickes. Wickes paper is highly personal, comprehensive and emotionally charged paper based on her Honours thesis entitled '"Never really heard of it": a study of the impact on identity of the Queensland certificate of exemption for Aboriginal people'. The second paper is by Aroha Harris, a member of the Te Rarawa and Ngapuhi tribes of Aotearoa New Zealand who describes to us the experiences she has had to go through in writing a biography about Maori elder Joe Hawke. The third paper written by Munzhedzi James Mafela, a Professor of African Languages at the University of South Africa is not a straightforward biography about Nelson Mandela, but a commentary about the Mandela biography and how traditional kinship bloodlines play a significant role in indigenous biographical storytelling. Finally the fourth paper in this section is by PhD candidate Maria Preethi Srinivasan who discusses the work of and attempts to link two indigenous women, Dalit writer Bama and Native Canadian writer Lee Maracle.

So as you read through the next four essays we ask that you might like to consider the context in which the papers were delivered at the conference and imagine the spirit that was shared by all those who came to tell their indigenous stories.

Frances Peters-Little

'Never really heard of it': the certificate of exemption and lost identity

Judi Wickes

When I first heard the call for papers for the 'Indigenous Biography and Autobiography' Conference earlier this year, I felt that I was being offered a unique opportunity to share the genesis and the findings of my Honours thesis entitled '"Never really heard of it": a study of the impact on identity of the Queensland certificate of exemption for Aboriginal people'. I came to research the certificate of exemption largely as a means of finding answers to questions that I have carried around all my life. These questions concern my identity, my family history and information relating to my cultural heritage. My journey to answer them involved a search for my own identity and the genealogy of my family. In a very real sense, this research reflects both my own Indigenous autobiography and biography.

Beginnings

From my earliest memories as a child in the late 1950s I recall asking my parents questions about my identity, in particular 'Who am I?' and 'Where do we come from?' I was curious about these issues, and about photographs showing that I was a blue-eyed blonde as a young child. Whenever I put these questions to my parents, my dark skinned brown-eyed mother and fair skinned blue-eyed father always gave me the same answer – 'You are an Australian, Judi'. This answer, however, always left me wondering: 'What did it mean to be an Australian?', 'What did an Australian look like?', 'Did I look like an Australian?' and 'Did my family look and behave like Australians?' I knew that I was different to all my friends but I could not compare myself with them as none had parents with the same mixed heritage as mine.

Later, as a teenager I felt driven to find out more, when I came to realise that my mother's heritage, which she denied, was Aboriginal. My father was of mixed European heritage.[1] His sister, one of my favourite aunts, cautioned me about my personal journey to find my mother's family. She asked: 'Why not say you are Italian, and therefore save yourself the heartache?' I wondered what she was really saying. Why did she think it was easier to claim Italian heritage rather than Aboriginal? At the time I was extremely upset to hear my aunt's words, because it seemed that she wanted me to deny or erase the Aboriginal part of my mixed cultural heritage. Alternatively, perhaps it was because she did not want to be seen to have relatives with any Aboriginal heritage; then again it may have been something else.

Recently when my aunt was reflecting about the relationship between my mother and herself, she said, 'I have known your mother for over 50 years and we have never had an argument'. Again, what was she really saying? Was it because they were really 'soul sisters' or was it that my mother chose not to say anything controversial and certainly nothing about the exemption certificate that had silently erased her parents' Indigenous heritage and her own? Nevertheless, in recent years I have come to comprehend the 'heartache' my aunt spoke about, as my work and research has meant confronting the impacts of my elders renouncing their Indigenous heritage.

By the late 1970s and again in the mid 1980s, when I was working within the Aboriginal community, first at Queensland Health[2] and later with the Aboriginal Health Service, I became increasingly aware that I had been cut off from my own kinship and homelands. I was constantly reminded of the fact that I did not know the answers to the questions Aboriginal people (Murris) were asking of me.[3] 'Who is your family?' and 'Where do you come from?' Many of the Murris I was working with were able to answer those important questions about their own biographies. Eventually, I found that the answers I was searching for had been lost, due to Queensland government legislation introduced in 1897.

After my grandfather passed away in 1980, my mother found his certificate of exemption while sorting through his belongings.[4] This piece of paper presented me with questions about my grandfather's biography. What was he doing with this certificate? What exactly was it? What did it mean? My curiosity was triggered by the discovery of this old document and inspired me to continue my personal journey of biographical research and discovery. It was during the early 1980s that I befriended an Aboriginal woman who was studying at TAFE in Brisbane. I decided to return to study the following year to enrol in the same welfare course for Indigenous people that she was undertaking. It was through this course that I started mixing with other Indigenous people for the first time, in the classroom, at community meetings and community social events. At that stage, I was like a sponge soaking up all the information I could to learn more about my Indigenous cultural background.

In the mid 1980s, to find out more about my Indigenous heritage, I made contact with various Queensland government departments via letter and telephone, even visiting some of them on a few occasions. Sadly, all my investigations failed to reveal anything about my Aboriginal heritage. At this time, access to government records and information was often restricted, especially to Indigenous people. Fortunately, Queensland's *Freedom of Information Act* 1992 has changed this situation to a degree, and opened the way for further Indigenous research.

During the early 1990s I enrolled at the University of Queensland and graduated with a social work degree. In the late 1990s and early 2000s I worked as a social worker with 'Link-Up', an organisation that engaged in re-uniting Indigenous families who had been fragmented by Stolen Generation legislation.[5] In time, I discovered that this work was subconsciously taking an emotional toll on me because, with each reunion I was involved with, I was always wondering if this family could perhaps be part of my family? Moreover, as I had been taught nothing of my Indigenous cultural and spiritual heritage, I felt lost and disconnected from my identity as an Aboriginal woman. This situation triggered a personal turning point in my life, re-directing me to resume my quest to discover my own lost identity. Taking up tertiary studies again in 2004 offered me an opportunity to further this quest, through researching the Queensland certificate of exemption and its impact on identity as my honours thesis topic.

The exemption certificate and the erasure of Indigenous identity

Initially I began by searching for scholarly literature about the Queensland certificate of exemption. I discovered only a very small number of publications about the exemption certificate and its repercussions. Some notable authors mentioned various aspects of the certificate of exemption.[6] These included the fact that once Aboriginal people gained the certificate they would in effect have to lose their Indigenous identity and culture, their family and their homelands, in exchange for living in the wider community. Yet the social impact on cultural identity for the certificate holders and their descendants remained largely unexplored by research and analysis.

This situation drove me into researching material about the legislative origins of the exemption certificate, 'The Aboriginals Protection and Restriction of the Sale of Opium Act, 1897 (Qld)', housed in Queensland's state archives.[7] The parliamentary debates in relation to the '1897 Act' reflected a range of political arguments and differences of opinion regarding the treatment of Indigenous Queenslanders that existed amongst the parliamentarians of the era. Several arguments were posed as justification for the 1897 Act, but three points detailed in the debates were specifically emphasised. The first concerned the establishment and enforcement of legislated penalties for supplying liquor to 'Aboriginals' and 'half-castes'. The second referred to similar provisions outlawing the supply of opium to 'Aboriginals' and 'half-castes'. The third referred to making it a punishable offence for non-Aboriginal people to possess government blankets that had been issued to 'Aboriginals' and 'half-castes' by the State appointed Protectors of Aboriginal Queenslanders.[8] As historian Rosalind Kidd has noted: 'Protectors were directed to see that they do not get any liquor or opium, that they keep their blankets'.[9]

In general, the focus of these parliamentary debates centred on the belief that a system of 'care and protection' for Aboriginal people would work for their betterment. The passing of the 1897 Act empowered the Queensland government to regulate, discipline and control every aspect of Aboriginal Queenslander's lives. It meant that the government dictated where Indigenous Queenslanders could live, where they could work, how they could spend their wages and whom they could marry. In many cases the government decided if they could keep their own children.

With the knowledge of hindsight, it is clear that in reality, 'care and protection' was in fact regulation through 'control and incarceration' most particularly via the removal orders of Section 9 of the 1897 Act. This Section 9 gave government officials the legal right to remove Aboriginal people from their homelands and elsewhere and place them onto reserves and missions.

> Section 9: It shall be lawful for the Minister to cause every aboriginal within any District, not being an aboriginal excepted from the provisions of this section, to be removed to, and kept within the limits of, any reserve situated within such District, in such manner, and subject to such conditions, as may be prescribed. The Minister may, subject to the said conditions, cause any aboriginal to be removed from one reserve to another.[10]

Other parts of the 1897 Act were equally oppressive and reveal the extensive powers of the Chief Protector in regulating Indigenous lives and communities. They included the authority to control and restrict all movements on and off reserves (Section 11), determine, regulate and revoke 12 month employment permits issued to 'Aboriginal and half-castes' (Sections 12 and 13), supervise all 'Aboriginal and female half-castes' in employment (Sections 15 and 16) and prevent any removal of Aboriginal people to other districts or outside the colony of Queensland (Section 17).

It is now recognised that the removal system created by the 1897 Act delivered a trans-generational impact on the lives of Aboriginal people that is still felt today. Many researchers and writers have noted that the process of removal resulted in the demise of Aboriginal societies, with the loss of homelands, kin, culture, language and identity.[11] Queensland's 'protectionist' system can be characterised by an ongoing multi-faceted and systematic attempt to transform Aboriginal societies and culture. With the many removals fragmenting families and kinship groups, numerous Aboriginal languages and sub-cultures were transformed to the point of extinction.[12] The certificate of exemption itself was introduced originally in Section 33 of the 1897 Act, which stated that:

> It shall be lawful for the Minister to issue to any half-caste, who, in his opinion, ought not to be subject to the provisions of this Act, a certificate, in writing under his hand, and that such half-caste is exempt from the

provisions of this Act and the Regulations, and from and after the issue of such certificate, such half-caste shall be so exempt accordingly.[13]

The exemption certificate represented the only legal mechanism by which Indigenous Queenslanders could live independently away from reserves or missions, out from 'under the Act'. However, it required severing all ties with their Aboriginal kinship and culture including connections with country, or the exemption could be revoked by the state.[14]

Historian Thom Blake has noted:

> Exemption Certificates were granted only to those Aborigines who demonstrated to the Chief Protector's satisfaction the capacity to survive in the outside world. In other words, they were imbued with capitalist values concerning money, time and work. But the standards required for exemption were high; certificates were not freely issued.[15]

In his view, exemption from the 'under the Act' was offered as an incentive, a reward for working hard and obeying the rules. He argues:

> As well as punitive measures; there was one incentive for workers to give faithful and diligent services – exemption from the Act.[16]

Castle and Hagen, in the only, albeit unpublished, article written entirely about the certificate of exemption, 'Turning black into white: the exemption system in Queensland 1908-1965', emphasise the economic situation concerning Aboriginal workers' labour relations and unionism issues, triggered by the government's 'protectionist' policy. They argue that '[t]he aim of the 1897 Act was to establish a system which would cover all Aborigines in the Colony and regulate their contacts with other inhabitants of Queensland'.[17] The financial and logistical advantages for government would be less Aboriginal people to care for. In effect the system established by the Act enshrined the distinction between Aborigines and 'half-castes'.[18]

My research into official exemption statistics found that over the 60 years from 1908 until 1967/8, a total of 4092 certificates of exemption were issued. This figure included 2520 males and 1570 females, as well as 1165 children on their mother's certificate. The age groups of exemptees varied from the very young (9 months, in 1908) to the very old (88 years in 1958). It is likely that the older applicants were seeking their certificates of exemption so that they could claim their entitlements as Age Pensioners. Prior to 1958, Commonwealth benefits for Aboriginal people were only given if the person lived off a 'reserve or mission'.[19] In another example, information found in the 1958 Register of Certificates of Exemption Issued involved Aboriginal people at the Lazaret on Fantome Island, where inmates applied for Invalid pensions and other Commonwealth benefits after being exempted.[20]

One personal highlight during my research was to actually hold the original *'The Aboriginals Protection and Restriction of the Sale of Opium Act,* 1897 (Qld)' document in my gloved hands for a few minutes. Whilst I realised that this was a great privilege, I also realised that I held in my hands the very document that had literally enslaved my family and countless other families over many decades. I was aware that this piece of paper was responsible for so much loss and heartache for thousands of Indigenous Australians. The loss of kinship, culture and traditional land, which also encompassed stolen wages[21] and even stolen children, was the painful legacy of this aging document. The 1897 Act had come close to achieving the genocide of Australia's original inhabitants and it was certainly responsible for generations of despondency and helplessness that persist to this day.

Aboriginal writers, when writing their autobiographies, typically seem to skip quickly over the issue of exemption certificates. Was the certificate of exemption something that they were not comfortable writing about? Or was it that they knew very little about the exemption? To leave a State Reserve or church mission required an application for a certificate of exemption. I can understand now why many Aboriginal people sought a certificate as the only possible path to freedom and independence. This has been explained by such writers as Marnie Kennedy, Jackie Huggins, Albert Holt, Regina Ganter and Ruth Hegarty.[22] Their writings illustrate the varied lifestyles each was forced to adopt in order to survive injustices and live within contemporary Australian society. For those still living 'under the Act' it meant to live a life of subjection and servitude, with very few, if any, of the freedoms enjoyed and taken for granted by the wider community.

Uncovering and reclaiming Indigenous identity

Sifting through large quantities of mostly undisturbed printed documents and records in the Queensland state archives inevitably meant uncovering the biographical material about Indigenous Queenslanders which has shaped my own identity. I found my grandfather, Roy, was born at Nanango, in the South Burnett region of Queensland in 1901. Daisy, my grandmother, also a Queenslander, was born on Boomarra Station, north of Cloncurry, in 1900. I also found out how that each had their young lives affected by state removal orders. The Queensland Government removed Roy, aged 13, from Taabinga Station near Nanango to Purga Mission near Ipswich in the south-east of the state in 1914. He was enrolled at the Mission school in 1914 and later sent out to work when he was 16-years-old.[23] At the age of 20, Daisy[24] was removed from the Hillcoat's family home at Teneriffe in Brisbane and taken to Purga Mission.[25] Roy and Daisy met there and were married in 1924, at the Purga Mission Salvation Army Church.

Figure 6.1: Daisy, baby Gwen and Roy Smith taken in 1926.

Roy, Daisy and my mother Gwen, aged 13 months, left Purga Mission after Roy gained his exemption certificate on the 25 March 1926. My grandmother did not herself require a certificate of exemption as she was exempt from removal orders under Section 10c of the 1897 Act as 'A female lawfully married to, and residing with, a husband who is not himself an aboriginal'. Therefore, after 25 March 1926, my grandfather and his family were legally no longer classified as Aboriginal and could reside away from the mission provided they upheld the conditions required of them by the certificate of exemption.

Uncovering this family genealogy, while it began to throw some light on my multiple identities, left me with mixed feelings. On one hand, I was happy to finally find information about my grandparents, but on the other hand, I was saddened to know that they suffered so much. My research uncovered documentation that both my grandparents were removed prior to my grandfather being granted a certificate of exemption, thus they were twice subjected to cultural identity loss.

Fortunately, prior to commencing this archival research, I had discovered diaries that my grandmother Daisy kept methodically during the 1940s and 1950s. These were a unique find and are possibly the only surviving records written by an Indigenous woman from this era in Queensland. They provide much insight into my grandparents' lives as exemptees after they left Purga Mission. From various family members, I have been able to obtain six of these diaries, each one recording the annual family events for the years 1942, 1944, 1945, 1947, 1949 and 1951.

The 1951 diary contained a brief entry written by Roy in 1979, on Daisy's birthday, four years after she had passed away: 'How I miss you Mum'. They were a very close couple throughout their married lives. Their closeness appears to have been an important aspect of successfully maintaining their exemption and overcoming the isolation from other family members that the exemption rules required.

Figure 6.2: Daisy with Mervyn and baby Maurice taken in the early 1930s.

Figure 6.3: Roy Smith and his football team taken in the 1940s.

Figure 6.4: Roy Smith and his beloved car – the Rigby.

Figure 6.5: Roy and Daisy Smith taken in the 1950s.

In these diaries, Daisy recorded in detail the Smith's daily family life in regard to housekeeping, work, education, housing, sport, travel, entertainment and community/civic life. Here is an example of her daily entry:

> Cleaned out all the house. Roy still out near the Plateau.
> Maurice mustering cattle for Tim Downing.
> Les. & Ruth. went up to the Hospital & then up to town.
> Valma. at school. All went to see 'Song of the Island'
> at night. No mail. Posted letter to Gwen.[26]

She also recorded major events in Queensland, national and international public affairs. The entry for the end of World War II, shown as:

> Roy and gang down at Wethern. Roy on tractor.
> NEWS came through at 9.15. Peace being Declared.
> And what rejoicing. I did my washing and hosed
> out the Kitchen. Val went up town but were too late
> to shop. All went to pictures.[27]

After reading through the diaries, I became aware of the things they did not mention. There were no references to any Aboriginal issues, social or political. For instance, Daisy makes no reference to 26 January in any of her diaries as being a day of significance for Aboriginal people. Neither did she mention Aboriginal friends or visitors, apart from immediate family members. Instead, the diaries reveal only the ordered law-abiding measured lives my grandparents lived to ensure that they maintained the exemption from living 'under the Act'.

For my grandfather, the decision to apply for the certificate of exemption must have been a difficult one to make. Choosing to either to live 'under the Act' or fend for himself and his family in the wider community was something that he had to consider carefully. I wonder if I could have gone down the same road as my grandfather and grandmother in 1926, and been as brave, progressive and enterprising as they? Today, however, I can see their reasoning, concerning what they wanted to achieve for their family. Again I wonder, if my grandfather could have looked into the future and seen the loss and heartache resulting from gaining the certificate of exemption, would he have taken the same road again? Nevertheless, it seems clear that he insisted his daughter and my mother, Gwen, always be conscious of the rules and regulations pertaining to the certificate of exemption, and the consequences for her family if they were not obeyed. Throughout her 82 years, Gwen has complied meticulously with the conditions of her father's exemption, and as the daughter of an exemptee has never seen or referred to herself as Aboriginal.

Making sense of exemption

In trying to make sense of the powerful impact of the exemption certificate, I was attracted to the work of the late French social theorist, Michel Foucault. A number of other researchers have adopted Foucault's theories regarding crime and punishment and his concepts of surveillance and self-regulation to analyse the various government policies that affected the Aboriginal population in Queensland.[28] In *Discipline and punish: the birth of the prison*, Foucault identifies two dimensions of discipline, both of which can be seen to have operated on the reserves and missions – 'the discipline-blockade' and 'the discipline-mechanism'. Foucault notes that:

> There are two images, then, of discipline. At one extreme, the discipline-blockade, the enclosed institution, established on the edges of society, turned inwards towards negative functions: arresting evil, breaking communications, suspending time. At the other extreme, with panopticism, is the discipline-mechanism: a functional mechanism that must improve the exercise of power by making it lighter, more rapid, more effective, a design of subtle coercion for a society to come.[29]

Searching some of the official correspondence written in the 1920s requesting advice or clarification clearly shows how closely Aboriginal Queenslanders were controlled and managed, through the authority of government officials charged with the responsibility for their well being. Here is an example:

> Only two of the six sets of correspondence related to females seeking exemption. They indicate a paternalistic and moralistic approach to the

treatment of Aboriginal women in the care of the Office of the Chief Protector. The first application, which was unsuccessful, contained seven pages of supporting documentation from the Protector in Cloncurry. The rejection was made without explanation despite the good references, the applicant's ability to 'read and write a little', a considerable savings account, and the applicant 'having had no association with coloured people. Even the fact that she had both a sister and a brother with certificates of exemption, and that she spoke good English without the slightest accent' counted for nothing. The applicant was advised, 'the girl should be assured that as long as she maintains her present good character she need not fear being removed to a Reserve'.[30]

Foucault's work provides a powerful theoretical explanation of the oppressive regulation dispensed by the state to Aboriginal Queenslanders who sought exemption. Those who successfully obtained and maintained exemption did so through a process of ongoing self-regulation, which involved sobriety, thrift, cleanliness, regular employment and disassociating from Aboriginal kin, culture and country. In effect, the laws and instituted policies resulted in a 'self' shaped by the domination of every aspect of the lives paradoxically exempted from 'under the Act'.

Foucault's work on surveillance pinpoints my mother's biography perfectly. As noted earlier, Gwen has lived a measured cautious life, like her parents, to avoid triggering the attention of authorities who could return her and her family to the reserve for violation of conditions of the exemption. In particular, avoiding association with Aboriginal people has been a quiet preoccupation for Gwen. For example, as far back as I can remember, Mum has always asked me questions like: 'Who are those [darkies] and do you know them?' It seemed that it was alright for me to enquire, but not her. As a teenager in the mid 1960s I remember our local church appointing a Torres Strait Islander as our Curate, but outside church and school we had no contact with him and his family. My mother's apparent fear of socialising with Murris probably best accounts for the small size of my family as a child and the almost total absence of Aboriginal people within the family's circle of friends. Foucault referred to this kind of management and control as 'biopower'.[31] In more recent years Gwen has claimed that she 'was always free', but what was she free from? To me her life has been highly regulated through disciplining of her self. Was she talking about the freedom from the strictures of life on the reserve? One can only guess as she has never discussed these aspects of her biography and does not wish to do so.

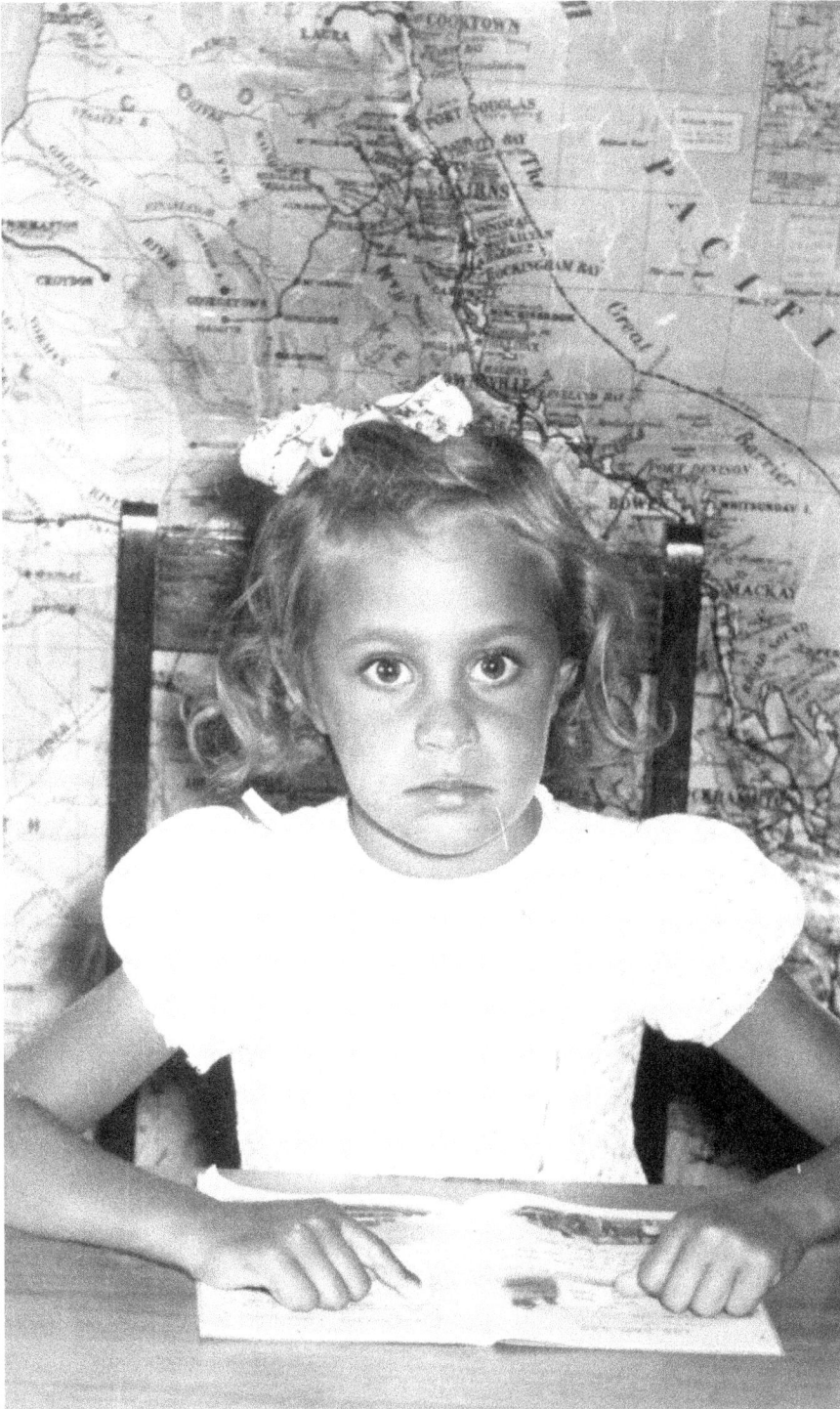

Figure 6.6: Judi Wickes.

Biographies of others descendants of exemptees

Originally, I planned to interview Aboriginal people who themselves were exemptees or descendants of someone who had an exemption certificate to gather material about the 'lived experience' of exemption. I found that the legacy of this regime evident in the erasure of Indigenous cultural identity amongst the greater percentage of those descendants of the exemptees interviewed for the thesis research.

I interviewed a total of six participants and found that the interview material fell short of my expectations, as the interviewees lacked knowledge about the exemption certificate. When I asked about this 110-year-old legislation, I discovered that almost all the interviewees had 'never really heard of it'. Most were not even familiar with the draconian conditions imposed upon Aboriginal Queenslanders who were forced to live under the 1897 Act for the next 70 years. When describing their own sense of self, the interviewees responded in different ways. Few of them shared commonalities in terms of their perceptions of personal identity. None identified as 'white' or non-Indigenous Australians and most reported experiences of racism as a result of being identified as Aboriginal people by non-Indigenous Australians.[32]

Nevertheless, what has become a journey of reclaiming my own Indigenous heritage as the descendant of exemptees has continued since completing and submitting my Honours thesis in December 2005. For example, recently more information about my family's biography has come to light as the result of attending a local historical and genealogy group. In particular, information about my grandfather's European family history, for which I have been searching for over 20 years, has emerged. I found that my maternal great-great grandparents were both Irish born, met and married in Brisbane in 1852 and went on to have 12 children. My great-grandfather was their eleventh child. He passed away in 1920 aged 43. I discovered that Roy's mother, Maud Taabinga, died in childbirth at Nanango. I have no further information about my great-grandmother other than her name on Roy's marriage certificate. Each new discovery, however, opens up more questions about my ancestors who were responsible for my mixed heritage. So far, I have no records of Roy from birth to age 13, when he was removed to Purga Mission. I wonder if Roy and his father were together on Taabinga Station during those 13 years until he was removed? One can only guess at this stage.

By Aboriginal standards, my family group is very small, consisting of those descended from my grandparents Roy and Daisy and my grandmother's sister Nancy.[33] When growing up I learned very little about my maternal grandparents' family history. There were no stories told of the 'old days' or who their families were or where they came from. Yet, I still have fond memories of visiting the Hillcoat family home at Teneriffe, a suburb of Brisbane. The Hillcoats were a non-Indigenous family who owned Boomarra Station in north-west Queensland, who my grandmother had known and worked for since she was a young girl. Interestingly, our two families have been intertwined for over 100 years, beginning as a friendly relationship between employers and employees. Later, the relationship continued as one established between good family friends. Finally, the third generation were to become as close as sisters. This relationship continues even to this day.

I am always looking for information about Daisy and Nancy's life prior to being removed to Purga Mission. Last year my mother gave me a Prayer Book with Daisy's name written on the inside cover. The book commemorates her confirmation in 1917 at the St Thomas Anglican Church, Toowong in suburban Brisbane suggesting that Daisy and Nancy were living in Brisbane with the Hillcoat family then. The Hillcoat sisters have subsequently confirmed that their family lived in the Toowong area prior to moving to Teneriffe. This also confirms that Daisy and Nancy lived with the Hillcoat family in Brisbane for at least three years prior to being removed to Purga Mission. When Daisy and Nancy moved initially to Brisbane with the Hillcoat family remains uncertain. More research is needed to fill the information gaps about my grandmother and her sister. It is worth noting that Daisy and Nancy and their families maintained a close lifelong relationship.

Another significant question in this jigsaw is: from what Indigenous nation or nations am I descended, and can claim connection to? Does knowing that my grandfather was born in Nanango and my grandmother born on Boomarra Station entitle me to say that my Indigenous heritage is Waka Waka and Kalkadoon? I can only guess. Whatever the answer to this question is, my exploratory research shows that the erasure of connection to kin and homelands required by the exemption certificate came at a high cost to exemptees and their descendants which reverberates into the present.

Further reflections

Biography and autobiography of people's lives is an important part of our 'lived experiences' and therefore, very much part of each individual's life journey and personal searches. I would like to think that my research might prove to be important and relevant to other Indigenous people who are searching for their family history, trying to establish their kinship ties and genealogy. Some of these people may discover that, like me, their grandparents or other members of their family were also issued with certificates of exemption. It appears that many of today's Aboriginal generation are totally unaware of the existence and consequences of this legislation. If attempts to trace their ancestry meet with a wall of silence, it may be due to the enforcement of the exemption certificate's requirements for complete separation from cultural and family ties. As noted earlier, my own research began as a journey to address questions which this silence created for me personally. It continues to grow as I uncover more and more information about the facts and injustices relating to the exemption certificate. For instance, a number of local organisations have approached me to be a guest speaker, giving a lecture on the certificate of exemption. Another outcome relates to my niece, who after reading my thesis, created an art installation and then displayed it at a successful two-week art exhibition at Southbank in Brisbane with the theme 'certificate of exemption'. I am sure that the topic of exemption will take on a life of its own and eventually become more of an issue within the wider community.

It is my hope that this research will help to fill the educational void that exists, concerning the loss of identity and culture experienced by exemptees and their descendants. It may also serve to educate the non-Indigenous population about the hardships and heartaches experienced by so many Indigenous Queenslanders who were forced to live for many years 'under the Act'.

In conclusion, I believe that all Australians need to be informed about the deeply puzzling and traumatic loss of identity, culture and traditional homelands suffered by those exempted Indigenous people and their families. I am concerned that the vast majority of people whom I have spoken with since the completion of my thesis ask, 'What is the certificate of exemption?' and then remark, 'I never really heard of it'.

Acknowledgements

The author would like to acknowledge the University of the Sunshine Coast for its provision of financial assistance and Dr Lucinda Aberdeen for her helpful comments and support of this paper.

References

Unpublished sources

Queensland State Archives

Chief Protector of Aboriginals 1923, Correspondence from Protector of Aboriginals and Aboriginal Queensland to the Office of the Chief Protector of Aboriginals, Brisbane 1921-1923, QSA-A/58734, 23/369.

Correspondence of the Office of Native Affairs, 'Commonwealth and States Native Welfare Conference. Department of Territories, Canberra. August, 1951', Queensland State Archives, Brisbane, SRS 10431/ Box 516 Batch 275.

Castle, R and J Hagan 1997, 'Turning black into white: the exemption system in Queensland 1908-1965', Mimeograph, University of Wollongong, Wollongong.

Smith, Daisy 1945, Unpublished personal diary.

Wickes, Judi 2005, '"Never really heard of it": A study of the impact on identity of the Queensland certificate of exemption for Aboriginal People', Honours Thesis, University of the Sunshine Coast.

Published sources

Aberdeen, Lucinda 2002, 'The Politics of Settlement', in *Social self, global culture: An introduction to sociological ideas*, 2nd edn, P Beilharz and T Hogan (eds), Oxford University Press, South Melbourne: 191–203.

AIATSIS 2000, *Guidelines in ethical research in Indigenous studies*, AIATSIS, Canberra.

Blake, Thom 2001, *A dumping ground: A history of the Cherbourg settlement*, University of Queensland Press, St Lucia.

Cuff, EC, WW Sharrock and DW Francis 1998, *Perspectives in sociology*, 4th edn, Routledge, London.

Donovan, Val 2002, *The reality of a dark history: From contact and conflict to cultural recognition*, Platypus Graphics, Brisbane.

Evans, Raymond 1999, *Fighting words: Writing about race*, University of Queensland Press, St Lucia.

Evans, Raymond, Kay Saunders and K Cronin 1993, *Race relations in colonial Queensland: A history of exclusion, exploitation and extermination*, University of Queensland Press, St Lucia.

Foucault, Michel 1975, *Discipline and punish: The birth of the prison*, Penguin Books, London.

Ganter, Regina 1998, 'Living an immoral life – "coloured" women and the paternalistic state', *Hecate* 24(1): 13-40.

Hall, Robert A 1989, *The Black Diggers: Aborigines and Torres Strait Islanders in the Second World War*, Aboriginal Studies Press, Canberra.

Hegarty, Ruth 1999, *Is that you, Ruthie?* University of Queensland Press, St Lucia.

Hollinsworth, David 1998, *Race and racism in Australia*, 2nd edn, Social Science Press, Katoomba.

Holt, Albert 2001, *Forcibly removed*, Magabala Books, Broome.

Human Rights and Equal Opportunity Commission 1997, *Bringing them home report of the national inquiry into the separation of Aboriginal and Torres Strait Islander children from their families*, Sterling Press, Canberra.

Huggins, Jackie 1998, *Sister girl*, University of Queensland Press, St Lucia.

Huggins, Rita and Jackie Huggins 1994, *Auntie Rita*, Aboriginal Studies Press, Canberra.

Kennedy, Marnie 1985, *Born a half-caste*, Aboriginal Studies Press, Canberra.

Kidd, Rosalind 1997, *The way we civilise: Aboriginal Affairs – the untold story*, University of Queensland Press, St Lucia.

Martin, Karen 2003, 'Ways of knowing, being and doing: a theoretical framework and methods for Indigenous and Indigenist re-search', *JAS, Australia's Public Intellectual Forum* 76: 203-15, 256-7.

Queensland Parliament 1897, *Aboriginals Protection and the Restriction of the Sale of Opium Act 1897, Proceedings of the Legislative Assembly*, Queensland Government Printer, Brisbane: 6173-6183.

Queensland Parliament 1897, *Queensland Parliamentary Debates on the Aboriginals Protection and Restriction of the Sale of Opium Bill (three Readings)*, Queensland Parliament. Queensland Government Printer, Brisbane.

Reynolds, Henry 1999, *Why weren't we told?: A personal search for the truth about our history*, Viking, Ringwood.

Rowley, CD 1970, *The remote Aborigines*, Penguin Books Australia Ltd, Sydney.

—— 1981, *A matter of justice*, Penguin Books Australia Ltd, Sydney.

ENDNOTES

[1] My father has English and German heritage.

[2] I was working as a casual employee in the Special Projects (Indigenous) of the then Department of Health, Queensland government.

[3] The regional term 'Murri' relates to Indigenous people who live in Queensland.

[4] My grandparents were married for 51 years when my grandmother passed away first in 1975 and then, exactly five years to the day later, my grandfather also passed away.

[5] Bringing them Home. A report into the removal of Indigenous children from their families was tabled in the Federal Parliament, Canberra on 26 May 1997.

[6] Rowley 1970; Hall 1989; Kennedy 1985; Evans et al. 1993; Kidd 1997; Hollinsworth 1998; Huggins 1994; Blake 2001; Donavan 2002; Aberdeen 2002.

[7] Public Acts of the Parliament of Queensland. Aboriginals: An Act to make Provision for the better Protection and Care of the Aboriginal and Half-caste Inhabitants of the Colony, and to make more effectual Provision for Restricting the Sale and Distribution of Opium [Assented to 15 December 1897].

[8] Queensland Parliamentary Debates on the Aboriginal Protection and Restriction of the Sale of Opium Bill 1897: 1541.

[9] Kidd 1997: 48.

[10] *Aboriginals Protection and the Restriction of the Sale of Opium Act* 1897 (Qld): 6175.

[11] See for example, Rowley 1981; Huggins 1994; Evans 1999; Reynolds 1999.

[12] Evans 1999: 116.

[13] *Aboriginals Protection and the Restriction of the Sale of Opium Act* 1897 (Qld): 6182.

[14] The system of exemption was incorporated in protectionist policies later elsewhere after the federation of Australia in 1901. For example, *NSW Aborigines Protection Act 1909-1943* and later the *NSW Aborigines Welfare Act 1943-1968* in New South Wales, the *Aborigines Act 1905*, in Western Australia and the *Aborigines Act Amendment Act 1939* in South Australia including the Northern Territory. Like the

Queensland legislation, the conditions of exemption included the requirement of severing family connections and could be revoked at any time.

[15] Blake 2001: 136-7.

[16] Blake 2001: 136-7.

[17] Castle and Hagen 1997: 2.

[18] Castle and Hagan also make the observation that, by substituting the word 'Aboriginal' for 'half-caste' in its definitions, the amended 1939 version of Act made it possible for 'full-bloods' to become eligible for the certificate of exemption.

[19] Correspondence of the Office of Native Affairs, Queensland State Archives, Brisbane, SRS 10431/ Box 516 Batch 275.

[20] Fantome Island Exemptions Register, 1958 cited in Wickes 2005: 61.

[21] Kidd 1997. As part of her PhD, Kidd uncovered Queensland government records revealing the widespread practice of misappropriation of Aboriginal people's wages, thus known as the 'stolen wages'.

[22] Kennedy 1985; Huggins 1998; Holt 2001; Ganter 1998 and Hegarty 1999.

[23] Roy Smith has government records of his work in the Chinchilla region of south-west Queensland. Included as well is a letter written by him stating the appalling living conditions he was living in. Recently, I found in Daisy's 1951 diary, Roy has written a few sentences about his teenage years. Also, entries for a few months, written about nine months prior to his passing away.

[24] Grandmother (Daisy) talked about being hidden in the downstairs rooms of the house when police came around on previous occasions.

[25] I discovered that the police forcibly removed Daisy from Teneriffe, Brisbane, where she has been working as a single 20-year-old housemaid. My research revealed that it had been decreed that single Aboriginal females living in suburbia represented a source of moral temptation for the (white) males. She was taken, along with her 10-year-old sister, Nancy, to Purga Mission near Ipswich, Queensland in August 1920.

[26] Smith 1945: Friday 9 February.

[27] Smith 1945: Wednesday 15 August.

[28] Blake 2001; Kidd 1997.

[29] Foucault 1975: 209.

[30] Chief Protector of Aboriginals 1923. This letter was in a box of correspondence: QSA-A/58734, 23/369. A total of seven pages of correspondence pertaining to this female applicant and her outcome: she was refused exemption. Location: Cloncurry. Date: 25 January, 19 February and 16, 23 March 1923.

[31] Cuff et al. 1998: 273.

[32] Knowing that Aboriginal people have been over-researched, especially by non-Indigenous researchers, I was very conscious of community protocols and the importance of anonymity and confidentiality in gathering and handling the data from interviews. Therefore, throughout the research and analysis, I strictly adhered to the principles of ethical research as set out in *Guidelines in ethical research in Indigenous studies*, AIATSIS 2000. Martin claims that non-Indigenous researchers usually conduct this kind of social research, as they tend to predominate in the field, Martin 2003. I believe that sharing a similar cultural background with the interviewees supported my research, as the participants felt they could freely discuss the culturally sensitive issues of impact and identity without the feeling of 'being judged'.

[33] Nancy married Jack Mittabong; they had one daughter, Gwendoline who only recently passed away in 2007. Nancy passed away in 2003 and Jack in 1991. Gwendoline was a widow for over 30 years and had no children.

Biography as balancing act: life according to Joe and the rules of historical method

Aroha Harris

The *papakainga* (homeland, community) of the Ngati Whatua people at Okahu Bay in Auckland is a place where the people and the land are so inseparable that each defines the other. It is also a place that signifies many familiar historical patterns: of colonisation, legislation and policy-making, attitudes and perceptions that rendered Ngati Whatua politically and economically powerless, wrested them from their lands, and devastated their culture and society. These patterns recur not only throughout Aotearoa New Zealand, but also throughout the indigenous world – coloured and embellished by variations within and between tribes and cultures.

By the end of the nineteenth century, the Native Land Court had irreversibly destroyed the customary tenure and therefore tribal authority that Ngati Whatua exercised over the entire area and the colonial government had compulsorily taken the first of several sections it would eventually acquire. Then, from the early twentieth century, Auckland City openly coveted Okahu Bay. It claimed the *papakainga* as an area into which the city would expand, and marked out its intention by constructing a sewer line right through the front of the *papakainga*. By 1951, Auckland was easily New Zealand's largest and fastest growing city. It had grown up and out from what is now the Central Business District. And, in 1951, one of the gravest consequences of that growth was the forcible removal of the Ngati Whatua people from their *papakainga*, their home.

Joseph Parata (Joe) Hawke would have been nine or ten years old at the time. His home, the home of his family, the home he was born into, was one of many deliberately burned to the ground in a government-sanctioned action that moved the people out of their traditional home and community, away from the beach and the public eye, and up the hill into state homes – that proud badge of post-war New Zealand citizenship. Twenty-six years later, Joe led *whanau* (family) and supporters in an occupation of Bastion Point on the ridge behind the *papakainga*. The occupation was a key event for the Maori land rights movement of the 1970s and 1980s. It was an attempt to stop the government of the day from selling land that Ngati Whatua asserted was rightfully theirs. That was an historical assertion, previously directed through so-called 'official' channels such as petitioning and litigation. The occupation ended spectacularly in May 1978, 507 days after it began. Police and armed forces removed the protestors and destroyed the temporary *marae* (tribal meeting house and associated land and facilities) they had erected there.[1]

In the aftermath, Joe, a builder by trade, found that his protest profile had rendered him unemployable. He was the subject of vicious and threatening vitriol. Ten years after the occupation the Waitangi Tribunal substantially upheld the Ngati Whatua claims to their lands, and a degree of tribal economic and community development has occurred since. Joe has been a part of those recent developments, but it is probably the younger, radical Joe, that older New Zealanders remember.

The very sketchy outline given here has cut through multiple detailed and nuanced layers to introduce Joe and his life. It also indicates some of the gristly problems that research and writing his biography presents, and into which this essay will delve. As the researcher and writer of Joe's story, by far the most gristly problems faced to date are those that attach to subjectivity – Joe's, his family's and mine. Subjectivity is arguably embedded in Maori research due to the obligations of *whakapapa* (genealogy, connections). Maori scholar Danny Keenan has unequivocally asserted *whakapapa* as the primary organising device for tribal histories.[2] Few Maori historians would disagree. Charles Royal, for example, maintains that there is no such thing as Maori history, there is only tribal history.[3] And Joseph Pere contends that only tribal members should be eligible to write tribal histories.[4] If *whakapapa*, tribal belonging, is subjectivity, then these and other scholars effectively advocate subjectivity as both the analytical frame and the authority for writing Maori tribal histories. In effect, Maori scholarship embraces and even demands subjectivity, and many Maori scholars aim to do what Maori academic Linda Smith urges: to 'reprioritize and reconcile what is important about the past with what is important about the future'.[5]

Though Maori scholarship values oral sources – the spoken accounts of life, of experience and of reality, it can and does use documentary evidence, especially the State's. But it does so critically, maybe even suspiciously, aware that the so-called official record is the record of the coloniser, of the legislator and governor who observed and wrote. Maori scholarship has also generated its own documents – some in relationship to the State and some indifferent to it – with access governed entirely by Maori protocols.

Maori scholarship has protocols that allow research participants an influential say about the projects to which they contribute. In the case of Joe's biography, that means his *whanau* (family) can, has and will continue to have a say about it. Before the research for Joe's biography even began, I asked Joe and a few of his family members what they wanted readers to get from reading his biography. He and his wife Rene responded quickly and clearly that the book must convey the government's progressive encroachment on Ngati Whatua territory and authority, the subjugation of Ngati Whatua in the name of modernity, and the *mamae* – the hurt – that it caused. This reflects the indivisibility of Joe's life from the land. Joe and Rene's daughter, Sharon, was also quick to respond. She said she just wanted people to see that Joe is human, a man with strengths *and* weaknesses. Her brother, Parata, made a similar remark, commenting on Joe as a father. Initially, this all sounded great, simple even. But it became more and more loaded with every interview, because when Joe speaks his human-ness speaks. In the inflections of his life I see and hear what I understand his children want depicted in words and images on paper. And I am struck by the enormity, difficulty and privilege of the biographer's job.

The *whanau* influence can easily be viewed as biased and constraining. It presents a tension that leads to the kinds of questions the 'Indigenous Lives' conference chose to address, like: who owns the story? Many more questions may be raised, cultivated by the risky admission of subjectivity into the already fraught activity of writing biography. Though I acknowledge the problems, the brevity of this essay precludes any resolution of them. Instead, it has the more modest goal of sharing a particular incident, one that demonstrates some of the difficulties faced in balancing the desires of Joe and his family with the demands of historical method.

Within the creative, academic, cultural and philosophical processes of researching and writing Joe's life is the recurring motif of the *mamae*, the hurt. Joe has talked about the *mamae* a lot. It occurs not only in his words and story-telling, but in his biting back tears; in his skirting around emotional scars that, years later, still smart; and in his conveniently finding distractions in the middle of the most poignant stories. The *mamae* also presents some of the project's greatest challenges, highlighting in particular the problems of subjectivity, both Joe's subjectivity *and* mine.

One of the earliest stories of *mamae* that Joe told me was from his childhood, a story about himself, his older brother Eddie and their sister, Patu. It is a story that began happily; so many children's stories do. The *papakainga* was the centre of Joe's childhood universe. He learned to fish, and loved to fish, from its shore. He ate from its gardens and orchards. He played war games and hide-and-seek in the long grass with his brothers and cousins, and though Orakei had transformed by the 1940s into a wealthy Auckland suburb, Joe's quintessentially *Ngati Whatua* life was largely indifferent to it.

The *papakainga* was joyful and rich, the social and cultural centre of its people, often filled with the music and laughter of family and relations – aunts, uncles, cousins. Joe remembers the meeting house had two pianos. Two aunties would commandeer one each and playfully compete, taking turns to play and rousing the whole house with song and dance. At the end of one of those nights, Joe, Eddie, Patu and their parents took the usual walk to their home nearby. It was a wonderful night, a comfortable familiar night. But it turned horribly wrong when Patu walked into a wire barb on a fence, which hooked straight into her throat. Joe and Eddie had to hold Patu still and aloft, one each side of her, while their father removed the barb careful not to let it tear. Fortunately, Patu recovered, and Joe said she has sung like a bird ever since. But she also still bears the scar tissue, as does the land, because the fence she walked into was the Crown's fence – a fence declaring the Crown's undefeatable authority over some sections within the *papakainga*, an authority that would eventually swallow the *papakainga* whole.

I cried the first time I heard this story. I cried for those three children in the past, their fortitude and their trauma. I cried for the many loaded meanings of fences and barbed wire, and their particular representation in Joe's story. And I cried for Joe in the moment he told the story. I saw him struggle with it, heard him talk over and around the *mamae* that came so immediately to him as he spoke. He seemed to cry without tears. I cried quiet, objective, academic tears, bowed my head so that Joe and Rene would not notice, tried to put some distance between my role as researcher-writer and my instinctive emotional response. I told myself it would be unprofessional and even unethical to cry in an interview, that it might become an intrusive distraction, and an obstacle to the freedom of Joe's expression. It is a view I stand by, the telling of life stories in research situations ought to occur openly, and not be constrained by concern for the researchers' feelings. However, my real emotions were pent up. A few minutes after leaving Joe and Rene's home that day I was overcome. I pulled over, unwittingly at the park that used to be the *papakainga*, and wept. I knew I had a difficult problem on my hands, one that would require me to find a way to express my human emotional responses but without impacting the interview process. I also knew it would be a problem I would face again and again as the research progressed, and this has proven to be the case as the story of Patu getting caught in the fence is but one of Joe's many stories of the *mamae*.

Joe's narration of the *mamae* brings forth the delicacies and indelicacies of his story. It makes apparent my privileged position of 'knowing' and hearing Joe as a gentlemanly grandfather, softer than his imposing frame suggests, and unfamiliar to the public's memory of Joe the radical activist. Once again I find myself in search of that happy but elusive equilibrium between telling Joe's story and 'doing' history, mining one man's past for solutions to methodological puzzles: How do I write the hard stuff? How do I academically distinguish between Joe's emotions, my emotions and the biography? How do I write over and around my own emotional responses? And on the other hand – on the Maori hand – should I? With its appreciation of subjectivity, does Maori scholarship actually seek some connection – not only to Joe in the present but also to Joe in his past? But then, if Maori scholarship calls me to embrace my personal responses, does it also call forth more problems, for instance, allegations of bias or of academic restraint to the detriment of academic freedom? I will not pretend I have the answers to all these questions, but I hope that laying them out allows for clarity about their existence. With the problems in the foreground, resolution of them may be able to follow later, perhaps in the simple act of completing the project effectively.

Acknowledgements

I am indebted to Nga Pae o te Maramatanga, the National Institute of Research Excellence for Maori Development and Advancement, who materially supported my attendance at the 'Indigenous Lives' conference, as well as the attendance of Joe Hawke's granddaughter, Koha Hawke, and his niece (and researcher), Tui Hawke.

References

Primary sources

Walker, RJ 1979, 'Bastion Point [papers compiled by Ranginui Walker …]', University of Auckland General Library, Auckland.

Published sources

Hawke, Sharon 1998, *Takaparawhau: The People's story*, Moko Productions, Auckland.

Harris, Aroha 2008, *Hikoi: Forty years of Maori protest*, Huia Publications, Wellington.

Keenan, Danny 2000, in 'Ma Pango Ma Whero Ka Oti: unities and fragments in Maori history', Bronwyn Dalley and Bronwyn Labrum (eds), *Fragments: New Zealand social policy and cultural history*, Auckland University Press, Auckland: 44-51.

Pere, Joseph 1991, 'Hitori Maori', in *The future of the past: Themes in New Zealand history*, Colin Davis and Peter Lineham (eds), Department of History, Massey University, Palmerston North: 29-48.

Royal, Te Ahukaramu Charles 1992, *Te Haurapa: An introduction to researching tribal histories and traditions*, Bridget Williams Books, Wellington.

Smith, Linda T 1999, *Decolonizing methodologies: Research and indigenous peoples*, Zed Books and University of Otago Press, London and Dunedin.

Waitangi Tribunal 1987, *Report of the Waitangi Tribunal on the Orakei Claim (Wai 9)*, Waitangi Tribunal, Wellington.

ENDNOTES

[1] Fuller accounts of the Bastion Point occupation and the history of the Ngati Whatua land in the area may be read in: Sharon 2008; and Waitangi Tribunal 1987. Newspaper clippings following the occupation as it unfolded throughout the late 1970s may be found in Walker 1979, 'Bastion Point [papers compiled by Ranginui Walker ...]', (available at the University of Auckland General Library).

[2] Keenan 2000: 44-51.

[3] Royal 1992: 9.

[4] Pere 1991: 45.

[5] Smith 1999: 39.

The revelation of African culture in *Long walk to freedom*

Munzhedzi James Mafela

Long walk to freedom is the autobiography of Nelson Mandela. The author recounts his life, but at the same time deals with those experiences of his people and events he considers most significant. Writers of autobiographies are concerned primarily with themselves as subject matter. As Abrams writes: 'Autobiography is a biography written by the subject about himself'.[1] This means that in an autobiography, the subject recounts his or her own history. The novelist Graham Greene says that an autobiography is only 'a sort of life'. Any such work is a true picture of what, at one moment in a life, the subject wished – or is impelled – to reveal of that life.[2]

Long walk to freedom recreates the drama of the experiences that helped shape Mandela's destiny.[3] Throughout his life, Mandela fought for justice, freedom, goodness and love. The narrative is therefore a story about Mandela as well as the struggle of Africans in South Africa. The autobiography can thus be categorised as a historical or political narrative because it deals with matters affecting not only Mandela, but the nation as a whole. Shelston says that this type of narrative appeals to our curiosity about human personality, and to our interest in factual knowledge, in finding out 'what exactly happened!'[4]

As indicated above, the life of Mandela holds for us not only the political events that took place in the country, but also a record of the cultural life of his countrymen at the time, especially of Africans. One can therefore regard Mandela's life as representative of political, cultural and educational expression. Besides revealing the oppression he and his people experienced, the narrative reveals many cultural matters such as those affecting the institution of marriage, running a homestead, the life of a boy in a rural area, the role of women in the family and kinship relations.

The focus of this article is on kinship relations among Africans, as revealed in the narrative. The use of kinship relations will be highlighted to enhance an interpretation of some of the actions which would otherwise be difficult for readers to understand. This will bring more clarity to the storyline.

Kinship relations

Kinship is the organising principle of a society as it provides a good idea of the prevailing system of social organisation. The family is certainly fundamental in this regard. Kinship plays a basic part in the upbringing of the human individual, and has a universal place in human society.[5] According to Grabun:

> In all societies, people are divided into categories to perform certain tasks that have to be done and, at the same time, all these tasks contribute in their own ways to the running of the society that we may call social integration.[6]

Kinship relations differ from one culture to another. According to Van Warmelo, 'The context of the nomenclature of kinship varies considerably in different parts of the world.'[7] Hereunder, the difference of kinship relations between Western and African cultures is provided.

Western Culture	English Meaning	African Culture
aunt	sister of one's father	✓
	sister of one's mother	✗ (mother)
brother	a man's male sibling	✓
	a woman's male sibling	✓
cousin	daughter or son of mother's brother	✓
	daughter or son of father's sister	✓
	daughter or son of mother's sister	✗ (sister or brother)
	daughter or son of father's brother	✗ (sister or brother)
nephew	son of a woman's sister	✗ (son)
	son of a man's brother	✗ (son)
	son of a woman's brother	✓
	son of a man's sister	✓
niece	daughter of a woman's sister	✗ (daughter)
	daughter of a man's brother	✗ (daughter)
	daughter of a woman's brother	✓
	daughter of a man's sister	✓
sister	a woman's female sibling	✓
	a man's female sibling	✓
uncle	brother of one's mother	✓
	brother of one's father	✗ (father)

Failure to grasp the differences in kinship relations between Europeans and Africans could make it difficult for the reader, both non-African and African, to understand the reasons behind some of the actions in the narrative. As Van Warmelo writes:

> There exist certain differences between native and Europeans' ways of thought, and the social behaviour of the natives is guided by the standards of the society, which is moulded on a plan much different

from ours. An understanding of social structure means insight into relationships.[8]

As indicated above, concepts such as brother, sister, uncle, aunt and cousin do not have entirely the same meaning as those found in English and other cultures. Those who may be called cousins may not necessarily be cousins according to African culture, as illustrated above.

In explaining kinship relations in African culture, Mandela writes:

> In African culture, the sons and daughters of one's aunts and uncles are considered brothers and sisters, not cousins. We do not make the same distinctions among relations practised by Whites. We have no half-brothers or half-sisters. My mother's sister is my mother; my uncle's son is my brother; my brother's child is my son, daughter.[9]

The extract above has been added in the narration of events by the author to show that kinship relationship is the foundation of social life, and the basis of custom and law among the Africans. The author introduces the above to emphasise the unity that prevails among Africans. When people are closely related they will care for each other. Therefore, the chance of one's human rights being violated by another is limited. African culture does not preach individualism, but encourages living together as communities.

Kinship relations played an important role in shaping Mandela's political life. It was through following the traditions regarding kinship that Mandela came to understand the political situation in South Africa. For example, Kaizer Daliwonga Matanzima played an important role in Nelson Mandela's life, especially when they were at the University of Fort Hare together. Matanzima, who was senior to Mandela in age and royal status, looked after Mandela. Both Matanzima and Mandela are the descendants of King Ngubengcuka. They all belong to the Thembu Royal House. However, Matanzima is from the Great House and Mandela from the *Ixhiba* house. As a result, Mandela's rank in the royal house is subordinate to that of Matanzima. The function of *Ixhiba* is that of counsellor to the king. As Mandela comes from the *Ixhiba* house his function was to fulfil the role of counsellor to the royal house. At the same time, however, Mandela is Matanzima's father's younger brother. It is indicated in the narrative that Nelson Mandela is KD Matanzima's uncle, which is correct in English. According to African culture, however, Nelson Mandela is Matanzima's father even if he is younger than Matanzima, and should be respected as such; Matanzima is not Mandela's nephew as stated in the narrative, but Mandela's child because they all belong to the Thembu Royal House. This is illustrated by the extract below:

> Fort Hare had only 50 students, and I already knew a dozen or so of them from Clarkebury and Healdtown. One of them who I was meeting for

the first time was K.D. Matanzima. Though K.D. was my nephew according to tribal hierarchy, I was younger and far less senior to him.[10]

The mention of *nephew* may be confusing to the reader because, according to African culture, a nephew is a man's sister's son or a woman's brother's son. Matanzima is not Mandela's sister's son, but his brother's son. This could be confusing to both African and non-African readers. As far as the term *nephew is* concerned, in English it means the son of one's brother or sister. The meaning of nephew in African culture is restricted to the son of one's sister (if one is male) and one's brother (if one is female). The son of one's brother (if one is male) is one's son, and the son one's sister (if one is female) is one's son. According to African culture, a nephew is not regarded as one's immediate family because he belongs to another family. Therefore he has no power to influence life in his mother's family. Matanzima, on the other hand, is Mandela's immediate family member, and has the power to influence Mandela's life. That is why he was responsible for raising Mandela's political awareness and for looking after him while he was at university. Matanzima's rank in the royal family dictates that he should guide Mandela and look after him, although he is Mandela's son according to African culture. Matanzima was Mandela's mentor but later Mandela's political views advanced beyond those of Matanzima, to such an extent that he practised his role of advisor by advising both Matanzima and Sabata to keep out of homeland politics. This is revealed when the author says:

> In many ways, Daliwonga still regarded me as his junior, both in terms of my rank in the Thembu hierarchy and in my own political development. While I was his junior in the former realm, I believed I had advanced beyond my one-time mentor in my political views. Whereas his concerns focused on his own tribe, I had become involved with those who thought in terms of the entire nation. I did not want to complicate the discussion by introducing grand political theories; I would rely on common sense and the facts of our history. Before we began, Daliwonga invited Mda, Letlaka and his brother George, to participate, but they demurred, preferring to listen to the two of us. 'Let the nephew and the uncle conduct the debate', Mda said as a sign of respect.[11]

Mandela did not agree with Matanzima's political views and this is why they planned to debate this issue. Although, according to African culture, Mandela is father to Matanzima, he is subordinate to Matanzima according to the Thembu hierarchy. The Thembu genealogy is explained by Mandela as follows:

> Ngubengcuka, one of the greatest monarchs, who united the Thembu tribe, died in 1832. As was the custom, he had wives from the principal royal houses: the Great House, from which the heir is selected, the Right Hand House, and the Ixhiba, a minor house that is referred to by some

as the Left Hand House. It was the task of the sons of the Ixhiba or Left Hand House to settle royal disputes. Mthikrakra, the eldest son of the Great House, succeeded Ngubengcuka and among his sons were Ngangelizwe and Matanzima. Sabata, who ruled the Thembu from 1954, was the grandson of Ngangelizwe a senior to Kaizer Daliwonga, better known as K.D. Matanzima, the former chief minister of the Transkei – my nephew by law and custom – who was the descendant of Matanzima. The eldest son of the Ixhiba house was Simakade, whose younger brother was Mandela, my grandfather.[12]

The genealogy explained above is diagrammatically represented in Figure 1:

THEMBU TRIBE

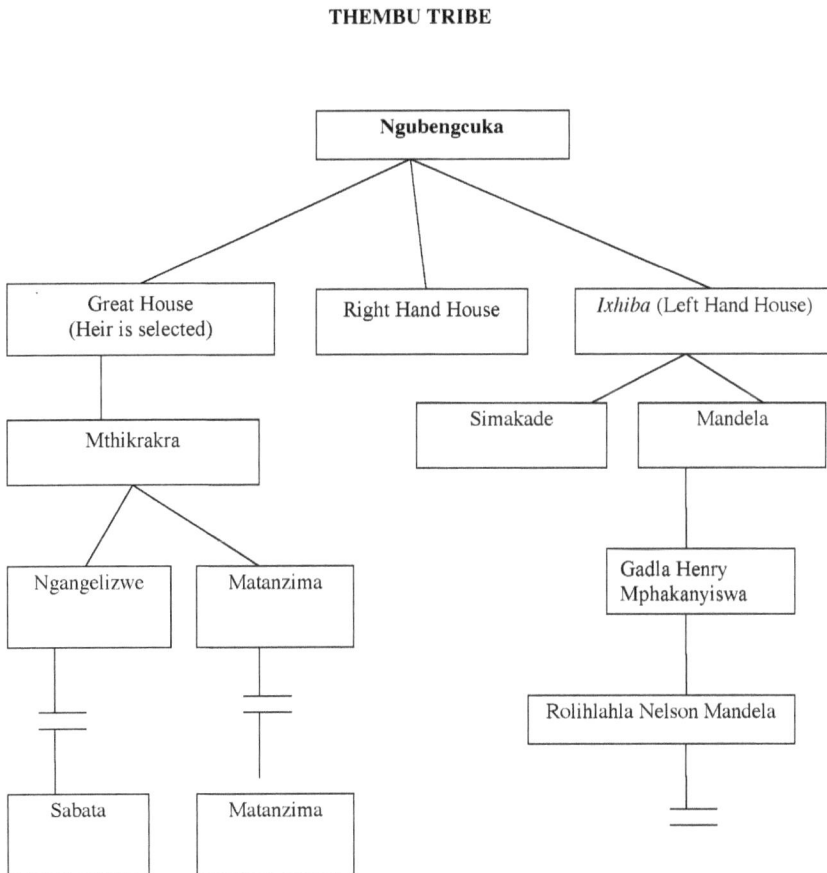

Figure 8.1: Genealogy of the Thembu tribe.

As indicated above, Matanzima is from the Great House, whereas Mandela is from the *Ixhiba*. It would therefore have been difficult for him to persuade Daliwonga to oppose the imposition of Bantu Authorities. However, it was within his rights to advise Daliwonga because he was counsellor to the royal house. Secondly, Matanzima and Mandela are nephew and uncle respectively. To take it at face value is confusing. According to African culture, Matanzima and Mandela are *son* and *father* respectively. In English, *uncle* denotes the brother of one's father or mother, and an aunt's husband.[13] In African culture and custom, the use of *uncle* is restricted to the brother of one's mother. The brother of one's father is one's father. It would be expected in African culture that Matanzima be considered subordinate to Mandela; but because of the houses from which they come, Mandela is considered junior, and as such might not be heeded.

The above extract reveals the relationship between Nelson Mandela, KD Matanzima and King Sabata. These three are descendants of King Ngubengcuka, King of the Thembus. As indicated above, both King Sabata and Chief Matanzima are Mandela's children according to the Thembu hierarchy because he is brother to their fathers. However, Mandela is from the *Ixhiba* house, and does not qualify to be the King of the Thembus. Both Sabata and Matanzima are from the Great House, but Matanzima does not qualify to be the King of the Thembu people because the rightful person is Sabata. So, Mandela was not in line to succession of the Thembu throne, and he served as the counsellor to Thembu rulers. Mandela writes:

> Although over the decades there have been many stories that I was in the line of succession to the Thembu throne, the simple genealogy I have just outlined exposes those tales as myth. Although I was a member of the royal household, I was not among the privileged few who were trained for the role. Instead, as a descendant of the *Ixhiba* house, I was groomed, like my father before me, to counsel the rulers of the tribe.[14]

It is not surprising that Mandela stayed at the Thembu Royal House under the guardianship of Jongintaba after his father's death. The main reason was to train him to counsel the rulers of the Thembu tribe. This is the function he tried to fulfil in advising King Sabata and Matanzima against accepting the imposition of Bantu Authorities. It was within his rights to counsel them and his behaviour was guided by African custom.

Another example of the confusion caused to readers by kinship terms involves the term *cousin*. Realising that they (Mandela and Justice) had failed to convince the regent (Jongintaba) not to force them to marry women chosen on their behalf, Mandela states:

> In retrospect I realised that we did not exhaust all the options available to us. I could have attempted to discuss the matter with the regent through intermediaries and perhaps come to some settlement within the framework of our tribe and family. I could have appealed to the regent's

cousin, Chief Zilindlovu, one of the most enlightened and influential chiefs at the court of Mqhekezweni. But I was young and impatient, and did not see any virtue in waiting. Escape seemed the only course.[15]

The abovementioned extract was uttered by the author after he was forced by the regent to take as his future wife a woman chosen on his behalf. Mandela did not accept the arrangement, and together with Justice, the regent's son who was also given a wife, he ran away. According to the Thembu law and custom, a father is responsible for choosing spouses for his sons. The regent had the right to arrange marriage for Nelson Mandela and Justice.

The main point under discussion here is the relationship between Zilindlovu and the regent, Jongintaba. According to African custom, Zilindlovu is not Jongintaba's cousin, but his brother, that is, either a younger or an elder brother to Jongintaba. This is why it is indicated that he is the most enlightened and influential chief at the court of Mqhekezweni. He could not have influenced the court of Mqhekezweni if he was just a cousin to Jongintaba. He could only exert his influence if he was an immediate family member. According to African culture, a cousin is the son or daughter of one's mother's brother or the son or daughter of one's father's sister. In English, children of one's father's brothers or sisters, or mother's sisters or brothers are all one's cousins. This is not the case in African culture; children of one's father's brothers or mother's sisters are one's brothers and sisters. Mönnig states that children of a father's brother are treated in much the same way as are a person's own brothers.[16] The meaning of *cousin* in African culture is restricted to the children of one's father's sister and those of one's mother's brother. A cousin is therefore not considered as a member of one's immediate family, and he or she has limited influence in one's family's affairs. If Zilindlovu were Jongintaba's cousin he would have had no power to intervene in matters affecting the royal house. The role of a cousin is minimal compared to that of a brother.

The point here is that, since Zilindlovu is a member of the Thembu Royal House and has the power to intervene in matters affecting it, Mandela and Justice should have asked him to speak to the regent about the arranged marriages. As a brother to the regent, he may have succeeded in persuading the King to abandon the idea of choosing spouses for his son and Mandela, or he could have convinced the two young men to understand the position of the King. This may have made it unnecessary for Mandela and Justice to run away to Johannesburg to avoid marriage. Had the events followed this direction, perhaps the political situation in South Africa would have developed differently from what it has today. Going to Johannesburg deepened Mandela's political involvement. If he had stayed in the Transkei homeland, as suggested by KD Matanzima, his political views would have been restricted to that particular homeland. Johannesburg exposed him to the politics of the nation rather than simply the politics of a tribe. To summarise, one could claim that if Nelson Mandela had not been forced to marry a girl he did not love, his movement to Johannesburg would have been delayed or may never have happened at all. Hence he would not have experienced the hardships as narrated in the text, the hardships which shaped his political views.

The same applies to the relationship between Nelson Mandela and Justice. Justice and Mandela are revealed as cousins in the narrative. The truth is, Mandela and Justice are not cousins but brothers according to African culture and custom. That is why Jongintaba indicated that he would treat Mandela as any of his children. He regards him as his own son. Referring to this, Mandela says: 'The regent and his wife No-England brought me up as if I were their own child.'[17]

It is important to understand the social structure of the society in order to have an insight into the relationships. Knowledge of African culture may assist one in gaining such insight into relationships between Mandela and his people.

Conclusion

The actions of Mandela's close relatives, in particular Matanzima and the regent, Jongintaba, exerted great influence in determining his destiny. Besides the fact that Matanzima was Mandela's mentor and that Jongintaba exposed him to national affairs through forcing him to migrate to urban areas, both these men kept reminding him about his role in the Thembu Royal House, i.e. as counsellor to the Thembu rulers. This is what Mandela achieved in his lifetime; in addition to being counsellor of the Thembu rulers, Mandela saw himself as counsellor to the rulers of South Africa. He advised the Thembu rulers and resolved disputes in the Thembu Royal House. This role encouraged him to advise South African leaders and to resolve disputes in South Africa. In line with African culture, he saw all South Africans as members of one big family – brothers, sisters, nephews, cousins, nieces, and so on.

It is vital that the reader understands the differences between kinship relations in African and in European cultures. Without this insight the reader will not be able to make sense of or correctly interpret the events and conduct of characters in *Long walk to freedom*. Certain privileges are attached to certain kinship positions and these in turn inform people's actions and their prerogative to intervene in the lives of members of the close family.

References

Allen, RE (ed) 1990, *The concise Oxford dictionary of current English*, Clarendon Press, Oxford.

Abrams, MH 1981, A *glossary of literary terms*, Holt, Rinehart and Winston, New York.

Grabun, N 1971, *Readings in kinship and social structure*, Harper & Row Publishers, New York.

Hsu, FLK (ed) 1971, *Kinship and culture*, Aldine Publishing Company, Chicago.

Mandela, N 1994, *Long walk to freedom: The autobiography of Nelson Mandela,*: Little, Brown and Company, London.

McHenry, R (ed) 1992, *The new encyclopaedia Britannica*, Volume 23, Encyclopaedia Britannica, Inc, Chicago.

Mönnig, HO 1978, *The Pedi*, J.L. van Schaik, Pretoria.

Shelston, A 1977, *Biography*, Methuen & Co. Ltd, London.

Van Warmelo, NJ 1931, *Kinship terminology of the South African Bantu*, Ethnological Publications, volume II, Government Printer, Pretoria.

ENDNOTES

[1] Abrams 1981: 15.
[2] McHenry 1992: 190.
[3] Mandela 1994.
[4] Shelston 1977: 3.
[5] Hsu 1971: 5.
[6] Grabun 1971: 3.
[7] Van Warmelo 1931: 8.
[8] Van Warmelo 1931: 6.
[9] Mandela 1994: 10.
[10] Mandela 1994: 51–52.
[11] Mandela 1994: 214-215.
[12] Mandela 1994: 5.
[13] Allen 1990: 1328.
[14] Mandela 1994: 5.
[15] Mandela 1994: 65.
[16] Mönnig 1978: 237.
[17] Mandela 1994: 21.

A Dalit and a First Nations Canadian speak of the women in their bones

Maria Preethi Srinivasan

> A nation is not conquered
> Until the hearts of its women
> Are on the ground
> Then it is done, no matter
> How brave its warriors
> Nor how strong its weapons
>
> Traditional Cheyenne saying[1]

My engagement with research on indigenous women's life writings with specific reference to the issue of 'gaining a voice', left me wondering about the singularity of 'voices' and the multiplicity of voices in 'a voice'. Bama's *Sangati* and Lee Maracle's *I am woman* presented themselves to me as texts that have many interesting points of intersection in their respective presentations about Indian Dalit women and First Nations women in Canada. Both Bama and Maracle seek to foreground through their narratives the 'difference' of the women of their respective communities from women of mainstream society and the irrelevance of mainstream feminist ideology in understanding the experiences of Dalit or Native women. It struck me as something amazing that two women writers from two geographical extremities should exhibit a similar approach to exploring and expressing issues that concern themselves and the group they represent. Another striking similarity was seen in their development as writers: each of them began their literary careers with the writing of their life stories/autobiographies and they moved on to narrating the lives of the women of their respective communities. Bama's autobiography *Karukku* was followed by the publication of *Sangati*; Maracle's *I am woman* followed the writing of *Bobbi Lee: Indian rebel*.[2] *Sangati* is committed to the purpose of exposing the ramifications of caste hegemony in the lives of Dalit women. Her preoccupation with caste and gender is complemented by Maracle's commitment (in *I am woman*) to explicating the connection between racism and sexism.

The road to Bama's *Sangati*

Karukku was published in Tamil in 1992, a significant period in the history of Dalit struggles. 1992 was a year of Dalit awakening with the Ambedkar centenary celebrations. It was Father Mark Stephen a Catholic priest who seized this moment to present Bama's story. My pursuit of 'how' Bama 'gained a voice' engaged me in interviews with the publisher of the English version, Mini Krishnan of

Macmillan and her translator, Lakshmi Holmstrom. A strong suggestion that I should interview Fr. Mark Stephen presented itself in the 'Author's Preface' to *Karukku*, in which Bama writes,

> Father Mark understood the nature and sources of this book, and urged me to write it. Not only did he encourage me to give thought to each separate topic, he supported me in the writing of it, he worked tirelessly to bring it out in the shape of a book.[3]

Fr. Mark Stephen said that I was the first person to interview him about Bama. From him I learnt the story of how *Karukku* came to be published. When Bama left her convent, after seven years of service to the Catholic church, she came directly to Madurai and met Fr. Mark Stephen who hails from her own village, Pudupatti. She shared with him her tragic story of disappointment with the church and the discrimination that she had to endure in the convent on the grounds of caste. At that time Fr. Mark Stephen (who is not a Dalit) was engaged in a battle to purge the church of caste conflicts and discrimination against Dalits. He was one of the pioneers of the Dalit Christian Movement which later came to be known as the Dalit Christian Liberation Movement. Against this backdrop and the Dalit awakening through the Ambedkar Centenary celebrations, he sent out a call to Dalits to participate in a life writing seminar. The objective was to record the experiences of Dalit Christians through their self-written life stories. There was no stipulation about the educational qualifications of the participants. The only requirement was their interest in writing. There was a good response to this. Just after this seminar was over, Bama arrived from the convent in Jammu. She approached Fr. Mark, as she had nowhere else to go. Fr. Mark was a close friend of her family. He had known her from the time she was a child. He asked her to write her story, suggesting each topic on which she might write. She wrote it in literary Tamil. He asked her to rewrite it in the dialect of her people. She did so. All the while, he did not disclose to her his desire to have it published. Describing that moment when he declared his intention to her, Fr. Mark Stephen says:

> Then she said: 'No!' She got a shock. She said, 'I thought you asked me to write to give vent to my feelings. You want to degrade our community'. I said: 'No, its not a question of degrading'. We [Bama and Fr. Mark Stephen] are from different caste backgrounds. I am a non-Dalit. But I have been working all along for Dalits and Dalit literature. Somehow I convinced her.[4]

Karukku proved a success not only because of the experience it presented but also because of the language it employed. Following the success of *Karukku*, Bama worked on a suggestion from Fr. Mark. He says in the interview:

Then I asked her to write about Dalit women whom she encountered in the village, ordinary women who are not educated, how they go to the field, how they are in oppressive situations, what is the thing that makes them live, and their struggle against the caste structure, their life in the family, their male dominated society. She was very interested in this and she wrote the second one, *Sangati* (1994). That also came out very well. I liked the second one better than the first [*Karukku*]. Till that time there was the view that all women have the same problem. But her writing showed that Dalit women have an entirely different problem compared to caste women. At the same time they enjoy a certain type of freedom which the caste women don't enjoy. That aspect she brought out very well.[5]

Karukku and *Sangati* were born of such mentoring and had a good reception due to their being published at a time when Dalit activism was upbeat. The English translations of *Karukku* and *Sangati* were published in 2000 and 2005 respectively.

From *Bobbi Lee: Indian rebel* to *I am woman*

The production and publishing history of *Bobbi Lee* has one point of intersection with Bama's *Karukku*, in that, like the Dalit movement in India, it is set against the backdrop of Native activism through the Liberation Support Movement (LSM) and Native Alliance for Red Power (NARP). Maracle's life story was recorded on a tape recorder as part of a life writing project by members of the LSM (a Marxist political group) to which she belonged. It was a part of their 'Life Histories from the Revolution Series'. Don Barrett and Rick Sterling transcribed and edited her words: 80 hours of tape and three inches of manuscript were reduced to a slim volume bearing the title, *Bobbi Lee, Indian rebel: Struggles of a Native Canadian woman*. A new edition was published in 1990 by Women's Press, Toronto. This incorporates additional material, including a foreword by Jeanette Armstrong, as well as a prologue and epilogue by Maracle.[6] The 1990 edition is presented with an introductory chapter, 'Oka Peace Camp – September 9, 1990'. Here she emphasises that 'We all know that we must talk. Really talk – from a position of wholeness, completeness – about building a sustainable movement in the country ... *The life of Bobbi Lee is about why we must talk.*'[7]

With regard to the history of production and publication, *Bobbi Lee* bears resemblance to *Karukku* in that there is the presence of Don Barret in its production, who acts as almost a mentor. Maracle dedicates 'both volumes' of her book to the memory of Don Barret. At the same time she expresses the discomfort she experienced in collaborating with him. She cites her own experience as an illustration of the fact that 'As-told-tos between whites and Natives rarely work.' Her verdict on the 1975 edition is summed up in these words: 'In the end, the voice that reached the paper was Don's, the information alone was mine'. (There is, in contrast, no hint of an overbearing presence in the 'support' given by Fr. Mark Stephen to Bama). Though Don Barrett was a leader who 'believed' in Maracle's 'potential' and tried 'to groom' her and encouraged her 'to get command of [her] voice' she could not cope with his 'centralist leadership'.[8] Nor was she convinced that his ideology could pull the Native people out of the mess they were in. Therefore she 'decided to seek out that "lonely attic" in which writing, theory, story and life is imagined and put on paper'.[9] In the epilogue to the 1990 edition of *Bobbi Lee*, Maracle states that through 'the long process of unravelling that began in 1975' 'missing pieces … came alive' and 'Some of those memories are partially accounted for in *I Am Woman*'.[10] Writing stories became an activity she indulged in to keep sane. She realised that all that tormented her 'had everything to do with racism and self-hate'.[11] She testifies to the transformative power of story-telling when she states:

> It took twenty-five years to twist me and only ten to unravel the twist. I still wrote for the demonstrations Native people held, but I began putting my need to write poetry and stories ahead of the political words that our people needed written. I became a woman through my words.[12]

Two hegemonies and the Woman question

Racism and casteism are beyond doubt dehumanising in their effects. Racism may be the offspring of colonialism while casteism owes its genesis to the caste system. Maracle draws attention to the fact that 'Racist ideology had defined womanhood for the Native woman as non-existent'.[13] She says that in her activism she failed to recognise and acknowledge her gendered self. The assertion 'I am woman' came through an awakening to this reality. On Women's Day, 1978, she declared in a video presentation made for the occasion, that it was irrelevant to her that she was a woman and what mattered to her was the fact that she was Native. A gentle nudge to her conscience came from a well-wisher who had watched this presentation. He praised her understanding of the colonial process and added, 'couldn't you see that perhaps it was because you were Native and woman that your insight was powerful?' He also asked another penetrating question, 'Don't you think you could have taken responsibility for being a woman and inspired our sisters, just a little?'[14] Some soul-searching and reflection led Maracle to realise that she was always conscious of convincing white colonial society that she was 'not like the rest of them … an alcoholic … a skid row bum … a stupid Native'.[15] She realised that racism had warped her sense of self. She examined the historical process – a whole set of dehumanising policies: before 1961 the Native people were considered 'wards of the government, children in the eyes of the law'. Rebellion against this attitude gave rise to remedial policies through Native self government and the Native land question. This being the case, 'The woman question still did not exist for us.

Not then', says Maracle.[16] She highlights the complicity of white women in the subjugation of Native women: even in the 'white women's movement' she observes, 'White women invite us to speak if the issue is racism or Native people in general. We are there to "teach", to "sensitize them", or serve them in some other way. We are not, as a matter of course invited as an integral part of "their" movement – the white women's movement.'[17]

Bama states that *Sangati* (which means 'news') is all about what it means to be Dalit and woman. Drawing attention to the fact that mainstream society which discusses the 'position of women', takes no notice of Dalit women, she states: 'We have all come across news, broadcast widely and everywhere telling us of the position of women in our patriarchal society, and of the rights that have been plucked away from them. But news of women who have been trapped not only by patriarchy but also by caste-hatred is often side-lined, hidden, forgotten.'[18] The tendency to 'side-line' Dalit women and matters pertaining to them is also addressed by Dalit writer Kumud Pawade.[19] For example, at conferences of the women's movement in India, she has had to challenge the upper caste women's assumption that 'the entire woman caste is dalit'.[20]

The urgent need to study and take affirmative action on the issues pertaining to Dalit women cannot be emphasised better than in the report in *The Hindu* about the Eighth National Conference of the All India Democratic Women's Association (AIDWA) held in Kolkata in November 2007 where a resolution was passed stating that the AIDWA would strongly take up the cause of Dalit women.[21]

Both *Sangati* and *I am woman* are charged with the writers' urge to communicate the 'difference' of Native/Dalit women from white/upper caste women. Maracle makes a clear bid for highlighting the fact that the white women's movement and their feminist ideology exists beyond the pale of the indigenous woman's experience. Australian Aboriginal theorist Aileen Moreton-Robinson focuses on this issue in *Talkin' up to the white woman: Indigenous women and feminism*. In her critique of the liberal feminist argument she writes:

> Because it centres white middle-class women as the normative position from which to judge the oppression, liberal feminism dehistoricises women and lacks an understanding of the different historical and material conditions that enable certain women to compete on the basis of merit. The invisibility of white race privilege and racial and class oppression is an outcome of giving primacy to gender oppression and sex difference.[22]

She observes that, even when white feminists engage with a politics of difference, 'the effect of such theorizing is to make a politics of difference colour blind in terms of whiteness and power evasive in that all differences are rendered equally significant'. On the other hand women of colour, indigenous women and Afro-American women who theorise on difference 'do include within their respective positions the idea that there is some fixity to difference in power relations which places limits on inter-subjective relations'.[23] Moreton-Robinson also observes that though bell hooks 'sees feminism as being fundamentally racist, she believes it has something to offer Black women in America'.[24] To use the language of information technology, feminism may be viewed as software that is infected with racism and therefore this software will not work on Native systems (individual and collective). In Moreton-Robinson's view feminism has something to offer, but 'what is required is a redefinition of feminism'.[25] This redefinition of feminism/feminism which is inclusive of Indigenous/Dalit women's experience, is one in which white race/upper caste privilege is interrogated.

Transnational feminism and a world space for women

The interesting parallels between the literary careers of Maracle and Bama, their identification with the women of their respective communities, their commitment to highlighting the difference of the Native/Dalit women from women of dominant society, and their celebration of difference, require for discussion a location that is not governed by temporal and spatial considerations. Bama and Maracle belong to two geographical extremities and yet there are so many interesting ways in which their work may be seen as intersecting. They belong to an imagined community.

The opportunity to present this paper at the Indigenous Biographies and Autobiographies Conference, held in Canberra, had for me a moment of truth when the objective of my presentation settled on me with a strong force and armed me with a strong sense of purpose. As a foreigner and one untrained in the use of maps to find locations, I realised quite suddenly that I could locate my 'position' on a map by looking for 'intersections'. The ways in which *Sangati* and *I am woman* intersect, gives each of these writers a 'position', a location and a shared space in the global arena. This venture, which draws from two texts and contexts, is a kind of mapping which is so significant at a time when Dalit people seek to internationalise their issues. Finding these intersections with Maracle's writing and her journey as a writer, creates a location, and a global one at that, not merely for Bama's *Sangati*, but for understanding the experience of Dalit women.

This concept of 'location', of creating a 'world space' for that which could be passed over as a regional issue, is theorised through 'transnational feminism', promoted by Caren Kaplan and Inderpal Grewal. In their view there is a need for women to 'work collaboratively in order to formulate transnational feminist alliances'.[26] Kaplan states that the transnational feminism they advocate should not be confused with Western feminists' ideas of 'a global sisterhood of women with shared values'.[27] They argue that '[t]he claiming of a world space for women raises temporal questions as well as spatial considerations, questions of history as well as of place.'[28] In applying the theory of transnational feminism we are warned against 'constructing similarity through equalizations when material histories indicate otherwise'.[29] Bearing this word of caution in mind, this paper turns the spotlight on intersections that function as sites of information flow: these intersections could be caused by either similarity or difference. There is therefore a 'politics of location' involved. Kaplan states that this practice should be viewed as 'affiliation' or 'coalition'. In her view 'a practice of affiliation, a politics of location identifies the grounds for historically specific differences and similarities between women in diverse and asymmetrical relations, creating alternative histories, identities, and possibilities for alliances'.[30] Maracle in her writing displays this consciousness of forging alliances with similarly displaced or marginalised peoples – 'Palestinians, Chileans, Filipinos, Eritreans, Ethiopians, El Salvadorans, Anti-apartheid activists and Black Canadian and American people who broadened [her] thinking and opened [her] eyes to the world of struggle and the joyous anticipation of new humanity that is being worked out in their countries'.[31]

Bama's transnationalism does not find expression in the text of *Sangati*. However, when I asked for her view on whether Dalit issues had to be internationalised she said:

> Take Sri Lanka. Such a small country and the separate Tamil Eelam that they are asking for, because it is internationalised it is getting attention and it is going on. I'm not equating the issues, but just using it to explain. The problems of Dalits' issue is for thousands and thousands of years. The history of this caste system is for many years. For many years we were kept like that and without abolishing this caste system. India cannot become equal to any other country in this world though it has all resources – economic, nuclear and intellectual, etc.[32]

She referred to the response received by her book in France and other countries. The French translation of *Sangati* was published in 2002. She noted her interaction with a scholar engaged in a comparative study of her stories and those of Alice Walker. She was very appreciative and excited about the points of intersection.

The internationalisation of Bama's work has taken it beyond the regional level to the international arena. It is through book fairs like the one she went to in France and the transnational studies of researchers, that Bama has been included in the 'world of struggle' of which Maracle speaks.

In the critical parlance of Caren Kaplan and Inderpal Grewal, colonialism and casteism may be described as 'scattered hegemonies'. We are yet to examine, in the light of Bama and Maracle's writing, how patriarchy allies with colonialism and casteism in subjugating Native/Dalit women. Maracle's *I am woman* and Bama's *Sangati,* when drawn together by a comparative study, occupy a 'location'. In this location there are some sites that present an alternative history that is not dependent on temporal and spatial considerations.

Love, sex and power

'Isn't love a given?' is a question that Maracle raises in her justification of lesbian relationships. Her defence of lesbian relationships draws attention to the question of love, and she juxtaposes this against heterosexual relationships which are characterised by aggression and violence from the male partner. In many cases of heterosexual relationship the home is the site of rape. Lee links this issue to lesbianism to suggest that if brutal, loveless, heterosexual relationships are accepted, why not a love relationship between two women. She brings home the idea that relationships are based on love and not the question of power. Her analysis of the abusive behaviour of both Native and white men towards the Native women reveals that rape of Native women has its roots in racism. The white man, the Native man, the white woman and the Native woman are subjected to Lee's psychoanalytic scrutiny. White male abuse of the Native woman is pinned down to her being 'the object of the kind of sexual release of white males whose appetites are too gross for their own delicate women'.[33]

In her view the Native man has a craving for white flesh and the brutality he inflicts on the Native woman is a result of frustration. In her study of rape she finds that fear in the woman excites the man. The Native woman, who subjects voluntarily to such brutality, reaches a point of self loathing which has its repercussions in the form of alcoholism and child abuse. It might be argued by some that rape in marriage is not exclusive to Native/coloured women/women from marginalised groups: it could very well be the case in the homes of white/upper caste women. Maracle's objective here is confined only to the 'why' of rape in the homes of Native people. Her analysis points to the frustration that is a result of ungratified attraction that Native men have towards white women. This kind of attraction of opposites can be seen in the white men's attraction to dark-skinned Native women. Describing the play of power in this eroticism, she says that they are 'frenzied by dark-skinned sensuality' and want for themselves 'the self-effacing surrender of dark women to white superiority'.[34]

In Bama's presentation of power relations, she does point out that Dalit women among whom she has lived are subject to sexual exploitation by upper caste men and are subject to brutal sex at the hands of their own husbands. However, Dalit women also employ strategies to cope with their situation. In this they show a marked difference from upper caste women whose torment is hushed within the walls of their homes. Bama states that the Dalit women of her community bring their domestic quarrels right onto the streets. Justifying their loud ways, she says that they work at home and outside the house and cope with almost no financial support from their husbands. Therefore, 'If he shows his strength of muscle, she reveals the sharpness of her tongue. Because she can't hit him back, she curses him roundly.'[35] This cursing is full of expletives. She seems to find a reason for the kind of language they use when she says, 'No matter what the quarrel is about, once they open their mouths, the same four-letter words will spill out. I sometimes think that because they have neither pleasure, nor fulfilment in their own sexual lives, they derive a sort of bitter comfort by using these terms of abuse which are actually names of their body parts.'[36]

A patriarchal religion

Religion is one of the forces that Bama identifies as being responsible for the subjugation of women. Bama's village is Dalit and Catholic. (It was the European missionaries who brought Catholicism to her village.) The festivals that they observe are Christian. In the midst of the excitement about the pageantry, about who is going to play Jesus and who will play Our Lady, the gender discrimination stands out glaringly. The women are not allowed to take any of the roles. They go to the ridiculous extent of men playing the roles of women. One of the women asks why a woman cannot play the part of Jesus. A conversation with Pecchi and Irulaayi who belong to another Dalit community, the *chakkilis*, brings her to realise that Dalits who have converted to Christianity are governed by Christian marriage laws in which marriage is binding for life. Irulaayi makes a statement on her people's position on the question of leaving one husband for another: 'it's quite common with us. It's only you Bible-people who can't do it. We are Hindus. But even amongst us, it's only the *pallar* and *chakkili* communities who can end one marriage and go and marry a second time. None of the other communities do it'.[37] The woman who wants to separate has the opportunity to present her case before the village headman and she is free to separate and marry again. Bama's resentment of institutionalised Christianity finds expression in her narration of how even the Catholic priest did not stand by the young lovers who defied the sanctions of caste and desired to be united in marriage.

A section of *I am woman* is devoted to presenting the erosion of Native culture that was hastened by the coming of Roman Catholicism into their communities. The 'black robes' (Catholic priests) brought Europe and her ways with them. Maracle observes that they made for the colonies in a bid to escape Europe and she asks this incisive question: 'why do they have to bequeath the very things they escape to us?' She presents this question through the voices of the Native grandmothers who accept the imposition of European education on their children and grandchildren. They encourage their children and grandchildren to 'Master their language' for 'hidden within it is the way we are to live among them'. It is a decision that they make with resignation because to them it has become 'clear that they [the Europeans] will never go away'.[38] It could also be viewed as a strategy for survival.

Maracle has not explicitly pointed out the patriarchal nature of Catholicism, but describes it in terms of a very masculine presence. One observes that it is the grandmothers who have engaged with Catholicism and contemplated the possibility of 'the coming together of ... histories'.[39] She acknowledges their subversion of colonial power with these words, 'I would not have had such thoughts if the grandmothers of this land had not battered themselves with this question [of mastering the colonisers' language], mused aloud in the presence of their granddaughters'.[40] The point of intersection that Bama has with Maracle with regard to religion is the feeling that the coming of the Christian missionaries into their community eroded their culture. Bama also points out that the Dalit Christians do not enjoy the privilege of reservation for jobs and other concessions that the government gives to other Dalits. She is also very sore about the hypocrisy and insincerity of the nuns and priests. She has expressed this strongly in *Karukku, Sangati* and in her interview with me.

The ways of the grandmothers

Interestingly Bama and Maracle foreground the presence of the grandmothers: they are repositories of the history of the community. They play an active role in the life of the community, stepping into areas of need. Time and again the narrator of *I am woman* recalls her grandmother's words of wisdom: the words of her grandmother help her learn about the history of her people. Maracle has to make a conscious effort to learn the ways of her grandmothers. Colonisation has eroded Native culture. Maracle states that she 'bent in the direction of European ideology' and 'hid for a long time from the teachings of the ancient ones'. She admits, 'When my sickened spirit needed to be healed though, I sought the teachings of my grandmothers'.[41] Maracle quotes a Native belief which states, 'If you live right the grandmothers will take care of you'.[42] A corollary of this is, 'if you live wrong they will forsake you. You will sicken and perhaps die'.[43] This Native proverb operates in her narrative to emphasise the significance of Native women in shaping the history of the Native people. Woven into the narrative are Maracle's own joys and yearnings as a mother. Her narrative betrays her preoccupation with the education of her children, not in the European sense, but in terms of life skills and values. As a committed writer she is conscious of expressing the concerns of the women and children who have been a part of her life. Her reflections on the role of Native women in antiquity and for posterity are expressed in the poem 'Creation':

I know nothing
of great mysteries

> know less of creation
> I do know
> that the farther backward
> in time that I travel
> the more grandmothers
> and the farther forward
> the more grandchildren
> I am obligated to both.[44]

The grandmother of the narrator of *Sangati* is a vibrant presence. She is a highly respected member of the community because she has served the community as midwife. She has a story to say about the birth of each child in the community. In Bama's *Sangati,* the education of her granddaughter takes place when the two of them are engaged in their favourite activity: the granddaughter picks lice from the grandmother's hair and through her seemingly endless store of stories she imparts to her granddaughter the ways of their people. In one such moment of communion with her *Paati* (grandmother), the narrator chafes with indignation at the humiliation of Mariamma, on account of the false charges framed against her by a lustful upper caste landlord. She is unable to brook the fact that neither Mariamma, nor any other woman could speak up against the injustice.

> Whether it is right or wrong, it is better for women not to open their mouths. You just try speaking out about what you believe is right. You'll only get kicked and beaten and trampled on for your pains. And it isn't just here that it happens, you know. It's the same throughout the world. Women are not given that kind of respect.[45]

This is what years of subjugation under patriarchy have taught *Paati*. The events she has witnessed in her life have led her to believe that '[i]f you are born into this world, its best that you are born a man'.[46] Though there is a kind of resignation in these words, there are many episodes which show that it is the grandmother who takes initiative to do something for the welfare of her grandchildren and other women in the community. In the story of Mariamma, it is the narrator's mother and grandmother who take her to the doctor because she has not reached puberty. Medical attention solves the problem by establishing that Mariamma's anemic condition is the actual cause. The grandmother steps into the lives of the women of the community, in their very hour of need, whether it be a matter of child birth, ill-health or domestic violence. They inscribe in the narrator's consciousness the value that, rather than single-handedly fight or resist male domination or aggression, a more effective strategy is that of women being together and being there for each other. This aspect of community life is stronger among Bama's people. Maracle acknowledges that this aspect has disappeared from the lives of Native people. Expressing her yearning she says, 'I am a hungry woman. I hunger for my homeland, ailing and sick, that it is.

Ka-Nata, "spirit of community." I hunger for an end to the robbery and hunger for the spirit of community to envelope my home again.'[47]

Native and Dalit women's souls and bodies

Maracle draws on the experiences of her people to define the ways in which what happens to the body affects the soul. Native women often find that in their relationships with their husbands or lovers they are objects of lust. Maracle dwells at length on the question of love and of how dehumanising it is to be the object of lust. Having to cope with a loveless life, the earning of their daily bread and the raising of their children, leads to withdrawal. In her presentation of the sad story of Rusty, Maracle writes of how Rusty's spirit withdrew and 'jumped into the ever-present wine bottles that men and her good looks brought'.[48] She reiterates in *I am woman* that her humanity, which was trampled on by the racism and sexism that she was subject to, was revived by the love she found in her second marriage. She brings her experience – past and present – to understanding and presenting the lives of Native women. She shows that Native women are viewed through the lens of racial prejudice and regarded as sub-human – 'the female of the species'.[49] This being the case '[they] are by definition, incapable of womanly love. It is aggressive sex that [they] get – a passionate body language but no spiritual affection'.[50] The result of such denial is an increased yearning, a vicious cycle of yearning and denial. Describing the despair in which they find themselves, she writes, 'Our life is lived out schizophrenically. Our community desires emancipation. The greater the desire, the more surely do we leap like lemmings into the abyss of alcoholism, violence and suicide.'[51]

In *Sangati*, which is a collection of episodes from the life of her community, Bama presents the myths about *peys* (evil spirits) possessing people and she notes that in all the stories she has heard from her grandmother the spirits only seem to possess women. She is suggesting that what is taken to be possession by evil spirits is actually a manifestation of the psychological stresses that women of her community have to endure. At the same time, she shows that her people are full of song and dance. They have songs for every occasion, from birth to death and it is the women who sing these songs. There are the *roraatu* (lullaby), *oppari* (dirge) and also songs sung at a girl's coming of age.[52] In an interview with me she described how the whole village stood by her when she lost her parents, one after the other in a matter of two days. In this excerpt she explained the necessity of song and dance even at the time of death:

> MP: As a non-Dalit I don't understand how that happens? Why the dance?
>
> Bama: Dance in the sense they have a particular song for that occasion and they sing and they dance, that says, 'Death is inevitable'. They don't

cling on to anything actually. That detachment. You may not understand or accept. It is paradoxical. One thing is that they indulge in life and pleasure.

MP: At that time.

Bama: No, no in the culture. Indulge. That is part of Dalit culture and detachment that also is part of Dalit culture. See, if they want to make love, they make it to the full and enjoy it. And if there is some pain they indulge in it to the last drop of it.

MP: That purges it out.

Bama: And singing is part of their life. While working. During death also they sing. At the time of birth they sing.[53]

Celebrating difference

When it comes to celebrating themselves, there is a resonance between *I am woman* and *Sangati*. When Maracle writes, 'I want the standard for our judgement of our brilliance, our beauty and our passions, to be ourselves', her voice resonates with Bama's who appreciates the robust dark-skinned bodies of the women of her community. In one of the episodes in *Sangati*, Devi, a Dalit child, wonders if the dark coloured *ragi kuzh* (gruel) which is the staple food of her community of Dalit people, is the reason for their being 'born coal-black in colour, just like crows', and wonders if the fair skin of upper caste people is due to the rice and milk that they consume. Rendupalli, a woman from the Dalit community rises in defence to reply: 'Black is strongest and best, like a diamond. Just go to their [upper caste] streets and look about you. Yes, they might have light skins, but just take a close look at their faces. Their features are all crooked … If they had our colour as well, not even a donkey would turn and look at them.'[54]

Maracle's celebration of Native womanhood comes from her assertion 'I am woman'. She aptly describes her writing as 'channeled through the pen of a recently decolonized woman'.[55] The awakening to self and life came only by getting rid of the colonial baggage and its attendant patriarchy. Her poem 'Fish-Wife' juxtaposes stereotypical images of the Native and white woman. One is 'loud, lean, raw', with 'no manners and no finesse … but very much alive'.[56] The stereotype of the white woman she sees on billboards is of a person for whom 'physical work is damning'.[57] In contrast Maracle's image of the Native woman is of a person 'for whom mobility, muscular movement, physical prowess are equal to the sensuous pleasure of being alive'.[58]

Native and Dalit men's subjugation

There is no opportunity for Mariamma to establish the truth about the lewd conduct and advances made by the upper caste man towards her. In a bid to silence her, he claims that he was an eyewitness to her improper conduct with a young Dalit man. His allegations are accepted by the men in the Dalit community. In another instance the narrator asks her grandmother, why *paraiya* women do not go to the theatre to watch a movie. She is told that it is so because they want to avoid caste men. Even in the village, the women go out together to gather firewood and so on. They fear that they will be preyed upon. The Dalit men cannot confront the upper caste men in such cases because of their economic dependence on them as landlords. Bama attributes the domestic violence in Dalit homes to the same cause of suppressed manhood of the Dalit male; she writes:

> Nowadays, when I reflect on how the men in our streets went about drinking and beating their wives, I wonder whether all that violence was because there was nowhere else for them to exert their male pride or to show off their authority. All that suppressed anger was vented when they came home and beat up their wives to a pulp.[59]

Maracle's writing about the erosion/corruption of the Native man's manhood is equally compelling. She ascribes the brutishness in Native men to the ill-effects of colonisation. She finds a kind of hierarchy in the present way of life where 'The dictates of patriarchy demand that beneath Native man, comes the female Native. The dictates of racism are thus that Native men are beneath white women and Native females are not fit to be referred to as women.'[60] Maracle expresses her resentment of Native men's practice of standing up when a white woman enters the room. It is a clear indication of the psychological conditioning about the place assigned to Native men. Colonisation has also conditioned them to behave 'like lesser white men of the brutish type'.[61] In the traditional culture of Maracle's people, 'men responded to women' and the woman's 'choice was sacred'. However, with the erosion of 'traditions that kept us human', many indigenous women endure rape at the hands of drunken husbands.[62]

The plight of the children

Both narratives reveal that girl children in Native and Dalit communities witness a great deal of domestic violence. Maracle speaks explicitly of the abuse that the child suffers at the hands of a brutal father/the mother's partner. The story of Maikanni in *Sangati* is heart-wrenching and very powerful. Dalit men are often irresponsible and do not bring their wages home. Maikanni is the bread winner as her father has deserted the family. She works, sticking on labels in the matchbox factory. She represents the problem of child labour in India, which affects Dalits more than other communities. Maikanni narrates an incident of how she was lured by a man to pick firewood in a lonely part of the forest. But she is wise in gauging his intent and flees from the scene. The narrator wonders what life has made of Maikanni. 'If she was required to work far harder than her years demanded, she also behaved with a commonsense far beyond her years.[63] The girl child in a Dalit community has a very brief childhood. The boys play freely. But the girl child is saddled with responsibilities – looking after her siblings, fetching water, firewood, helping with other domestic chores, and to top it all, many are like Maikanni, bringing home a wage.

The story of Maikanni finds a point of intersection with what Maracle's account of an episode concerning a L'ilwat child. As a volunteer parent on a school trip she notices that the European girls did not speak to the L'ilwat girl. On the return trip the little girl was standing while two European children occupied a three seater. The teacher was reduced to physically moving the European children and even then they gave her the bare minimum place to sit. The Dalit child Maikanni tells her aunts in the community of a caste-clash that takes place in the matchbox factory. Children from Maikanni's village are called *paraiya* and abusive names by children from a higher caste. It is strange that although their economic condition is the same as these Dalit children – they have also been driven to work in the matchbox factory – they have pride of caste. She holds her listeners in thrall as she narrates: 'If you had been there yesterday, you'd have seen a real fight going on. All the children from our streets refused to work; we even picked up our tiffin carriers and were ready to walk out.'[64] They resume work with pleas from the employer and assurance that he will not allow this to happen again.

Narrating difference: effecting transformation

Bama and Maracle's identification with the women of their communities is so deep that the phrase, 'the women in their bones' seemed an apt expression to bring into the title. It is due to this aspect of identification that Lakshmi Holmstrom, in the introduction to *Sangati,* describes this text as 'the autobiography of a community'.[65] Moreover, the focus of Maracle and Bama is the difference of the women of their respective communities from women of mainstream society. This consciousness of difference has influenced their narrative style. To put it in Gopal Guru's terms, Bama and Lee Maracle's writings bear witness to the fact that Dalit/indigenous women 'talk differently'. Speaking to Manoj Nair about what the Cross Word award for *Karukku* meant to her, Bama says that what gave her 'most satisfaction' was the fact that the language of her people got recognition. The dialect that she employs in her writings was 'a language that was not recognized by the pundits of Literature, was not accepted by any literary circle in Tamilnadu, was not included in the norms of Tamil Literature'. But the success of *Karukku* 'forced the critics to accept the users of the dialect into their fold'. Bama says that she was proud of being 'instrumental in bringing about this change in Tamil Literature'.

This aspect of 'talking differently' creates genres that are different from conventional mainstream productions. In their work on Vankar, Bhangi and Koli-Patel, women of the Bhal region of Gujarat, Franco Fernando and others have identified genre as a cultural production. They reiterate that the work of anthropologists and folklorists has helped to break genre's 'exclusive association with literary criticism' and regained its original meaning of class or type (Latin: *genus*, class). Gary Gosses, who worked with Chamula Indians in the 1970s, suggested that the organisation of genres reflects a world view. Franco Fernando et al. endorse this view: 'they [the genres] tell us something about the group's cultural grasp of the world. Genre thus becomes a social phenomenon rather than a formal one'.[66]

In her essay 'Oratory: coming to theory', Lee Maracle states that in writing *I am woman*, she intended to write theory and that her quest took her through hundreds of books on capitalist theory, decolonisation, philosophy, Indigenous law, philosophy and culture. She puts the whole effort in perspective when she states:

> My understanding of the process of colonization and decolonization of Native women is rooted in my theoretical perception of social reality, and it is tested in the crucible of human social practice. The stories and the poetry bring the reality home and allow the victims to devictimize their consciousness. For native women, and a good many white women, *I Am Woman* is empowering and transformative.[67]

Bama also emphasises this transformative, empowering effect of the stories of her people when she states that *Sangati* 'changed' her.[68] 'What liberated you?' was a question that I posed to her in my interview. Her spontaneous response was 'Dalit culture'. The following excerpt brings home the transformation associated with the production of *Sangati*:

> MP: Okay, I want to ask you, 'Where does your strength come from?' In *Sangati* you say: 'To bounce like a ball that has been hit became my deepest desire and not curl up and collapse because of the blow'. When did you arrive at this philosophy? When? How?
>
> Bama: When I wrote *Sangati*. I wrote about different women.
>
> MP: So it was at that point. Not *Karukku*.
>
> Bama: No, not *Karukku*.
>
> MP: Would you say that you became more vociferous, more confident after Karukku?
>
> Bama: Not after *Karukku*. After *Sangati*.
>
> MP: After *Sangati*?

Bama: Not after, while writing *Sangati*. See at the end of *Karukku* I have written, 'Like a bird whose wings have been broken, I am now'.[69] That was the condition when I wrote *Karukku*. I wanted to fly freely but my feathers were cut. But while writing *Sangati*, the women who were against this oppressive system, that was in me.[70]

The word that captures the spirit of Bama and Maracle's story-telling is 'transformation'. Kay Schaffer and Sidonie Smith's study titled *Human rights and narrated lives: The ethics of recognition*, enhanced my understanding of the transformative power that operates in and through the texts *Sangati* and *I am woman*. Their study ranges from the stories of 'comfort women' in Japan to 'the stolen children' in Australia and the stories of Tiananmen Square in China. The authors of *Human rights* endeavour to present story telling's link with human rights campaigns: their study shows that the narratives undergo transformation and gain greater efficacy through their connection with the human rights discourses, platforms and campaigns. The reception of their stories and the wide audience they sometimes gain also enable this process of transformation. With avenues for telling their stories and participation, especially in cross-cultural exchanges and exposure to human rights discourse, comes transformation. 'These confident narrators reveal astute political awareness, utilizing a language of human rights'.[71] It is the language of human rights that informs the narratives *Sangati* and *I am woman*. Tracing the journeys of these two women, Bama and Lee Maracle, reveals that their coming into contact with human rights activists was responsible for the recording of their life stories – *Karukku* and *Bobbi Lee*. The progress of each of these women from their first publication to presenting through autobiographical fiction a compelling case for the recognition of the 'difference' of the women of their respective communities from women of mainstream cultures, bears witness to the forces of transformation at work. They have discovered that committed writing is their vocation. The revolutionary intent in writing *Sangati* is expressed by Bama in her acknowledgments: '*Sangati* grew out of the hope that the Dalit women who read it will rise up with fervour and walk towards victory as they begin their struggle as pioneers of a new society.'[72] Maracle's writing is also governed by her consciousness of being in 'the world of struggle' that works towards 'a new humanity'.[73] She articulates the journey that she made from the frontlines of activism to the lonely attic of a writer and her conviction that writing was what she was meant for. Her writing is replete with the discourse of human rights.

There is however a marked difference between the register that each of these writers employ. In Bama's stories one does not encounter the terms feminism, casteism or patriarchy: she uses the words caste and patriarchy only in the acknowledgements. However, the narrative is unmistakably informed by the zeal of a crusader for the rights of Dalit women and an assertion of their uniqueness and their humanity. Maracle's writing on the other hand is more academic.

Conclusion

Transnational destinations: moving voices, finding spaces

The efficacy of transnational feminism became tangible when Bama explained to me, as shown in the excerpt below, the impact of a researcher's cross-cultural study of Bama's short stories and those of Alice Walker:

> MP: You were talking with great passion about Alice Walker.
>
> Bama: Yeah because Alice Walker ... There is a lady in Stella Maris College, there is an English lecturer, Agnes, she has done this comparative study. Her thesis was titled 'Celebrating Life' and *I just love* it because for me also life is to be celebrated and for Alice Walker too. Most of her stories are from the Christian background, about how those people were treated within the Church by the whites. In spite of all those things they celebrate life. Some such similarity when I find, I'm interested to read. Even poetry. That is the thing. We may face a hundred and one atrocities and things like that. But still we rise above these things.[74]

This aspect of 'rising above' is what characterises Maracle's and Bama's work. This study is presented with the hope that the voices of these marginalised women who have already taken wing, will soar to many more transnational destinations by means of which more locations for dialogue and exchange of information will open up.

References

Bama 1992, *Karukku*, IDEAS, Madurai.

—— 1994, *Sangati*, IDEAS, Madurai.

—— 2000, *Karukku*, Trans. Lakshmi Holmstrom, Macmillan, Chennai.

—— 2005, *Sangati*, Trans. Lakshmi Holmstrom, Oxford University Press, Chennai.

Bataille, Gretchen and Kathleen Mullen Sands 1984, *American Indian women telling their lives*, University of Nebraska Press, Lincoln.

Chattopadhyay, Suhrid Sankar, 'AIDWA to take up the cause of Dalit Women', *The Hindu*, 4 November 2007, accessed at <http://www.hindu.com/2007/11/04/stories/2007110456401500.htm>

Franco, Fernando, Jyotsna Macwan and Suguna Ramanathan (eds) 2000, *The silken swing: The cultural universe of Dalit women*, STREE, Calcutta.

Grewal, Inderpal and Caren Kaplan 1994, *Scattered hegemonies: Postmodernity and transnational feminist practices*, University of Minnesota Press, Minneapolis.

Guru, Gopal 'Dalit Women Talk Differently', *Economic and Political Weekly*: 2548-2550.

Holmstrom, Lakshmi 2005, 'Introduction', in *Sangati*, Bama, Trans. Lakshmi Holmstrom, Oxford University Press, Chennai: xi–xxiii.

Maracle, Lee 1975, *Bobbi Lee: Indian rebel: struggles of a Native Canadian woman*, Liberation Support Movement Press, Richmond, B.C.

—— 1988, *I am woman*, Write-on Press, North Vancouver, B.C.

—— 1990, *Bobbi Lee: Indian rebel*, revised edn, Women's Press, Toronto.

—— 1994, 'Oratory: coming to theory', *Essays on Canadian Writing* 54, Winter: 7.

Moreton-Robinson, Aileen 2000, *Talkin' up to the white woman: Aboriginal women and feminism*, Unversity of Queensland Press, St Lucia, Queensland.

Rege, Sharmila 2006, *Writing caste/writing gender: Reading Dalit women's testimonios*, Zubaan, New Delhi.

Schaffer, Kay and Sidonie Smith 2004, *Human rights and narrated lives: The ethics of recognition*, Palgrave Macmillan, New York.

Warley, Linda 1996, 'Reviewing past and future: postcolonial Canadian autobiography and Lee Maracle's Bobbi Lee, Indian rebel', *Essays on Canadian Writing*, 60, Winter: 59.

Interviews

Interview with Father Mark Stephen, conducted by the author, 9 and 10 September 2006.

Interview with Bama, conducted by the author, 15 August 2006.

Interview with Bama, conducted by Manoj Nair, 'Recognition of the language of my people is the biggest award I can win', 26 April 2001, accessed at: <http://www.ambedkar.org/entertainment/RecognitionFor.htm>

ENDNOTES

[1] Cited in Bataille and Sands 1984: vi.

[2] Bama 1992, 1994; Maracle 1988, 1975.

[3] Bama 2000: xiv.

[4] Interview with Father Mark Stephen, conducted by the author, 9 and 10 September 2006.

[5] Interview with Father Mark Stephen, conducted by the author, 9 and 10 September 2006.

[6] Warley 1996.

[7] Maracle 1990: 11.

[8] Maracle 1990: 19.

[9] Maracle 1990: 20.

[10] Maracle 1990: 201.

[11] Maracle 1990: 229.

[12] Maracle 1990: 230.

[13] Maracle 1988: 16.

[14] Maracle 1988: 17.

[15] Maracle 1988: 16.

[16] Maracle 1988: 17.

[17] Maracle 1988: 20-21.

[18] Interview with Bana, conducted by the author, 15 August 2006.

[19] Rege 2006 presents excerpts in translation.

[20] Rege 2006: 235.

[21] Chattopadhyay, *The Hindu*, 4 November 2007.

[22] Moreton-Robinson 2000: 35-36.

[23] Moreton-Robinson 2000: 63.

[24] Moreton-Robinson 2000: 50.

[25] Moreton-Robinson 2000: 50.

[26] Grewal and Kaplan 1994: 1.

[27] Grewal and Kaplan 1994: 137.

[28] Grewal and Kaplan 1994: 137.

[29] Grewal and Kaplan 1994: 139.

[30] Grewal and Kaplan 1994: 139.

[31] Maracle 1988: iv.

[32] Interview with Bama, conducted by the author, 15 August 2006.

[33] Maracle 1988: 18.

[34] Maracle 1988: 61.

[35] Bama 2005: 67.

[36] Bama 2005: 68.

[37] Bama 2005: 92.

[38] Maracle 1988: 85.

[39] Maracle 1988: 86.

[40] Maracle 1988: 86.

[41] Maracle 1988: 43.

[42] Maracle 1988: 5.

[43] Maracle 1988: 5.

[44] Maracle 1988: 8.

[45] Bama 2005: 29.

[46] Bama 2005: 6.

[47] Maracle 1988: 155.

[48] Maracle 1988: 59.

[49] Maracle 1988: 24.

[50] Maracle 1988: 77.

[51] Maracle 1988: 24.

[52] Holmstrom 2000: xx.

[53] Interview with Bama, conducted by the author, 15 August 2006.

[54] Bama 2005: 114.

[55] Maracle 1988: x.

[56] Maracle 1988: 18.

57 Maracle 1988: 19.

58 Maracle 1988: 19.

59 Bama 2005: 65.

60 Maracle 1988: 20.

61 Maracle 1988: 29.

62 Maracle 1988: 29.

63 Maracle 1988: 75.

64 Bama 2005: 74.

65 Holmstrom 2005: xv.

66 Fernando et al 2000: 132.

67 Maracle 1988: para 16.

68 Bama 2005: viii.

69 This part of her speech coincides with the raucous, jubilant cawing of crows returning to their nests. There is also a shrill sound, almost like a whistle from an unidentified creature in the greenery around.

70 Interview with Bama, conducted by the author, 15 August 2006.

71 Schaffer and Smith 2004: 113.

72 Maracle 1988: ix.

73 Maracle 1988: iv.

74 Interview with Bama, conducted by the author, 15 August 2006.

Principles and Protocols

From this point the themes already taken up by the Indigenous writers grow even more complex. Each scholar is seeking answers to questions about appropriate protocols in biographical writing that seem so straightforward in theory but sometimes so murky in practice. First, quoting Frances Peters-Little, Michael Jacklin notes the difficulty of deciding who or what is the community one is supposed to consult, and what the benefits may be to that community when the biographical project deals with only one individual. Ethical Clearance Committees, without whose approval no fieldwork is supposed to proceed from within a university, should be able to tell us. From my observations such Guidelines that seem so absolute and demanding on paper leave unexplored important ethical issues that researchers face in their practice. For instance, no Guidelines require a researcher, having presumably built a warm relationship with a biographical subject, to maintain that warm relationship after the biography is complete. How could they? Yet an ongoing relationship may well be desirable from the point of view of the subject. Again, a biographer writing about an indigenous person of the early nineteenth century, probably would not consider submitting a research plan for ethics clearance. Yet for a conscientious biographer, to carry out such work without informing that individual's living descendants of the work in hand, would be unthinkable. So to literary studies. Michael Jacklin tells us that literary critics of indigenous texts are not required to consult with anyone. Until recently they have deliberately avoided speaking to an autobiographical author, not out of discourtesy, but because 'at least since the poststructuralist overthrow of authorial intention, seeking elucidation of a text through interlocution through its author has had little credit'. He argues persuasively that critics should join oral historians and anthropologists and get out into the community.

But having consulted appropriately, Jacklin found himself with information that he did not need, and indeed, did not want to know. This happens frequently amongst biographers who consult widely, and the complex ethical issues that emerge are often difficult to disentangle. Nowhere is this dilemma expressed more acutely than in the anguished discussion of Kristina Everett. Her title encapsulates the problem neatly: 'Too much information: when the burden of trust paralyses representation'. In one sense her problem is a new version of a familiar (but nonetheless difficult) conflict, that is, when the individual's wishes are at odds with those of many other community members. More seriously, as an anthropologist, Everett foresees that the act of editing and publishing the autobiography of her friend will create the potential for damage to a *future* claim by the author's community and beyond for reparation for past injustices by the Australian state. Where does Everett believe her responsibilities lie? It is only in the final sentence of the last paragraph that we learn her decision.

Simon Luckhurst's intriguing project carries the discussion in a different direction. From 3500 pages of personal documents ranging from diaries to bills, he seeks to create a biography or is it an autobiography of the Stolen Generations victim and children's storyteller Pauline McLeod. Though his interventions are arguably much less intrusive than those of other biographers in this monograph, Luckhurst still feels the need to justify his editorial practices. At the outset, though, the documents were in the possession of Pauline's brother Michael. Luckhurst needed Michael's permission to begin, and presumably he will ask for comments, and perhaps permission to publish, at the end of the project.

In her biographical account of her husband Jimmy Pike, Pat Lowe follows the opposite tack. In describing her decision-making processes in preparing her biography of Pike as a young man, Lowe consulted no one, except, significantly, her own memories of what Pike had said or her feelings of what he would have wanted. Each possible inclusion required individual consideration. Some of Pike's surprisingly frank accounts she or he had already published. Others she suspected might be at variance with the wishes or memories of his relatives. Quite possibly they might disagree amongst themselves. Reasoning that asking permission to publish certain accounts would imply a willingness to comply with the response, Lowe elected to consult nobody living. She took responsibility for her decisions about which stories to include and how to present them: 'Despite my occasional misgivings about one story or another, I deliberately didn't conceal anything, or dilute it to make it more acceptable, or try to explain it away'. The most controversial of Pike's autobiographical stories, perhaps, is the brief account of how as a young man he pretended to ravish a younger cousin. He reportedly retold the story with humour rather than shame, so Lowe included the story. Lowe's critics may insist on more contextual information about such stories and the circumstances of their retelling. They may reject altogether Lowe's decision to include them. Nevertheless Lowe's interesting defence of her editorial practice provides a further instance of the wide variety of ethical principles that guide biographers, in this case one who writes from the level of the personal knowledge and intimacy that exists between husband and wife. She reveals the resolution of her dilemmas in ways that many biographers shirk or avoid discussing publicly for fear of critical censure.

The ethical, moral and practical issues of entering, not another life, but another-life-in-community are endless. In these last four papers we catch a glimpse of where ethically aware biographers have been travelling and what challenges they may face in the future.

Peter Read and Anna Haebich

Consultation and critique: implementing cultural protocols in the reading of collaborative indigenous life writing

Michael Jacklin

Anyone working towards the publication of indigenous life narratives is aware of the significance of cultural protocols to both the narrative exchange and the writing and editing process. In the telling and the writing of an indigenous life story, protocols determining what gets told – where, when, to whom, or for whom – influence and sometimes complicate decisions regarding the final published narrative. This is the case whether the subject of the life narrative is the writer or whether the narrative is mediated by others. Indigenous protocols – including authority and moral rights over indigenous narratives and culture, kinship rights and obligations, care for country, mourning protocols, restricted knowledge, and reciprocity in the form of a return of benefits to indigenous communities – will significantly shape the production of the text. Negotiating protocols is often challenging, sometimes fraught, but always, in some form, an aspect of the writing of indigenous lives.[1]

This need to acknowledge and negotiate cultural protocols may also extend to the reading of indigenous life narratives, especially when those readings are published in the form of literary analysis and criticism. This is the basis of my own involvement with indigenous life stories. My academic training is in literary studies – a discipline which defines itself as working not with people in face-to-face exchanges but with texts. Engagement with producers of texts or with the families and communities of narrators and writers is not standard or even valued practice within the discipline. At least since the poststructuralist overthrow of authorial intention, seeking elucidation of a text through interlocution with its author has had little credit.[2] This disciplinary insistence upon texts as objects of study, separate, distinct and removed from the persons or communities of their making, sets literary studies in sharp contrast to other fields of academic research into indigenous cultures and knowledge, where respect for cultural protocols is one of a number of ethical guidelines to which the researcher must comply. Anthropology has long been forced to grapple with the ethics of its engagement with indigenous narratives, knowledge and belief systems. Oral historians, likewise, in their interaction with and dependence upon human subjects as sources of narrative have for decades contended with the dilemmas of producing scholarly work from narratives obtained in lived relationships. My argument, then, is not with historians or anthropologists. It is with literary critics who turn to indigenous narratives, often produced with the involvement of historians or anthropologists, for their objects of study. Elsewhere I have suggested that respect for cultural protocols ought to apply to the reading of indigenous literature in ways similar to other avenues of indigenous research and scholarship.[3] Reading indigenous lives and publishing those readings situate the literary critic in an ethical engagement with indigenous subjects not dissimilar from other academic disciplines, and fundamental to both academic and indigenous protocols is consultation. The purpose of this article, then, is not to reiterate that previous argument but to demonstrate some of the benefits and to indicate challenges that arise from consultation with the producers of indigenous life narratives. To do this I will make reference to experiences gained and dilemmas faced over the course of my PhD study on collaborative indigenous life writing in Australia and Canada.

There is a great deal of critical work which theorises the dynamics of collaborative life writing; most of this focuses on issues of power dissymmetries and how the voice of the narrating subject is shaped or altered – or alternatively how the integrity of that voice is maintained – in the process of reaching the printed page.[4] Because literary critics restrict their engagement to available texts, much of this theoretical work on collaborative writing is, by necessity, speculative. Critics will use paratexts – the surrounding or framing texts such as introductions, prefaces, afterwords, and so on – to gain some insight into the collaborative process.[5] Occasionally, an interview with the editor or writer will be available, or she or he may have published a separate academic article on the writing process. Literary theorists will then use this supplementary material to reflect upon the dynamics of collaboration and the effects of these dynamics on the published outcome. In some cases, the critic moves from commentary on perceived power differentials to a ready dismissal of the published text as failing to move beyond the colonialist framework that underlies its production. In my encounters with this type of criticism of selected indigenous life writing, I began to experience a sense of uneasiness as I wondered what the indigenous contributors to these texts, or – if they had passed on – their families or communities, would make of such critical work. This uneasiness moved me towards a commitment that if I were to publish readings of indigenous texts, I should try to contact and to consult the makers of the texts.

I was encouraged in this direction by remarks from Jeremy Beckett who, in an address given to his fellow anthropologists, spoke of the ways in which anthropology had changed over the previous decades, largely in response to theoretical shifts and critical insights in other disciplines, but also as a result of the tension between anthropology and postcolonial and cultural theory. This tension, Beckett suggests, is related to the disciplinary divide which marks literary and cultural studies as 'text based', while anthropology, through its practice of fieldwork, is necessarily a process of human engagement in which researchers work with individuals and communities in the production of knowledge. This difference, '[t]hat we have actually talked to the people we write about', Beckett says, 'seems particularly to get under the skin of our critics, which I of course believe conceals their insecurity about their own text-based speculations'.[6]

My belief that consultation could aid my reading of indigenous life narratives may have been prompted by the kind of anxiety Beckett suggests, but my understanding of the role of consultation and its potential to enrich the reading of indigenous life writing grew tremendously in the very process of undertaking it. For my PhD research I had identified 12 indigenous texts – both Australian Aboriginal life narratives and Canadian First Nations texts – that I would read and critique. In Australia, I spoke with Ruby Langford Ginibi and Penny van Toorn; with Patsy Cohen and Margaret Somerville; with Roy and June Barker and Cilka Zagar; with Jackie Huggins; and with Jennifer Isaacs.[7] In Canada, among the many people I met were Maria Campbell and Linda Griffiths; Daisy Sewid-Smith and Thomas Sewid; Yvonne Johnson and Rudy Wiebe; Freda Ahenakew; Heather Hodgson; Julie Cruikshank; Wendy Wickwire; and Beverly Hungry Wolf.[8] Over the course of these interviews, what started out as a rather theoretical concept – that indigenous protocols for meeting and exchanging knowledge might extend to reading and commenting on indigenous texts – became more thoroughly grounded and reinforced with each encounter and conversation that I became involved in. Australian author Kate Grenville has acknowledged that talking to Aboriginal people whose lives, or whose ancestors' lives, are implicated in one's writing is, at the very least, 'a matter of courtesy'.[9] Meeting with both indigenous and non-indigenous contributors to indigenous life writing – whether writer or editor, storyteller or family member – helped me realise that visiting and consulting was the foundation of good relations, and the beginning of ethical engagement. In reading and then writing about a published indigenous life narrative, consulting is a sign of respect – respect for the person and her or his authority over the narrative and knowledge that had been published. The question of 'Who owns the story?' is directly relevant here. Once published, a narrative moves beyond the control of its author or authors, and is open to commentaries, reviews, criticism, interpretations and re-contextualisations that its authors could not have imagined. All published work shares this fate and clearly it is neither possible nor necessary for literary critics to contact the author of each book they review or analyse. It is essential, however, that when a non-indigenous critic enters indigenous territory, represented here in indigenous life narratives, they should be aware of the protocols that guide other forms of research into indigenous lives and cultures, and be willing to respect these protocols in their own engagement with indigenous narratives and knowledge.

Respect for cultural protocols and a willingness on the critic's part to engage in dialogue with the makers of indigenous life-writing texts can contribute significantly to the understanding of a text, often in unexpected ways. Two examples will illustrate this potential. The first of these is in relation to the Indigenous life story *The two worlds of Jimmie Barker*.[10] In the early stages of my PhD, I wrote an article in which I pointed towards the degree of Indigenous agency in the production of the narratives upon which this book is based.[11] Jimmie Barker had been responsible for the majority of the recording process, having begun tape-recording well before he met with the non-indigenous researcher, Janet Mathews. His narratives provide a powerful account of Aboriginal identity and the struggle to maintain culture and language under the pressures of colonialist policies and practices of subjugation in north-west New South Wales. Although written by Mathews after Barker's death – based upon his tapes as well as letters and conversations – the book, I believed, was significant for the way it placed into question assumptions regarding non-indigenous control of interviewing and recording. However, my subsequent meeting with Roy Barker, Jimmie Barker's son, cast another light upon this collaborative text. As Mathews saw the book through to publication after Barker's death, she claimed copyright of the text. Roy Barker feels that, because of this, his family and the Muruwari nation have lost control of Jimmie Barker's life story. Although I was aware that Mathews held copyright, I had assumed that the Barker family's interests had also been respected. I cannot account now for why I thought this; perhaps I had naively assumed that the basic principle of Indigenous authority and moral rights over Indigenous narratives and culture had been respected. However, Roy Barker was emphatic that this was not the case.[12] Consultation here led me – a non-indigenous reader – to a deeper understanding of issues that continue to impact upon the way this published Indigenous life narrative is viewed by those close to, and affected by, its production.

A second example relates to the difficulties faced by a non-indigenous researcher looking at books published from a diverse range of indigenous cultures. Reading collaboratively-produced narratives from regions including Yolngu country in Arnhem Land, Anaiwan country in northern New South Wales, from the Kwakwaka'wakw territories of north-eastern Vancouver Island, and from Tyendinaga Mohawk Territory near the shore of Lake Ontario, meant that there was no way I could fully comprehend the culturally specific codes and practices that had contributed to any one text's making. Consulting provided an opportunity to learn something of how the narratives and texts were shaped by the cultural beliefs and practices of their makers. Specifically, I learned from speaking with Yvonne Johnson, who along with Canadian novelist Rudy Wiebe co-wrote her life story titled *Stolen life: Journey of a Cree woman*, that their book was designed so that the cover, and the book's opening and closing prayers would represent a medicine bundle, a power object of tremendous significance in Cree culture.[13] A medicine bundle is something in which sacred objects are wrapped to hold their power, both to protect that power from exposure to forces from without, but also to protect the unwary or unprepared from the force within. A medicine bundle can only be opened with due ceremony, respect and protocols. That Yvonne Johnson's life story is one of sexual abuse endured from the earliest years of her childhood, and one that culminates in her involvement in a murder for which she received a 'life-25' sentence, underscores the significance of wrapping her narrative as a medicine bundle, an object of power and potentially an object of harm.[14]

Consulting with the indigenous contributors, the narrators or co-authors, or their families, in this way allows for critical reading enhanced by some measure of cross-cultural understanding. Native American critic Greg Sarris points out that without such insight, and without engagement with those involved in the text's production, critics

> would not have any opportunity to know any story about the text except that of their own invention. Little, if anything, would inhibit their culture specific projection, which, in turn, can engender further discussion about the projection and spin the discourse further and further from the Indian narrator and her narration.[15]

Indeed, the unease I had experienced when reading some critical analyses of indigenous texts had been prompted by exactly this: non-indigenous critics devoting the majority of their attentions to editing and framing issues, to the neglect of the indigenous narrative, their putative object of study. Stephen Muecke made this same observation more than 20 years ago. A common approach to collaborative indigenous writing, according to Muecke, 'is to direct all critical attention to the linguistic strategies of the editors, as if these were the most salient features of the works'.[16] In two decades much has changed in other disciplines, yet in literary criticism the fixation upon the non-indigenous frame remains common. Consultation, on the other hand, could help literary critics enter into more meaningful engagement with the indigenous narratives they read and comment upon.

Consultation, however, brings not only deeper understanding of indigenous texts but also moves the literary critic into sometimes ambiguous issues of research and knowledge circulation. Frances Peters-Little has written about the near impossibility of fulfilling all aspects of cultural protocol requirements in indigenous research. Particularly she has commented on the difficulties involved in protocols such as community permissions and the return of benefits to community. Deciding 'who is community' and 'what benefits a community is not straightforward', she says, and guidelines provide little help.[17] Notions of community are complicated by issues of migration, by who has left town and who has remained, sometimes by forced separation from family and country, and by competing or overlapping family claims to status or to land.[18] In my own limited involvement in matters relating to indigenous communities, the same complex issues arose. Consultation, as argued above, can provide knowledge or information that the literary critic might otherwise fail to appreciate. A critic, of course, realises that an important aspect of a life narrative is selection, determining what is included and what is left out; this is how meaning is created. For the critic, awareness of who or what is absent and why they are absent is essential to any comprehensive reading. I found, however, that in consulting with those who knew much more than was included in published texts, I was sometimes given more information than I had anticipated. In some cases I felt that the information being relayed to me, if I included it in my published critical readings, had the potential for harm. I felt especially unsettled as a non-indigenous researcher being given information relating to conflict within indigenous communities – in some cases inter-family conflict, in others disputes between family members – that if circulated could have unforeseeable consequences. And to believe that publishing in academic journals entails little risk of commentary returning to community in quite unpredicted ways is both false and, in itself, harmful. Publishing in any forum has consequences. What gets written stays written, and can return to communities in unexpected ways.[19]

Avoidance of harm is an ethical responsibility of research which engages with human subjects. As I have argued throughout, such ethics and protocols may very well be extended to the literary critic's engagement with indigenous texts. In other research fields, another important consideration is the return of benefits. What is it, however, that a literary critic gives back to indigenous writers, narrators, or community in a published critical reading? How does consultation regarding the production and reception of indigenous life narratives work in terms of reciprocity? In this, I take my cue from First Nations writer Daisy Sewid-Smith, from the Kwakwaka'wakw people of north-eastern Vancouver Island and daughter of James Sewid. In a rejoinder to an American anthropologist who had been invited to attend her father's potlatch – a significant event in Kwakwaka'wakw culture and one that plays an important role in Pacific Coast First Nations life writing – Sewid-Smith took issue with the non-indigenous academic's subsequently published account of the event.[20] She writes that in answering this academic publicly, but outside the ceremonial space of the Big House where potlatches are performed, she is breaking with her cultural tradition, but she feels if she does not answer then the academic's words would become 'the only written record of this historic event in the academic world'.[21] Sewid-Smith takes issue, especially, with outsiders' interpretations of her family's, her community's, her nation's representational practices. Sewid-Smith refers to these outsiders as 'academic adjuncts', who, although perhaps invited into indigenous territory, when they leave, publish accounts without maintaining due process of consultation and respect for indigenous authority. I take Sewid-Smith's words seriously and accept that at most, whatever reading I offer will be that of an academic adjunct, an adjunct, however, who has made an effort to maintain relationships with those whose life narratives have provided the material for critical commentary.

This certainly has not been without difficulties. There were 29 people involved in my interviews. Maintaining relationships has been a matter of letters, phone-calls, emails, and with those close by, personal visits. For each chapter of my PhD I sent the finished material to contributors and asked for their comments. For some chapters, this meant the involvement of four or five people. Most responded positively; some took issue with the commentary, or with the arrangement, and asked for changes, which I respected. In one case, disagreement resulted from the conflicting responses of the indigenous and the non-indigenous contributors to one book. Through emails, I was able to work this through so that my chapter was satisfactory, although I felt considerable anxiety about becoming a mediator between the book's makers. In another case, however, a First Nations writer broke off our email exchanges because of a misunderstanding that I could not set right. Here, my mediation was not between co-writers, or narrator and editor, but between the indigenous writer and a number of published academic responses that she had not been aware of, but which I had discussed. The writer was dissatisfied with the implications she read between the commentary of these other critics, the placement of material from her interview and my analysis. I modified the chapter, removing the offending material, although I could not help feeling this to be an unfortunate outcome, as I had been attempting to critique the work of others who had, of course, not consulted with this indigenous writer before publishing their critiques. I remembered Eric Michaels expressing dismay at the difficulties of consultation and community vetting of his work in Yuendumu, particularly when the work of other researchers, 'who never submit[ted] a thing for comment or vetting', could be published unchallenged.[22]

This, however, is what the literary critic can give back. In every academic discipline it is acknowledged that 'research involving Indigenous knowledges and peoples needs to be conducted in culturally appropriate ways that fit the cultural preferences, practices and aspirations of Indigenous peoples'.[23] There is no reason why this could not, or should not, be the standard for academic work in literary studies which draws upon and publishes readings of indigenous life narratives. As mentioned throughout, published readings of collaboration in life writing often focus on power dissymmetries. It is necessary to acknowledge, however, that power dissymmetries are central not only to cross-cultural collaborative writing but also to the academic interest in such texts. The right to publish one's reading of another's life story is a privilege created by and contributing to existing structures of power. Aileen Moreton-Robinson's challenge to white feminists – that they need 'to theorise the relinquishment of power' – perhaps should be extended to literary studies, and to those who critique indigenous life writing.[24] Honouring protocols and consulting is a way of acknowledging that 'Who owns the story?' bears upon the reading of a narrative as well as its production.

References

Ahenakew, Freda and HC Wolfart (eds and trans) 1992, *Kohkominawak otacimowiniwawa: Our grandmothers' lives, as told in their own words*, Fifth House Publishers, Saskatoon.

Beckett, Jeremy 2002, 'Some aspects of continuity and change among anthropologists in Australia or: "He-who-eats-from-one-dish-with-us-with-one-spoon"', *The Australian Journal of Anthropology* 13(2) August: 127–139.

Blackman, Margaret B 1992, 'Returning home: life histories and the Native Community', *Journal of Narrative and Life History* 2(1): 49–59.

Brettell, Caroline B (ed) 1993, *When they read what we write: The politics of ethnography*, Bergin & Garvey, Westport.

Cohen, Patsy and Margaret Somerville 1990, *Ingelba and the five black matriarchs*, Allen & Unwin, Sydney.

Couser, G Thomas 2004, *Vulnerable subjects: Ethics and life writing*, Cornell University Press, Ithaca.

Cruikshank, Julie 1990, *Life lived like a story: Life stories of three Yukon Native Elders*, in collaboration with Angela Sidney, Kitty Smith, and Annie Ned, University of Nebraska Press, Lincoln.

Genette, Gerard 1997, *Paratexts: Thresholds of interpretation*, Trans. Jane E Lewin, Cambridge University Press, Cambridge.

Ginibi, Ruby Langford 1999, *Haunted by the past*, Allen & Unwin, St Leonards.

Grenville, Kate 2006, *Searching for the secret river*, Text Publishing, Melbourne.

Griffiths, Linda and Maria Campbell 1989, *The Book of Jessica: A theatrical transformation*, Coach House, Toronto.

Heiss, Anita 2002, 'Writing about Indigenous Australia – some issues to consider and protocols to follow: a discussion paper', *Southerly* 62(2) Summer: 197–206.

Hodgson, Heather (ed) 1989, *Seventh generation: Contemporary native writing*, Theytus Books, Penticton.

Huggins, Jackie 1994, 'Respect V Political Correctness', *Australian Author* 26(3) Spring: 12–14.

Huggins, Rita and Jackie Huggins 1994, *Auntie Rita*, Aboriginal Studies Press, Canberra.

Hungry Wolf, Beverly 1982, *The ways of my grandmothers*, Quill, New York.

Jacklin, Michael 2002, 'Collaboration and resistance in indigenous life writing', *Australian Canadian Studies* 20(1): 27–45.

—— 2004, 'Critical injuries: collaborative indigenous life writing and the ethics of criticism', *Life Writing* 1(2): 55–83.

—— 2005, 'Cross talk: collaborative indigenous life writing in Australia and Canada', PhD Thesis, Deakin University, Geelong.

—— 2007, 'What I have done, what was done to me: confession and testimony in *Stolen life: Journey of a Cree woman'*, *Kunapipi* 29(1): 19–33.

Janke, Terri 1998, 'Our culture: our future: report on Australian Indigenous cultural and intellectual property rights', Michael Frankel & Company, Surry Hills. Available online at: <http://www.frankellawyers.com.au/media/report/culture.pdf>

Marika, Wandjuk 1995, *Wandjuk Marika: Life story*, as told to Jennifer Isaacs, University of Queensland Press, St Lucia.

Mathews, Janet (ed) 1988, *The two worlds of Jimmie Barker: The life of an Australian Aboriginal* 1900-1972, rev. edn, Aboriginal Studies Press, Canberra. First published in 1977.

Michaels, Eric 1990, *Unbecoming*, EM Press, Sydney.

Moreton-Robinson, Aileen 2000, *Talkin' Up to the white woman: Indigenous women and feminism*, University of Queensland Press, St Lucia.

Muecke, Stephen 1984, 'The Scribes', *Meridian* 3(1): 41–48.

Neate, Erica and Marie Wilkinson 1997, 'Listen with your heart', *Oral History Association of Australia Journal* 19: 10–15.

Newton-De Molina, David (ed) 1976, *On literary intention*, Edinburgh University Press, Edinburgh.

Peters Little, Frances 2000, *The community game: Aboriginal self-definition at the local level*, Aboriginal Studies Press, Canberra. Available online at: <http://www.anu.edu.au/caepr/iwepapers/Peters-Little.pdf>

—— 2003, 'The impossibility of pleasing everybody: a legitimate role for white filmmakers making black films', *Australian Humanities Review* (January). Available online at: <http://www.australianhumanitiesreview.org/archive/Issue-Jan2003/peterslittle.html>

Rigney, Lester-Irabinna 2006, 'Indigenist research and Aboriginal Australia,' in *Indigenous peoples' wisdom and power: Affirming our knowledge through narratives*. Julian E Kunnie and Nomalungelo I Goduka (eds), Ashgate, Aldershot: 32–48.

Robinson, Harry 1989, *Write it on your heart: The epic world of an Okanagan storyteller*, Wendy Wickwire (ed), Talonbooks/Theytus, Vancouver.

Sarris, Greg 1993, *Keeping Slug Woman alive: A holistic approach to American Indian texts*, University of California Press, Berkeley.

Sewid-Smith, Daisy 1997, 'The continuing reshaping of our ritual world by academic adjuncts', *Anthropology and Education Quarterly*, 28(4) December: 594–602.

Spradley, James (ed) 1972, *Guests never leave hungry: The autobiography of James Sewid, a Kwakiutl Indian*, McGill-Queens University Press, Montreal and Kingston.

Theisz, RD 1981, 'The critical collaboration: introductions as a gateway to the study of Native American bi-autobiography', *American Indian Culture and Research Journal* 5(1): 65–80.

Torres, Patricia Mamajun 1994, 'Interested in writing about Indigenous Australians?' *Australian Author* 26(3) Spring: 24–25.

Wheatley, Nadia 1994, 'Black and white writing: the issues,' *Australian Author* 26(3) Spring: 20–23.

Wiebe, Rudy and Yvonne Johnson 1998, *Stolen life: The journey of a Cree woman*, Alfred A. Knopf, Toronto.

Wimsatt, WK and MC Beardsley 1976, 'The intentional fallacy', in *On literary intention*, David Newton-De Molina (ed), Edinburgh University Press, Edinburgh: 1–13.

Wolcott, Harry F 1996, 'Peripheral participation and the Kwakiutl potlatch', *Anthropology and Education Quarterly* 27(4): 467–492.

Zagar, Cilka (ed) 2000, *Goodbye riverbank: The Barwon-Namoi people tell their story*, Magabala, Broome.

ENDNOTES

[1] There are numerous publications outlining cultural protocols and their application to research in areas of indigenous knowledge. For the most comprehensive coverage, see Janke 1998; also, Huggins 1994; Neate and Wilkinson 1997; Torres 1994; Wheatley 1994; Heiss 2002.

[2] Rejection of authorial intention in literary analysis pre-dates poststructuralism, of course, with Wimsatt and Beardsley's article 'The intentional fallacy' signalling the textual turn in New Criticism in the 1940s: Wimsatt and Beardsley 1976. For an excellent collection of articles on the conundrum of intention, see Newton-De Molina 1976.

[3] This was the primary outcome of my PhD thesis, 'Cross talk: collaborative indigenous life writing in Australia and Canada', submitted to Deakin University in 2004. Based on a process of both reading and

consultation with the makers of indigenous life writing texts, I argued that literary criticism needs to take into account the co-operative aspects of textual production as well as the constraining factors that shape the outcome of collaborative texts. The thesis also insists upon the importance of non-indigenous critics acknowledging the centrality of indigenous protocols in both the production and reception of collaborative indigenous life writing. For a condensed version of this see Jacklin 2004.

[4] See especially the work of Couser 2004.

[5] Paratexts is a term borrowed from Genette 1997. For an early and important work on the use of introductions and other 'threshold' material in the analysis of collaboratively produced texts, see Theisz 1981.

[6] Beckett 2002: 129-130.

[7] See Ginibi 1999; Cohen and Somerville 1990; Zagar 2000; Huggins and Huggins 1994; Marika 1995.

[8] See Griffiths and Campbell 1989; Spradley 1972; Wiebe and Johnson 1998; Ahenakew and Wolfart 1992; Hodgson 1989; Cruikshank 1990; Robinson 1989; Hungry Wolf 1982. With each text read, I attempted to contact both the Indigenous and non-Indigenous contributors. This was not always possible, due to distance, or non-replies, or in some cases to the passing on of one or the other participant. From the list of contributors given above, 12 are Indigenous and eight non-Indigenous. For example, Ruby Langford Ginibi is a pre-eminent Aboriginal author from Bun djalung country in New South Wales, while Penny van Toorn is a non-Indigenous academic who edited Ginibi's book *Haunted by the past*, a biography of her son Nobby Langford: Ginibi 1999.

[9] Grenville 2006: 130.

[10] Mathews 1977.

[11] Jacklin 2002.

[12] Interview with Roy and June Barker, recorded 23 April 2002, Lightning Ridge, New South Wales.

[13] Wiebe and Johnson 1998.

[14] For a detailed reading of Wiebe and Johnson's book as a spirit bundle, see Jacklin 2007.

[15] Sarris 1993: 45.

[16] Muecke 1984: 45.

[17] Peters Little 2003: para 12.

[18] Peters Little 2000: 15-20.

[19] Amongst the works relating to the return of academic writing to a community of origin, see especially Brettell 1993; also Blackman 1992.

[20] The American anthropologist is Harry Wolcott. See Wolcott 1996.

[21] Sewid-Smith 1997: 598.

[22] Michaels 1990: 102.

[23] Rigney 2006: 46.

[24] Moreton-Robinson 2000: 186.

Too much information: when the burden of trust paralyses representation

Kristina Everett

This story is not a simple one, nor, very likely, an unfamiliar one to anyone who has conducted research in Indigenous contexts. It began when a long time Aboriginal friend, 'Alma',[1] asked me to help her to write her story so that her children, grandchildren, future descendants and the general public could know about her life. Due to the educational conditions Alma experienced in her childhood, she believed that her literacy skills were not up to the task of doing justice to her complex and compelling story, so she asked me, a white friend with a tertiary education and a sympathetic ear, to undertake the job. We agreed that this was to be a collaborative work based largely on an account and analysis of our relationship and the ways in which our stories as 'inter-racial' friends are intertwined, vexed, segregated and silenced. A difficult enough task I thought, until I realised after years of writing and further research, that it may well be an impossible one. I have come to understand that what began as a project to help write my friend back into Australian history could have dire ramifications for many different people, including myself. Some of the information in the biography could undermine the claims of Alma's community and of some other Aboriginal people. It could not only damage future claims for reparation of past injustices by the Australian state, but could impair some people's claims to 'authentic' Aboriginal identity according to the rules of native title in this country. It could make it impossible for me to ever work in this area again. But having accepted the job of telling someone else's story, do I now have the right to refuse to seek its publication which is much desired by Alma and her community? Is this my choice?

Introduction

Much has been said about the rightness and especially the wrongness of relatively powerful, educated whites writing the stories of black people. Many authors including Stuart Hall, Henry Louis Gates, Mudrooroo, bell hooks and Aileen Moreton-Robinson, to name a few, question the possibility of any kind of non-colonial representation being possible in the process of cultural translation that must necessarily occur when a white author presumes to write someone else's story.[2] Mari Rhydwen while acknowledging the kinds of problems raised by these authors, was among the first to also acknowledge that, in the era of native title and land claims, many Indigenous people not only accept the interest of white authors in compiling their biographies, autobiographies and life histories, but actively seek such attention.[3] For many Indigenous people, biographies written by white authors have become an essential part, not only of their claims against the state, but of writing themselves, their families and their communities back into an Australian history out of which they were previously written. Gaynor Macdonald reminds us, however, that data obtained from informants with a vested interest in having their story told can only be a reflection of a moment in time, cannot tell 'the whole story', require that Indigenous participants represent themselves within particular 'frames' (authentic, traditional people) and more-over, co-opt researchers in the service of a specific cause for a particular group of people.[4] In this paper I am concerned with these problems, especially the last two: that Indigenous participants in biographies and research generally *must* represent themselves as authentic, traditional people and that researchers are co-opted to reproduce these representations.

I was not naïve to the broader political ramifications of writing biography when Alma asked me to help her to write her life history. In 2001 I began collecting material – interviews, stories, copies of paintings, photos, maps and other documents. Alma and I had been close friends for many years, I knew her family, friends and was conscious of the wider community to which she belonged and was aware of some of their political concerns. Alma is a senior woman who belongs to a group called 'Galba' who claim traditional Aboriginal ownership of a large part of a modern Australian metropolis. I thought at the time that helping Alma to write her biography may support some of the claims of the broader community, contribute to the literature on urban Aboriginal identity, and, equally importantly, be an affirming and empowering document recognising Alma's personal history as an Aboriginal woman within the Australian state over the last 60 years or so. I had just begun my PhD candidature in anthropology at the time and I asked Alma and other community leaders for permission to use the material I gathered for the biography to be also used in my anthropological research.

Galba can prove that they conform to the official definition of 'Aboriginal' in Australia. This definition is formulated in most state's Native Title Acts, and is the same as that used in the *Commonwealth Native Title Act* 1993 and in Section 51(26) of the Australian Constitution. In all this legislation 'Aboriginal' is defined as: 'a person of Aboriginal or Torres Strait Islander descent who identifies as an Aboriginal or Torres Strait Islander and is accepted as such by the community in which he or she lives'. So, in Australia, self and community cultural identification, as well as genetic descent, determine who is Aboriginal. The Australian legal definition is a social category conflated with genetic heritage.

But identification as Aboriginal is not the same as being recognised as Aboriginal Traditional Owners. Under the *Land Rights Act* (NSW 1986), for example, Aboriginal people who have been alienated from their traditional, pre-contact countries may gain access and benefits to land with which they now have various kinds of connections. Under the Act these 'connections' do not need to pre-exist white settlement and may be related to histories of pastoral or industrial relationships with a particular tract of land or to long term settlement in a particular area. If, however, a group claims Aboriginal Traditional Ownership, the land is claimed under either the *Commonwealth Native Title Act* 1993 or one of the state's Native Title Acts. Under these Acts claimants must prove that they remain connected to a 'body of traditions, observances, customs and beliefs of Aboriginals or of a community or group of Aboriginals whose traditions, observances, customs and beliefs are applied to particular persons, sites, areas of land, things or relationships'.[5] In other words, claimants must prove that they remain, and have continuously been 'connected' to customs and beliefs that were existent before white people came to Australia. Proving ongoing connections to pre-contact Aboriginal traditions in the face of colonisation seems a most difficult task for any Indigenous group, but for people like Galba, whose traditional country is now an urban centre, this is virtually impossible.

What I was completely naïve about when I began researching the biography was the precise nature of the community to which Alma belonged: its unusual composition, its uncommon social structure and its difference from another group of people, also called Galba, who make similar claims in very different and competing ways. I knew that 'Alma's mob' may have once become a community in response to what they perceived to be the benefits of native title. But I did not completely grasp the serious repercussions of their more recent claim that their contemporary cultural expressions, such as singing, dancing and ceremony, are now such values in themselves that making land claims is now a secondary concern to them.

Alma's mob often perform public expressions of their group identity including 'welcome to country' speeches using a version of a pre-contact Aboriginal language, site smokings in which gum leaves are added to a fire to cleanse a particular space and the people inhabiting it of evil spirits, and Aboriginal dancing by performers wearing lap-laps with their bodies painted in white ochre. These performances are most often performed at the invitation of white officials at occasions such as opening ceremonies for exhibitions, local, state and federal government occasions, school functions and conferences. Alma's mob also engage in certain 'private' expressions of group identity including ceremonies that are not always meant to be observed by 'outsiders'. One of these is a ceremony performed after the death of a community member and involves the ritualised carving of a symbol of group identity into sacred trees.

The various representations of 'Aboriginality' and articulations of group identity employed by Alma's mob are drawn from many different sources. They are part of ongoing political-cultural processes of conservation and restoration, even when what is being preserved and renewed does not necessarily 'belong' to the people engaged in those practices. These practices come at least partly, as Sissons has found in urban indigenous contexts in Aotearoa/New Zealand and North America, from academic literature, popular culture such as books, films and even advertisements.[6] They may be 'borrowed' or 'shared' by other Aboriginal groups in Australia and international Indigenous groups in what is now a global Indigenous exchange. These cultural forms may also come from memories, dreams and imaginings for which there can be no accounting or tracing. But no-one could successfully argue that this is a brand new genesis, a made up identity, or a nostalgic post-modern 'simulacrum'. The identity produced by Alma's mob is the product of political strategising and manoeuvring, as well as extensive social relations. This is a political-cultural process of group identity formation and development.

The group of Galba who compete with Alma's group for the attention of white authorities (henceforth referred to as Group X) have based their claims to authentic Galba identity and ownership on genealogies and on academic research on language, archaeological sites and historical documents. This research is used to make native title and other kinds of claims against the Australian state, a very different form of identity making from Alma's mob who make public spectacles of their cultural practices. Group X do not claim, and in fact emphatically disparage any claim to ongoing cultural practices such as the dance, art production or language use which are important expressions of identity used by Alma's mob. Group X claims are connected to a modern political identity but one which still must have at its root the 'authenticity' that the Australian state demands for native title claimants: that is, ongoing connection to Aboriginal traditions and customs. This kind of political emphasis on Indigenous identity in a Native American context has been labelled 'political nationalism' by Gerald Sider.[7] Group X, the Galba political nationalists, claim that such displays of culture as dance, art and language-use damage their own claims to an authentic, modern, political Galba identity, further emphasising a schism between the two Galba groups.[8]

I was also unaware at that time that in being Alma's long term friend I had already been identified by both groups of Galba and their various supporters and detractors as a supporter of Alma's mob rather than as a supporter of Aboriginal people generally as I had perceived myself. Moreover, in conducting the research related to the biography I was affirming the position of 'Alma partisan'. It was not until I had conducted participant-observation fieldwork that I realised the extent of the schism between the groups and the impossibility of working with them both due to my history of working with Alma and her community.

This impossible positioning of researchers as supporters of one group or the other results from competition between groups for the attention of whites and is as true for government agents and private stakeholders as it is for researchers (both Indigenous and non-Indigenous). It is a result of a phenomenon that is common in many postcolonial contexts; Jeffrey Sissons calls it 'oppressive authenticity'.[9]

'Oppressive authenticity' is largely a result of the ways that courts determine Indigenous groups' eligibility for land claims, and in Australia, especially native title, arguably the ultimate recognition of Indigenous 'authenticity'. As Francesca Merlan explains, the incomparability of Aboriginal land rights with other kinds of property rights is legislatively managed in the *Aboriginal Land Rights Act* (NT 1976).[10] This is done by elaborate codification of what needs to be demonstrated to succeed as well as the creation of a new form of property title. The *Commonwealth Native Title Act* 1993, however, leaves what counts as 'custom' or 'tradition' for determination by the court. This is necessary because whereas land rights are a new form of land title in Australian law, native title is part of Australia's common law. From a legal point of view the basis for the existence of native title is the presentation of evidence that native title has *always* existed over a given place for specific people. Indigenous Australians can only demonstrate their continued relationship with a specific place by demonstrating their association with that place in terms of the court's interpretation of what counts as tradition because it is on the very different traditions to those of other Australians that their distinctiveness is grounded. Indigenous peoples' claims to prior occupation of Australia are based on their difference, and their difference is demonstrated in their traditions.[11] Because of this, Indigenous subjects of biography are compelled to present their stories in terms of their 'connections' to these traditions.

Courts, as Merlan demonstrates, have recognised sufficient evidence of ongoing Aboriginal tradition for the purposes of native title using highly essentialised notions of the term. That is, courts have used an immutable, static model of 'tradition' and 'custom' to demonstrate that claimants have *always* had a connection to the place they claim under common law, or one that recognises some change in the nature of cultural objects but constancy in the underlying social processes associated with those objects: guns instead of spears, acrylic paint instead of ochre, and motor bikes instead of walking, for example.[12] For native title to succeed, authentic Aboriginal tradition needs to consist in static essences and an ontology of fixed and unchanging meanings so as to demonstrate the immutable character of traditional Aboriginal ownership. The trouble with this is that the character of tradition as lived by people in the here and now is not consistent with a model of tradition as fixed, immutable and situated in a primordial moment before whites came to Australia. Indigenous Australians are faced with an impossible double bind. On the one hand, the courts require evidence of Aboriginal tradition and custom as unchanged, on the other, forced and voluntary participation in modern Australian life has required drastic and virtually total change from traditional (pre-contact) life ways. Biographers of Indigenous subjects are similarly placed in this double-bind. How can the dynamic circumstances of an Indigenous biography be represented while preserving legal requirements for static tradition?

The courts demand demonstration of fixed and unchanging traditions being performed by specific people in relation to a particular place to allow native title, yet, it is the Australian state (represented by that same court) which is primarily responsible for the kinds of radical cleavages with tradition that are used as evidence of a group's alienation from their traditional lands. I agree with Kalpana Ram when she says that 'authenticity' becomes virtually impossible to obtain in such circumstances, but because ongoing connection to land is a state imposed criterion for demonstrating collective identity, questions of authenticity become impossible to avoid.[13] Indigenous Australians who want to be recognised as authentic traditional owners must therefore demonstrate evidence of continuing reproduction of traditions associated with the claimed land even if this means that such traditions could only have survived as a result of being subversively performed during eras when traditional Aboriginal cultural practices were prohibited by Australian law. Such traditions must also be demonstrated even if current social conditions make them irrelevant or redundant. 'Connection' to these traditions can often only be substantiated by exhaustive, long term and ongoing research requiring the support of sympathetic white researchers often creating hostile relations with competing groups. State regimes of 'oppressive authenticity' only recognise the claims of a shrinking category of Indigenous peoples who are considered authentic because they can demonstrate ongoing traditional practices in relation to a place, and deny the claims of an ever growing group judged inauthentic because they cannot.[14] Biographers and their Indigenous subjects are thus placed in the position of both wanting and needing to 'tell the story', but to make that story one that does not undermine illogical and oppressive demands to demonstrate 'ongoing connections' to pre-contact traditions.

This has led, as it has in the Galba case, to many Indigenous groups splitting into factions that have different ideas about how to best demonstrate their authenticity. Group X base their claims to authentic Galba identity and ownership on genealogies and academic research on language, archaeological sites and historical documents. This research is used to make native title and other kinds of claims against the Australian state: another form of identity making. Alma's mob, as well as using genealogical evidence based on family history research practice a kind of 'strategic essentialism', which I explain below, to make claims to authentic Aboriginal identity and ownership.

Although courts use a highly essentialised notion of 'tradition' and 'custom' to determine a group's eligibility for native title, Francesca Merlan points out that public and academic understandings of Indigenous tradition do recognise that change in the form of adaptations, discontinuities and reconfigurations are inevitable, especially in colonial regimes which inflict such change.[15] Clearly, 'we' (academics and the general public) take a different view of the terms 'authenticity' and 'tradition' from that of the courts; biographers of Indigenous stories can play a role in further stretching the boundaries of these clearly flawed categories. But, as I will argue below, 'we' still retain at the core of our understanding, a conceptualisation of tradition as a bridge between past and present or the continuation of the past in the present.[16] As Ram reminds us, the relatively recent and pervasive postmodern critique of 'truth' still leads us to understand 'tradition' as a kind of 'essentialism', but an essentialism which only allows us to see traditions and the authenticity they claim to represent as political strategies.[17] These postmodern critiques are rightly based on an argument that any version of 'authenticity' and 'truth' which sees reality as essence, fixed and persistent over time, is illogical. But, 'we' (western thinkers) are not free from this tradition of thought, we *must* engage with this tradition because we are part of the history of western logic. Ram draws on Derrida to explain that although 'we' (westerners) know that tradition is changing and negotiable, we still need to engage with a metaphysics which sees tradition as immutable because such an understanding is part of 'our' intellectual heritage.[18]

It is not, however, only 'us' who need to engage with this contradiction but also minority groups who are not necessarily heirs to this tradition of thought, but who are dominated by it. Such groups, Indigenous Australians being one of them, need to politically manage such a questionable metaphysics by strategically engaging with it. That is, by recognising terms such as 'authenticity' and 'tradition' as contradictions of lived experience and using those contradictions to their advantage. 'They' (the colonised) need to take 'our' (the colonisers) ideas about 'their' traditions and use those ideas in ways which will benefit them politically and culturally. Indigenous subjects of biography can and do collaboratively strategise with their biographers to do this.

Alma's mob certainly make strategic use of essentialism. They use certain motifs in their paintings which are familiar to 'us' (the dominant culture) in central desert 'dot' paintings to represent their Aboriginality. They draw from various, but recognisably Aboriginal styles of dance in their performances. They ritually use a version of a pre-contact Galba language, which even if it is criticised as inauthentic, sounds like an Aboriginal language as such languages are represented in films, radio and how 'we' might imagine a 'primitive' language to sound. These practices are then represented in biographies and other texts as examples of the ways in which Alma's mob are 'connected' to past Aboriginal cultural practices.

But we need to be careful about the way strategic essentialism is theorised. It can, indeed, be understood as a manifestation of 'oppressive authenticity' if people are forced to behave in ways prescribed by a dominant culture in order to be recognised as possessing a particular identity. But it is often not recognised that people who have been previously dispossessed and have only been left with fragments of their culture do not always understand 'essentialised' cultural practices as solely political. In the case of Alma's group and many others I suspect, strategic essentialism is not all that is at the heart of their (re)invented culture. Older, more socially senior community members teach younger people and new-comers how to perform traditional practices 'properly' – they need to be performed by an appropriate person in an appropriate setting and they need to be performed to a standard. It is not enough to merely perform ceremonies, paint, make speeches or dance. These things need to be learnt and done with panache. A successful performance of a Galba tradition produces a relationship between the performance and the knowledge and social conditions from which the performance is drawn. It is not a performance by a detached artist, but a relationship between performers and audience which, in the case of Alma's community, is usually (but not always) between them and white people. These performances are aimed at representing sentiments, different versions of stories, experiences and traditions which are part of the relationship between community members and between them and 'outsiders'. This is, of course, highly political, but it is also very much about expressing and asserting self-respect, dignity and pride. This is something else that biographers can help Indigenous people express and record.

So, in contrast to Group X, who aim to conform to state ideas about how they should represent themselves as authentic with the goal of a successful native title claim, Alma's mob aim for popular recognition of their existence as authentic Aboriginal people with arguably less concern for their success or failure in the courts.

Clearly, Alma's group define themselves differently from the ways in which they are defined by 'us' (the dominant society). This is more than resistance and more than opposition to state rules and regulations, although it is certainly this in part. Alma's mob use 'strategic essentialism' to (re)invent traditional cultural practices and biography can be used to represent these practices in a way that can be taken seriously by 'us' without recourse to the courts. This is regardless of the fact that such behaviour could undermine their own and Group X's native title claims. Because they try to do this a schism has been created between Alma's mob and Group X.

As I said earlier, I had little appreciation for these politics when we began to collect material for the writing up of Alma's biography, or even after we had drafted it. It was not until I had begun to analyse the data I had collected for the ethnography that I realised some information Alma had divulged during our interviews for the biography contradicted some claims to genealogical and cultural continuity which is essential for successful native title claims according to the *Commonwealth Native Title Act* 1993. While writing the biography I had no idea what was at stake for Alma's mob, for myself, and particularly for Group X in publicly revealing certain information. Later I realised that Alma's mob have become, if not blasé about state definitions of 'authenticity', then at least philosophical about not always conforming to them. A senior member of Alma's mob told me that Galba people have nothing to hide. The problem, according to him, is with native title rules concerning who and what counts as real, not with how people think about themselves.

Group X undoubtedly also think about themselves in their own ways, but their public articulations of authentic Aboriginal identity are inextricable from the process of making native title claims.

Of course I am concerned about not representing the new, dynamic, self-determining identity that my friends assert. I am also embarrassed and worried about breaking a promise and straining relationships, but I am also concerned for the representations of Group X. In native title claims both groups are joined together. My work could, potentially, diminish the claims of both groups.

Where does this leave Alma's and my relationship? What can and will happen to the biography? It has now been seven years since we wrote the first draft and in that time Alma and I have negotiated too many personal crises in our relationship to re-count. But Alma and her community are adamant. Together we *must* work out a way to publish her story which is also the story of the (re)emergence of traditional Aboriginal cultural practices in the metropolis. But, of course, the colonialisms that have vexed relationships between Aboriginal and white people in Australia are not over. Alma and her community's story of self-determined identity making is suppressed by my reluctance to damage the state determined identity of both them and Group X. 'Oppressive authenticity' makes the representation of state-determined Aboriginal identity dominate self-determined Aboriginal identity.

Conclusion

So, were those who criticise the colonising agendas of white authors in writing other people's stories right all along? I do not think so. This is less an issue of misrepresentation and appropriation than it is a moral and ethical dilemma. It is also a dilemma that applies equally to white authors of black people's stories and to black authors of their own stories.

Is this merely a question of courage, or is it a question of needing creative new writing strategies to resist such oppression? I would rather think it is the latter. For myself, my personal ethics make seeking the publication of Alma's biography impossible in the short term, so at least for now, Alma, her community, our readers, and I must be satisfied with theorising our predicament and presenting it in the abstract terms I offer in this paper.

References

Hall, Stuart (ed) 1980, *Culture, media, language: Working papers in cultural studies, 1972-79*, Hutchinson in association with the Centre for Contemporary Cultural Studies, University of Birmingham, London.

hooks, bell 1994, *Outlaw culture: Resisting representation*, Routledge, New York.

Louis Gates, Henry 1989, *The signifying monkey: A theory of African-American literary criticism*, Oxford University Press, New York.

Macdonald, Gaynor 2002, 'Ethnography, advocacy and feminism: a volatile mix. A view from a reading of Diane Bell's *Ngarrindjen Wurruwarrin*', *The Australian Journal of Anthropology* 13(1): 88-110.

Merlan, Francesca 1995, 'The regimentation of customary practice: from Northern Territory land claims to Mabo', *The Australian Journal of Anthropology* 6(1-2): 64-82.

—— 2006, 'Beyond tradition', *The Asia Pacific Journal of Anthropology* 7(1): 85-104.

Moreton-Robinson, Aileen 2000, *Talkin' up to the white woman: Indigenous women and feminism*, University of Queensland Press, St Lucia.

Mudrooroo 1990, *Writing from the fringe*, Hyland House, Melbourne.

Nash, Manning 1989, *The cauldron of ethnicity in the modern world*, University of Chicago Press, Chicago.

Ram, Kalpana 2000, 'Dancing the past into life: the *Rasa*, *Nritta* and *Rāga* of immigrant existence', *The Australian Journal of Anthropology* 11(3): 261-73.

Rhydwen, Mari 1993, *Writing on the backs of blacks*, University of Queensland Press, St Lucia.

Roosens, Eugeen 1989, *Creating ethnicity: The process of ethnogenesis*, Sage, London.

Shils, E 1971, 'Tradition', *Comparative Studies in Society and History* 13(2): 122-59.

Sider, Gerald 1976, 'Lumbee Indian cultural nationalism and ethnogenesis', *Dialectical Anthropology* 1: 161-72.

Sissons, Jeffrey 2005, *First peoples: Indigenous cultures and their futures*, Reaktion Books, London.

Williams, Raymond 1977, *Marxism and literature*, Oxford University Press, Oxford.

ENDNOTES

[1] I use pseudonyms throughout this paper to protect the privacy of individuals and groups.

[2] Hall 1980; Louis Gates 1989; Mudrooroo 1990; hooks 1994; and Moreton-Robinson 2000.

[3] Rhydwen 1993.

[4] Macdonald 2002.

[5] *Commonwealth Native Title Act* 1993.

[6] Sissons 2005: 7.

[7] Sider 1976.

[8] Contrast with Roosens 1989 in a Canadian context.

[9] Sissons 2005.

[10] Merlan 1995: 65.

[11] Merlan 2006: 86.

[12] Merlan 2006: 88.

[13] Ram 2000: 257.

[14] Sissons 2005: 59.

[15] Merlan 2006: 93.

[16] See Merlan 2006: 86-88; Nash 1989; Williams 1977; and Shils 1971: 123 for some useful definitions.

[17] Ram 2000: 258.

[18] Ram 2000: 258.

Pauline McLeod: *The Magpie who became a Swan* – finding salvation in culture

Simon Luckhurst

Pauline McLeod was an Aboriginal performer, writer and storyteller who, at the time of her death at the age of 43 in 2003, left an archive of 34 boxes of writing: poems, diaries, notes, playscripts, film ideas and letters. Amongst the completed scripts and story drafts were also many examples of jotted notes and ideas, phrases and paragraphs, mostly undated. Also amidst the ephemera of her life were bus tickets, electricity bills and birthday cards, as well as a few letters, reports and reviews pertaining to Pauline but authored by other people. After she died her brothers cleared her flat, packing her things into the boxes. They were hoping that someone would use this material to tell Pauline's life story, and after being contacted by a mutual friend I have now spent some time working on the project.

It is my intention to use only material found in the boxes to tell Pauline's life story. To complete this process I have been literally 'unpacking' Pauline's work, scanning anything I think could be included in a biographical construct.

The story that will emerge will describe how she was fostered and later adopted, what life in her adopting family was like, how she met her natural family and how her adopting family disowned her after this took place. It will also cover her subsequent battle with mental illness which sometimes left her institutionalised, as well as her discovery of Aboriginal culture. I intend to explore how she came to rely on these experiences both for strength and for her career as a storyteller and writer.

In this paper I will describe some of these facets of Pauline's life, as well as attempting a brief discussion of some of the theoretical aspects I have been exploring as part of the compilation process.

The material

Given the possible reasons Pauline had for writing, and the likelihood of omissions of other aspects relevant to her 'complete' life story, it is appropriate that potential readers be given information on the nature of the text in advance of their reading it so they understand that they do not have the 'complete' version of something that was not complete in the first place. It is important, too, that the reader knows something of me – at a minimum, that I am male and non-Indigenous. They should know how I came to the project, the length of time I worked on it and what I hope will be the final result. They should understand my arrangement of Pauline's life, and that it is my attempt to convey what I understand to be the meaning of her words. My hope is that the presented life is recognisable to those who remember her, yet is also capable of offering new insights.

Pauline was born in March 1960 and wrote throughout her life. She kept much of her work, with the earliest surviving piece appearing to be a diary written in early 1976. The following extract is from the 1976 diary, New Years Day.

> We came home today after a week at our cousin's place. Last night we stayed up till 2 o'clock. It was fun. We had a little party and music. At 9 o'clock we started home and at 3 we reached home. It was hot and we went to sleep as soon as our jobs were done. Our TV broke. Pappa is going to try and get it fixed. My Bible verse for today:
>
> *Our Lord and our God. With joy in thee. Without, Thy heir we could not face unafraid the year before us.*
>
> God, please help me. Amen.[1]

As well as journals Pauline also wrote plays, poems, stories, letters and notes, while keeping miscellaneous other items including drawings, sketches, cartoons and photographs. The challenge for me in assembling this material is to create a cohesive narrative from the fragments, to let Pauline tell 'her own story' but in a myriad of forms, to allow the whole to become clear from the sum of many parts. I am still transcribing the material to be included in Pauline's story. Having read through all the documents I have found that there is enough to give a thorough account of her life, told in her own words, or through words that Pauline herself collected, either as letters written to her or as reviews. The challenge is how to determine not only what to include, but in what order to place the chosen extracts. In total there are over 3500 pages of documents, far more than most people wanting to find out about Pauline would be willing to sift through if left unedited. My intention is to construct a familiar autobiographical-type life story, with a beginning, middle and end.[2] This will require a solid period of assembly, as well as some editing to create a satisfactory narrative structure. While the cultural and gender-related content of this story requires discussion outside the scope of this paper, it is appropriate to here discuss some aspects of the editorial process used to create the story.

What Pauline wrote in her diaries was probably not intended for verbatim reproduction. It is arguable whether her creative work, too, would have undergone some sort of editorial process prior to publication. Although there are arguments against editorial intervention of Indigenous texts, including 'gubbarising'[3] it, I have taken the approach that this process is, to some degree, a valid methodology for the kind of story I am creating in this case. In his book,

A shared authority, Michael Frisch argues that if necessary, the process of editing material obtained from oral history can sometimes require 'a relatively aggressive, even manipulative approach to the "actual" text (being) the best way to faithfully convey its real meaning and essence'.[4] While Pauline's work is not oral history, I feel that some editorial intervention is appropriate to present her story to an audience unfamiliar with her life and writing.

Pauline's papers are a unique glimpse into her own experiences, much of them written as diary entries. In examining her journals, Pauline made the following notes:

> Notes on Diary and Journal Writing from 'The New Diary'[5]
>
> Diary uses:
>
> Developing creativity
> Problem solving
> Self discovery
> Self reliance and self help[6]

Like many diaries and other works written in the form of a journal there is no indication that what remains is indeed an accurate reflection of the life. Indeed, if the criteria above represent how Pauline saw her diary writing, then it is possible to conceive of her diaries as material created only when she needed to develop her creativity, had a problem to solve, was looking inwardly or was suffering from self-doubt. The *weighting* of particular accounts also deserves examination. What, for example, are we to make of the fact that Pauline mentioned her personal relationships so infrequently, and then almost flippantly? The absence of a serious examination of something most people consider important to their lives demands its own interpretation.

Some significant events in Pauline's life

Pauline was removed from her natural family when she was two years old, and she often repeated the story of how her mother went for help to the 'welfare' to find food and accommodation for herself and her six children. Instead she had all her children removed from her and was not to see her family again for more than two decades. Pauline was initially placed in a children's home before being fostered to a German family when she was four. She then moved with them to the mid-north coast of New South Wales, where she began to attend school.

The following extract is from Pauline's play, *The stolen one*, in which the central character, June, appears to experience some of things that Pauline herself underwent:

> June is now depicted as a child of six, wearing white stockings, carrying a skipping rope with her arm heavily bandaged.

June: I wish I could play, but they would laugh, make fun of me all da time. I don't know why. I am a good girl, I am. (June looks guilty.) But I had to hit Martin Farrell, cos he said I eat widd... widdgidy grwads.[7] (Pause.) I don't. He make me so mad. I hit him real hard. Like so. (She demonstrates.) He should have fall down, but he didn't. So I hit him again, like so. (She demonstrates a more powerful punch.) He still wouldn't fall down, so I told Mr Jamerson ... He gave me and Martin Farrell the cane! Why dey laff at me? I wish I could wash it off with soap or water or something.[8]

The family matriarch was 'Mutti', a strong-willed German woman who had taken it upon herself to raise six Aboriginal children as a promise to God. (She believed He had saved her life when she was ill.) In an unnamed story, Pauline wrote:

Being the eldest in our large family meant that I had little time or space to myself. When the chance came I always took it. Like when I had to look for a missing cow in the bush paddock ... It was during one of those times I was alone in the bush. I couldn't hear anyone. I was by myself, with no responsibility for anyone else except me. I loved those times. I started to explore, and during my exploration I started to have an adventure. Like I was in the darkest part of Africa, where there could be danger at every turn. At anytime a crazed wild animal might come charging towards me. Then, as I jumped over a fallen tree, I came across a little glen. It took my breath away. It was the most beautiful sight I had ever seen. A sunbeam lit up a small area near a crystal clear creek. The grass looked like it had been mowed. It was as if I was in the front yard of some little pixies or fairies, some little spirits who lived there. I had found a special, magic place. I lay down in the sunlight and for a second I even thought I had seen one of the pixies running behind some rocks. It was peaceful, warm and comfortable. And I forgot all the sorts of problems a twelve-year old girl might have had.[9]

The sorts of problems a 12-year-old girl might experience had sadly gone beyond even those of someone removed from their natural family. As well as Mutti's strict discipline, something more sinister was occurring, not noted by the Department of Youth and Community Services officers who came regularly to check on the family.

The foster family and the children that comprise the family are a very close unit. The parents are of German descent having come to Australia 22 years ago and since that period of time have been very keen on getting and caring for state wards, in particular Aboriginal state wards. The strangest facet of this foster placement is the ability of these foster parents to instil a family life atmosphere into all of the children in their care and to work so successfully with a wide age range of children of aboriginal descent. Pauline is extremely happy in this setting basically because she has foster parents who have reasonable expectations and are very geared to the problems that this girl has. She is also very secure and happy to the fact that she is with other state wards of Aboriginal descent.[10]

Pauline later wrote more extensively on the reality of her life at the time:

As we grew older and started to develop sexually I remember that my foster sister and I would be in the bathroom and often we would see eyes looking at us through windows or keyholes or holes in the walls. Mr Flory was watching us. I know this as a fact as he called out as we tried to cover the holes. We became very anxious and guarded about even undressing ourselves or being naked in our bedroom, as we on occasion could see someone outside looking in. We mentioned to Mrs Flory what was happening. She told us not to be promiscuous. Our foster brothers started to do as Mr Flory was doing, such as looking into the bathroom and bedroom. We had no privacy at all. My foster sister and I became ashamed of our bodies and could not even undress or change in front of each other. Whenever the welfare department officers attended the Flory's home, not one of us children was ever allowed to be alone with the department officers. Mr and Mrs Flory made certain that we were always supervised by them during any Departmental visits. Both Mr and Mrs Flory scared us. One of the punishments Mrs Flory used on us was to put the person to be punished in the centre of a circle and made the other children gang up on that person. It was a form of divide and conquer. Even if you didn't agree with it you still had to take part in it.[11]

On leaving school, Pauline attended Technical College, then worked as an enrolled nurse before joining the NSW Department of Youth and Community Services. Here she became a District Officer, one of the first Aboriginal people to do so. It was in this capacity that she was able to view her own ward file. She wanted to meet her natural family, but had fears she might lose her foster family in the process. She told the story in her play:

June: I wonder what my natural parents are like. I am going to meet them one day, not just yet though. Mother and Father would flip. I can talk to them about anything except my natural family, or how I feel about them and miss them. Father already says I am ungrateful for what they done for me when he is angry with me. I already lost one family. I couldn't lose another one.[12]

Despite the fear, the desire to know her family remained strong. Her eventual reunion with her mother, sister and three brothers in 1986 generated many conflicting emotions for Pauline. Her diary records:

> The experience was brilliant. For the first time I belonged somewhere. I really fitted in. I learnt about my history. I met my mother and family. I met aunties, uncles, cousins and other relatives beyond my wildest dreams. I was scared of not belonging, of rejection. Of losing.

> After the reunion I started getting lost in a maze of grief, hurt, pain. I was confused. The dream became a nightmare, I was slowly drowning in depression, suicide and despair. The loss became too great and for a period I wandered, looking for answers that no-one had.[13]

Pauline did not initially tell Mutti and Pappa she had met her natural mother, but wanted to be honest with them and to let them know what she was going through. This traumatic experience later recreated in a dialogue form:

> Mutti/ Pappa: You never told us.

> Pauline: I had to do this one thing on my own, and I am telling you now.

> Mutti/ Pappa: You went behind our back and did this. Why? What did we do wrong to deserve this treatment from you?

> Pauline: I didn't do this to deliberately hurt you. They are my natural family. I just wanted to meet them.

> Mutti/ Pappa: You betrayed us. It wasn't them who sat up all night when you were sick. Or kissed you better when you hurt yourself. Of fed you or clothed you for all these years. They didn't encourage you to get where you are today.[14]

Sadly, Pauline's natural mother died within a year of their meeting. Her death was followed a few months later by that of her brother, Robert. Her mother's death she portrayed in verse

> I loved her straight away
> She had no anger or hatred
> Only peace and wisdom.

> A gentle kind woman
> Whose patience paid off
> She got to see her grown children
> And her four granddaughters too!

> Now her journey's over
> She can rest at last
> She showed in the end
> That love would win.[15]

By this time Pauline had resigned from her job as a Welfare Officer and left Dubbo. She moved to Sydney, where she continued to suffer from depression, and in 1988 admitted herself to Prince Henry Hospital's psychiatric ward. It was not the only time she found herself there, for after she discharged herself her mood swings and depression continued. Her diary notes:

> Still feeling down. I am feeling very lonely. I know it's not good to sit in my flat by myself, but how often do people want me at their places. If I had a gun I'd probably … No, I wouldn't. I mean, I think of it all the time. Different methods and plans, but when it comes to the brass tacks, I couldn't go ahead. I'd be scared shitless I'd get caught. Last night, for example, I thought, 'why not empty that last lot of pills I have', but then I thought, 'No. Forget it'. At this point I don't want to die. Maybe sleep, but not die. It takes forever for the sun to rise, 5 to 6am is a long, slow time to wait. Cry, you jerk, just cry![16]

For Pauline the pain and angst of her situation continued through the subsequent years to the early 1990s. The following passage, extracted from a letter draft probably never sent, is by no means unusual in its depiction of the grief she felt during this period.

> Pauline Elizabeth McLeod died last night. She no longer is. Her body is breathing. She eats and sleeps. She continues on as if all is well, keeping up the pretence of life. Pauline Elisa Flory is dead. She died last year, when Mutti looked her in the eye and told her she was no longer her daughter. Both Paulines are dead. What is left? A shell of her former self, an image that will soon die. But not alone … no, not alone. Why can't they help? Why don't they try? Why haven't things changed? I feel like a walking time bomb that is due to explode very soon. Nothing and no-one can stop me. I have tried. Dear GOD, I have tried. I went for help, but there is nothing there. These arses don't know what the fuck is going on, and she doesn't know how to tell them. She is a boiling pit of anger, and soon she will show them all the extent of her pain. A silent sufferer will start to talk, and spill like a psycho. Nothing can touch her. Nothing will. She lies awake waiting for the right trigger to be pushed. It's coming. Slowly she can see it, and once it hits, it will do so with much vengeance and destruction. No-one will be able to contain her, or stop it.[17]

Pauline blamed many people for her situation, including herself. Mostly, though, it was the government or her foster family to whom she directed her anger. Her diary:

> I wonder if it's wrong to kill people? Mutti and Pappa are number one on my hit list. I feel they have cursed me and my family. The very first

time I told them about meeting my family, Mutti came out and asked me what I called her, my mother. I was honest and told her, 'I call her Mum.' In an instant I saw all of Mutti's hate and hurt. She hated Mum and I had hurt her. I figure it was then that she cursed me. I don't know why GOD listened and granted her wish, but tell you what, it's very unfair and the only way to stop all of this, is to kill them. It'll reverse the curse. Once I buy the gun I'll have enough ammo to destroy them all. Make me look like a fool, will they? Treat me like shit? Fuck them all.[18]

Sometimes it was expressed more simply:

Knock knock.
Who's there?
Madness.
Madness who?
You![19]

Pauline's diaries show a range of emotions. There were pages of plans, while others described her wretched unhappiness, her pleas to her foster family to take her back in,[20] and the times when it became apparent that it had all become too much, and when even her writing offered no solace.

Nor was her relationship with her natural family as smooth as she had hoped. Her father had died long before the reunion, her two surviving brothers and one sister had all undergone some form of trauma following their own removal. All were now coping with the repercussions of this in their own ways and sometimes they were not able to provide Pauline with the support she wanted. Possibly no-one could have done so.

After the reunion, Pauline heard a story which was to change her life which, at different times, she said was told to her both by her mother and her brother, Rick. It was the story of how the kangaroo got its pouch. She described this event in a poem

Throughout this doom and gloom
There was a shining light
A story my brother told
From the Dreaming late one night
It gave me hope once again
The beauty that shone through
To share the stories with others
Telling them culturally, entertainingly
And true.[21]

It was not the content of the tale which inspired Pauline, but its form. From it Pauline began to develop a new view of her life in which her lost Aboriginal culture took a central role. She wrote as a diary entry:

> In 1988 I moved to Sydney wishing to spend time with my natural family, and to try to overcome severe depression and start life anew. I went to the Eora Visual and Performing Arts Centre in Redfern and enrolled in the Performing Arts Course. From 1988 till 1991 I was a student and held a few jobs. I decided to become a performing artist and blues singer, a poet and writer as well as an Aboriginal Studies teacher and actor.[22]

By this time Pauline saw herself as a performer with the capacity to live a very different sort of life from that she had previously known. Another poem:

> There was a girl who had a dream
> That she was on the silver screen
> Was seen by many near and far
> As she became a famous star
> She was followed everywhere
> By fans who gave her googly stares
> She thought it fun and it made her laugh
> When people asked for her autograph.[23]

Pauline had found her calling and intended to become 'The Storyteller'. She believed that for thousands of years the Dreaming had been passed on in the oral tradition, and had produced 'an incredible culture and people'. This had not been done through books and electronic media, but through dance, music, art and storytelling. Pauline found what she thought were the best Dreaming stories that could be accepted by mainstream society. Her notes describe how she sought various elders and was granted permission by them to tell the stories. Her hope was that the stories would allow all those who listened to them the chance to finally understand and learn about Aboriginal culture.

> Everyone in Australia knows the stories of Cinderella and Little Red Riding Hood, yet ... Australians do not know one Dreaming story.[24]

Pauline began to build a world view based on her perception of her culture. For her, the paradise that had existed in Australia for tens of thousands of years ended on 26 January 1788 when the Europeans arrived. This extract is taken from the lyrics of an opera which she co-wrote

> Boorea:

> Life is simple
> Living in harmony with the land
> Each day we hunt for food
> And there is plenty of that

The ancestors have provided well
Here the ancestors still dwell
In the animals
In the land
Listen, you can hear them.
Animals tell us.[25]

In yet another fragment of an unpublished story, she described what happened next:

Strangers came to the land. Ghosts, not spirits, who were flesh and blood. Not our ancestors but strangers from another land, far away. For the first time in memory, nightmares came alive. Death and destruction arrived: to the people, the animals, the plants and finally the land itself. It occurred in only a short time, a drop in a millennium. The wars left survivors amongst the rubble. No longer was the land maintained, no longer was there a possum in every tree. Many of the languages disappeared, and the lullabies going to the sky went silent. The Bora rings were empty, in their place came concrete and steel. The new laws are strange, ever changing and never the same. The strangers made their mark and never admitted to their fathers' sins. The idea of reconciliation is like the sparkling glass jewels on string bead necklaces and diseased blankets. Promises which remain to be carried out turn into lies. We are strong, though. We have been here since the beginning of time, and no matter what we will survive. The Dreaming is still here, waiting to be seen again. To be dreamt by the descendants of those from long ago.[26]

Her understanding of Aboriginal culture helped Pauline cope with the continuing depression she felt. She missed her mother and brother, and understood that they had bird totems, in which, whenever she saw them, she would find some solace, as the following writing fragment illustrates.

Crow! I know you are there looking over me. Helping by watching and calling. Mother crow, Brother crow. Stay with me always as I learn and grow, and when I trip and fall. Mother Crow, Brother Crow, looking after me. Give me the strength to stand again. When I despair, search for me, Mother Crow send Brother Crow into the sky. Search until you find me. I come back and there they are again. Come close so we can meet and see into each other's eyes. The spirit of the crow. My mother's totem.[27]

The personal salvation she found in her culture had the potential to save the entire planet, which, she believed, was in pressing need of saving. Her diary:

We have fifty years, and then it's going to happen. What? The end of the world – the earth – and we, the Aboriginal people, the first born, the custodians of the kind earth have to now spend all our energies to stop what is happening to the earth at the hands of 'man' and re-educate them and teach them the way. They are lost beyond reason and we are not to hate them or seek revenge, as what goes around comes around. But we have to teach them as you would a stubborn, AUTISTIC CHILD, because really, that's all they are. 'Lost, lonely and scared'. We have to 'Be Noahs, not Jonahs'.[28]

Her belief in culture became a source of great strength to her, even in what she described as manic phases, or highs. Her diary again:

My brain is working overtime, and I'm about to burst with ideas to really start getting ahead financially. As well as helping others get a start and to return to the community some of the things taken from them. So much happening, life is like a roller coaster. No complaints. Just hanging on, sometimes thrilled with pleasure, sometimes filled with fear, and wondering why. Once I saw life only in terms of a few hours, hoping to make it through the day. Now I plan for the years ahead. A future and career is here to stay. Dare I say, 'Things are GOOD!'[29]

As her reliance on her interpretation of Aboriginal culture deepened, so did her resolve to understand it and transmit it in a way she felt was appropriate.

Not a 'fad' for one generation but a long term cultural goal. Pauline tells the stories:

With respect
Accurately
In a culturally correct manner
Entertainingly[30]

Pauline saw that one way of changing the wider community's understanding of culture was by its transmission in a positive and socially useful form. As the new millennium approached, her ideas for a business enterprise began to emerge.

P.E. McLeod Enterprises Outline

1. Tanda Tents (markets)
2. Wirra Parru Foods (bush foods)
3. Parra Tours (cultural tours)
4. Kirka Marri Theatre (performers)
5. Nallawilli (storytelling)
6. Wobbly Wombats (children's shows)
7. Yanakirri Kurrumin Studios (animation)
8. Bangada Products (jewelry/ ornaments)
9. Gurung Products (baby items)
10. Yerthoappendi Products (educational)

11. Thalangay Products (new inventions)
12. Watha Kampi Designs (fashion, clothing)
13. Writing Projects
14. Wirra Yarta (bush land farms)[31]

Aims and goals of P.E. McLeod Enterprises:
To set up fourteen companies by 2000.
To employ
75% Indigenous people
25% non-Indigenous people

Logo: Promoting Indigenous, cultural and natural products. Developing new industries for the new millennium. Training the new masters of humanity, philosophy and the environment.[32]

Pauline was going to participate to make her culture not only relevant, but economically viable.

> A mouse who never spoke
> Just sat back and watched and learned.
> And then one day, a change
> Big way. No longer meek and mild.
> Now I open my mouth and shout
> With all my might
> The mouse who never spoke
> Opened her mouth
> And everybody heard her shout.[33]

Pauline had now confirmed to herself not only the importance of culture, but the imperative of authenticity emerging only from Aboriginal people, whom she defined in her diary as being:

1. Must be a direct descendant of Aboriginal parents
2. Acknowledge self to be such and accept such
3. Before you can start to speak out as an Aboriginal person you must be accepted in the Aboriginal community
4. You must have experienced what an Aboriginal person faces on a daily basis, racism in all its ugliness.

Can one say they are Aboriginal if their direct line is a grandparent five generations ago, and they've not ever experienced racism or disadvantage because their family has followed the non-Aboriginal bloodline, until someone in recent times found a skeleton in the closet and decided to run with it? Does this make you an Aboriginal entitled to the resources available to Aboriginal communities and people? Interesting question, no easy answer.[34]

The debate on authorial integrity and authenticity was one which Pauline followed closely. She noted that:

> As Aboriginal culture becomes very popular, every aspect of the culture if looked at, studied, used and abused. For example, the inappropriate use of language, (like the example of the cosmetics company in Victoria, 'Biamee's Cosmetics'). Or the use of our art, the didgeridoo, bush foods and medicines, and now our stories. The publication of Dreaming stories is still done mainly by non-Aboriginals who attempt to explain the stories in their own words. Some are done sensitively, others are totally misinterpreted, and even made up. A new trend in storytelling, especially the telling of Dreaming stories, is growing and the sad thing is that some of these new storytellers are making up stories and calling them Traditional Dreaming stories, or are just hearing or reading a story and liking it and telling it.
>
> The rules of telling a Dreaming story are simple.
>
> 1. Find out where the story comes from and confirm.
> 2. Get permission from the elders of that region to tell the story.
> 3. With the elders, tell the story you want to tell and check whether your version is correct.
> 4. Learn the lessons and meanings behind the story.
> 5. When telling the story always acknowledge where it came from and the lessons and meanings behind it.
> 6. Never change the story or its meaning.
> 7. If you want to take it further, into publication, recording etc, get permission from the elders from where the story comes from.
>
> Follow these rules to tell Dreaming stories correctly, culturally and for the next generation.[35]

Pauline's battle with what had by this time been diagnosed as bi-polar disorder continued to be the other defining component of her life, and she found herself again hospitalised for six months in 1997.[36] At this time she was writing about alien abduction and the coming 'culling' of the human race which she believed would occur with the arrival of the new millennium. She still found strength in culture, and her position within the Aboriginal community, however, as another fragment illustrates:

> I am THE storyteller. The custodian of stories, particularly those from the south east coast of Australia, NSW. I am a cultural elder. It is my job to keep an eye on the Dreamtime stories, particularly when they're being put into a modern context with modern materials, it is important they are done so correctly. I have the authority and of the power of the

National Cultural Elders of this country. I have to do my job and do it well.[37]

By 2000 she came to believe that Aboriginal people had a different way of thinking, which she referred to in her diary as bi-lateral thought.

> Considered rare in the modern world, the bi-lateral thinker is gifted in their ability to 'see the many' in the modern world. Western societies teach their citizens to become structured, one-thing-at-a time thinkers. Whereas in Indigenous cultures, such as in Aboriginal Australia, people are taught to think bi-laterally and see the many at the same time. The bi-lateral process has to be taught, as few people are born natural bi-lateral thinkers. The see the whole and not just the part requires teaching and training. To understand Aboriginal Australia you must become a bi-lateral thinker – which means you must be trained to do so.[38]

Pauline's believed that the concept of bi-lateral thinking offered the capacity to change Australia's entire political structure.

> The Democratic/communist/Royalist systems of control don't work. They all got it wrong from the start, and have tried to fix them instead of scrapping them. I sit and wonder why the masses keep voting for individuals they have never met to control their lives. You can't fix what is already broken with band-aids. A new political party, a new republic, based on the traditional Circle of Elders ideology. For the people, by the people. Environment, land, creatures, water, plants. Environmental industries. Eventual abandonment of land now used for criminals/ lawyers/ jails/ defence forces. A new judicial system. Peace officers are footmen, local. Lawmen are the ones who track down criminals and bring them back to the Circle of Elders for trial, and an appropriate punishment. The Circle both protects and defends. The crimes of individuals include the effects not just on victims, but on families and communities.[39]

In conclusion

Pauline's story is as complex as it is moving. With the benefit of her entire archive to choose from, I have selected two pieces of her writing to place near the end of her story.

The first is an affidavit prepared in conjunction with a legal case brought by her foster sister, harking back to the days so long before when Pauline had witnessed her being abused by the man they both knew as Pappa.

> My memories of this time disappeared for several years and only in 1986 when I was reunited with my family did the memories come back. Around this time I rang my foster sister to find out if what I was

remembering was true. She confirmed it all, although she swore me to secrecy over the foster father on the farm. I kept the secret as long as I could, but around 1996 I confronted Mrs F. about our past, with severe consequences. I am so sorry I was never able to stop what happened. As I was the eldest I was supposed to protect my brothers and sister. Sorry, sis. I am so sorry.[40]

Pauline's heart, known to be weak already after an attack of rheumatic fever when she was a child, stopped beating on 22 May 2003 – just eight days after she completed the affidavit.

The second of the two pieces I conclude Pauline's life story with is drawn from a video recording Pauline kept of her appearance on a panel discussion which aired on SBS Television.

> Vivien Schenker: What do you believe happens to you when you die?
>
> Pauline: I believe we go back into the land. As an Aboriginal person I believe that we go back into our totem, and we stay as our totem animal until we decide to get reborn and then we come back and live another life.
>
> Vivien: What's going to happen to you?
>
> Pauline: I'm going to go back to a black swan and hang around down the river for a while until I decide, 'Oh, it's a good time to be born again and see what it's like to be a human again'. But I'm going to be a black swan for a while.[41]

References

Primary source

The Pauline McLeod Archive (34 boxes of material which are held at the home of Michael McLeod, Pauline's brother.)

Published sources

Heiss, Anita M 2003, *Dhuuluu Yala (To talk straight)*, Aboriginal Studies Press, Canberra.

Frisch, Michael H c1990, *A shared authority: Essays on the craft and meaning of oral and public history*, State University of New York Press, Albany.

Rainer, Tristine 1980 c1978, *The new diary: How to use a journal for self guidance and expanded creativity*, preface by Anais Nin, Imprint and Angus & Robertson, London and Sydney.

ENDNOTES

[1] McLeod: Diary extract, 1 January 1976. Pauline created many documents, of which a large proportion are undated or are fragments. All those presented in this document come from the collection held by her brothers. The archive is informal, and this is reflected in the structure of the citations for them. Some of Pauline's observations relate to events earlier in her life, so it should not be assumed that her comments were made contemporaneously with the events they describe.

[2] Exploration of cultural content, authorial authority and other aspects of the compilation process not discussed in this paper are also part of my PhD research, and will be explored in greater detail in my forthcoming exegesis.

[3] Heiss 2003: 66.

[4] Frisch 1990: 56.

[5] Pauline's notes from Rainer 1980 c1978.

[6] McLeod: Diary extract, undated, possibly c1990.

[7] Witchetty grubs – traditional 'bush tucker' of some Aboriginal people, which are actually insect larvae about four to six centimetres long.

[8] McLeod: Play, *The stolen one,* c1988. This short play appears largely autobiographical, although most characters appear to have different names to those in Pauline's own life story. It appears that Pauline kept no program notes for it, so possibly it was never performed.

[9] McLeod: Extract from short story, c1985.

[10] Report on State Ward, Youth and Community Services file extract, 29 April 1976.

[11] McLeod: Statutory Declaration extract, 14 May 2003.

[12] McLeod: Play, *The stolen one* extract, c1988.

[13] McLeod: Diary extract, c1986.

[14] McLeod: Fragment, c1986. Pauline recreated the conversation in script form.

[15] McLeod: Poem, *Mum* extract, 17 August 2001.

[16] McLeod: Diary extract, 16 October 1986.

[17] McLeod: Extract from letter, April 1989.

[18] McLeod: Diary extract, 4 April 1989.

[19] McLeod: Diary extract, undated, c1990

[20] It is unclear whether these letters were ever sent, or if Pauline sent them but retained a copy of them.

[21] McLeod: Poem extract, 17 August 2001.

[22] McLeod: Diary extract, undated, c1990.

[23] McLeod: Poem extract, c1990.

[24] McLeod: Notes for a performance of 'Nallawilli', undated, c1990. 'Nallawilli' was a collection of stories told by Pauline and frequently performed, however it also referred to a production in the late 1980s of a series of stories and performances by Kooris in Theatre.

[25] Opera libretto, *Garden of dreaming* extract (1st draft written with Melle Amade), April 1996. The opera has never been performed.

[26] McLeod: Story fragment, undated, c1995.My understanding is that this is what Pauline believed and how she lived, or at least tried to live her life.

[27] McLeod: Fragment, undated, c1995

[28] McLeod: Diary extract, c1997.

[29] McLeod: Diary extract, undated, c1998.

[30] McLeod: Notes for a performance of 'Nallawilli', undated, c1990.

[31] McLeod: Diary extract, 24 October 1997.

[32] McLeod: Diary extract, undated, c1998.

[33] McLeod: Poem, *Mouse,* undated, c1995.

[34] McLeod: Diary extract, c1998.

[35] McLeod: Fragment, c1998. It is worth noting that Pauline's earliest reference to telling Dreaming stories in the late 1980s had also included this caveat.

[36] Pauline's bi-polar disorder seemed to manifest itself more towards the late 1990s, at least it appeared to be diagnosed as such after this time, presumably prior to this she had assumed it was 'reactive' to the earlier events in her life. To what extent her condition was clinical and what extent it was reactive is impossible to say.

[37] McLeod: Fragment, undated, c2000.

[38] McLeod: Fragment, undated, c2000.

[39] McLeod: Fragment, undated, c2000.

[40] Statutory Declaration extract, 14 May 2003. Addendum to bottom of first draft of statutory declaration.

[41] Transcript of SBS Interview regarding Religion extract with Pauline McLeod, Vivien Schenker (moderator), Jon Casimir (atheist) and Fiona Horne (witch), broadcast date unknown.

The dilemmas of knowing too much: writing *In the desert – Jimmy Pike as a boy*[1]

Pat Lowe

I wrote the first draft of a manuscript about the artist Jimmy Pike's childhood in the late 1980s. For various reasons, the manuscript was never published during Jimmy's lifetime, and sat for a long time in my files.

A few years ago my editors at Penguin wanted to know if I had any manuscripts in preparation. I mentioned the draft biography, which they were keen to have a look at. I sent it away and they offered to publish it. We agreed that the manuscript needed more work.

It was many years since I had looked at the draft, and I did some rewriting including, at my editor's request, a number of flash-forwards to my own time in the desert with Jimmy. I had some notes of conversations and recordings in Jimmy's own words, but I also remembered many stories he had told me casually in the course of our 16 years together. Naturally, I drew on them as well.

As I worked through the manuscript again, mining my notebooks and memory, I occasionally had misgivings. Some of the stories were highly personal in nature: how would Jimmy have felt about my putting them in? I knew that he had quite a different attitude to privacy from me. Early on in our relationship, a film crew came out to our camp to interview him. I warned him that they would ask him about his years in prison. He wasn't fazed at all. Going to prison was all in a life's work to him, and he answered the anticipated questions unabashed. In later life, he often referred casually to his years in prison, and once, when we had joined a historical tour of Fremantle Prison, Jimmy took over from the official guide, pointing out features and telling anecdotes of his own. He simply didn't feel that having been to prison was something to be ashamed of.

Many times Jimmy had surprised me with his tolerant attitude to things I wanted him to be indignant about. When Elizabeth Durack was found to have offered for sale a whole exhibition of her own work under the name and persona of a fictitious Aboriginal male artist, Eddie Burrup, and entered the work in an Aboriginal art award, the art world expressed outrage. For a while, the media were full of it. People wanted to know what Jimmy felt about the imposture, but he just said: 'We can't down her, that old woman.' I read this as a reluctance to criticise someone he knew, or to take up the cudgels over something that didn't concern him. His disregard for such matters often caused me to reconsider my own society, and to notice how we love to express opinions, especially negative ones, about what other people do. Jimmy's culture seemed much less censorious.

Closer to home, I hated mining and exploration companies encroaching on Jimmy's desert country and wanted him to feel the same. But no: mining companies put in tracks, making remote waterholes more accessible; their rubbish tips were a good source of useful building materials. So long as they didn't trash significant places, mining companies were welcome.

So, what sorts of incidents in Jimmy's childhood was I worried about?

I didn't think Jimmy would mind mention of his early sexual experiences, such as jumping onto one of his young relations and pretending to ravish her. He had recounted this incident with amusement rather than shame.

Then there was his tendency to bully his younger brother, and other boyish bad behaviour. I already knew he wouldn't mind my retelling those incidents; he had previously illustrated some of those very stories, which I had written in fictional form.[2]

Then there were instances of other people's bad behaviour: Jimmy once told me a story about a relation tormenting a blind man with a smouldering stick. Years later, the relation he had accused told me exactly the same story, but with Jimmy as the perpetrator. Who was telling the truth? Probably both of them, I decided: clearly, they were both present and neither intervened on the blind man's behalf.

I worried more about telling stories that could be used as fuel for prejudice by those critics who seize on any information they think reflects badly on Indigenous culture: Jimmy's mother abandoning him on an antbed, for instance; the practice of killing one of a pair of twins; the story of a child left to perish in the desert after her mother died; any number of spearings; and, finally, Jimmy's aunty who claimed to have eaten human flesh. But the writer can't allow the ill-disposed to inhibit one's writing.

Of even more concern were matters touching cultural beliefs. I wasn't worried about retelling a couple of traditional stories, because Jimmy had made these public through his paintings. However, as a child he had broken a taboo. Would he have minded me writing about that? I remembered that he told me the story in a matter-of-fact way and didn't ask me to keep it to myself, as he did with some things. He is beyond being blamed for that incident now. However, I didn't know whether his relations would like that story.

They might not have liked other stories, either. All those abductions and murders and retaliatory spearings; all that violence. I think it is more likely to be people from my culture who would find that hard to stomach; we have become very squeamish about personal violence, especially when it entails the shedding of blood, though we have less compunction about wreaking all kinds of havoc on foreigners, preferably from the safety of the skies.

I could have gone to the family and read them the stories I wasn't sure about and asked their permission to retell them. But the very asking would have seemed to invite a refusal. I am reminded of one woman, quite closely related to Jimmy, who had contributed a lot of words and information to a dictionary of her language. She had supplied a number of words for parts of the body and its functions. However, when asked by a conscientious linguist if certain words should go into the dictionary or not, the woman said: no, they shouldn't go in. Asked then if doctors and nurses should know such words, she agreed that they should, and so the words in question went in after all. It was the linguist's selection of bodily function words as questionable that invited this woman to deem them inappropriate, probably more in deference to her notion of white people's sensibilities than her own.

If members of the family had raised objections to what I proposed to write, I would have argued my case as forcefully as I could, but in the end I would have had no option but to honour the implied contract: if one asks permission, one has to be prepared to accept the answer 'no'. In reality though, I am confident they would have respected the story as Jimmy's rather than theirs or mine, which I could never have written without his collaboration.

Then again, ever since I first went into the desert with Jimmy, I had felt privileged to be learning so much about the desert way of life, both through his teaching and incidentally, from observation and hearing casual stories. What should one do with a privilege – keep it to oneself, or share it with others? I chose to share it.

In so doing I was encouraged by how I have seen people react to collections of old photographs, such as those of Spencer and Gillen; how the younger generation of Jimmy's extended family have pored over other books I have contributed to about their parents' generation and way of life; and what Rolf De Heer said about Yolngu people's excited response to the Donald Thompson photographs that inspired his film *Ten Canoes*. I dare to think that future generations of Jimmy's people will be glad to have books such as this one, to tell them what their forebears were like and how they lived. They might have preferred them to have been written by the forebears themselves, but those people went in for oral history, not literature, and, as we know, the oral story lines have been disrupted. Besides that, people who grew up in the desert take for granted the conditions and details of daily life that so fascinate those of us who grew up in modern towns, and it takes an outsider to provide that sort of background.

So in the end I didn't consult anyone. I wrote down just about everything I could remember that Jimmy had told me about his childhood, feeling most secure when I could find a voice recording from him, or more-or-less verbatim notes I had written at the time. Despite my occasional misgivings about one story or another, I didn't deliberately conceal anything, or dilute it to make it more acceptable, or try to explain it away. It is all there for readers to enjoy or not, and to make of what they will. I believe it is more important to document this ancient but soon-to-be forgotten way of life, and to retell the precious stories of the last people to have lived it, than it is to censor oneself for fear of what the neighbours will say.

References

Djigirr, Peter and Rolf De Heer 2006, *Ten Canoes*, 87 min, Palace Films.

Lowe, Pat 1992, *Yinti: Desert child*, Magabala Books, Broome.

—— 2007, *In the desert: Jimmy Pike as a boy*, Penguin Group, Camberwell, Victoria.

ENDNOTES

1 Lowe 2007.

2 See Lowe 1992.

www.ingramcontent.com/pod-product-compliance
Lightning Source LLC
Chambersburg PA
CBHW061246270326

41928CB00041B/3439